Camden

Historical Archaeology in the South Carolina Backcountry

Kenneth E. Lewis
Michigan State University

 Case Studies in Archaeology: Jeffrey Quilter, Series Editor

THOMSON
━━━━✦━━━━™
WADSWORTH

Australia • Canada • Mexico • Singapore • Spain
United Kingdom • United States

THOMSON

WADSWORTH

Anthropology Editor: *Lin Marshall*
Assistant Editor: *Nicole Root*
Editorial Assistant: *Kelly McMahon*
Marketing Manager: *Wendy Gordon*
Project Manager, Editorial Production: *Christine Sosa*
Print Buyer: *Doreen Suruki*
Permissions Editor: *Stephanie Lee*
Production Service: *Mary Deeg, Buuji, Inc.*

Copy Editor: *Cheryl Hauser*
Cover Designer: *Rob Hugel*
Cover Image: *Historic Camden Revolutionary War Site*
Cover Printer: *Coral Graphic Services, Inc.*
Compositor: *Interactive Composition Corporation*
Printer: *Courier Corporation/Stoughton*

The logo for the Archaeology series is based on ancient Middle Eastern and Phoenician symbols for house.

All photos are reprinted with permission of the author except where noted.

Printed in the United States of America
1 2 3 4 5 6 7 09 08 07 06 05

For more information about our products, contact us at:
Thomson Learning Academic Resource Center
1-800-423-0563

For permission to use material from this text or product, submit a request online at http://www.thomsonrights.com.

Any additional questions about permissions can be submitted by email to thomsonrights@thomson.com.

Library of Congress Control Number: 2004115132

ISBN 0-534-51323-9

Thomson Higher Education
10 Davis Drive
Belmont, CA 94002-3098
USA

Asia (including India)
Thomson Learning
5 Shenton Way
#01-01 UIC Building
Singapore 068808

Australia/New Zealand
Thomson Learning Australia
102 Dodds Street
Southbank, Victoria 3006
Australia

Canada
Thomson Nelson
1120 Birchmount Road
Toronto, Ontario M1K 5G4
Canada

UK/Europe/Middle East/Africa
Thomson Learning
High Holborn House
50–51 Bedford Row
London WC1R 4LR
United Kingdom

Latin America
Thomson Learning
Seneca, 53
Colonia Polanco
11560 Mexico
D.F. Mexico

Spain (including Portugal)
Thomson Paraninfo
Calle Magallanes, 25
28015 Madrid, Spain

To Stanley South, colleague, mentor, and friend, whose imagination, open and inquiring mind, tireless energy, and zeal for discovery opened new pathways in historical archaeology. Emphasizing the methodology of science without losing sight of the humanist values on which it rests, Stan's work essentially set the course for the discipline in the second half of the twentieth century.

Contents

Foreword

ABOUT THE SERIES

These case studies in archaeology are designed to bring students in beginning and intermediate courses in archaeology, anthropology, history, and related disciplines insights into the theory, practice, and results of archaeological investigations. They are written by scholars who have had direct experience in archaeological research, whether in the field, laboratory, or library. The authors are also teachers, and in writing their books they have kept the students who will read them foremost in their minds. These books are intended to present a wide range of archaeological topics as case studies in a form and manner that will be more accessible than writings found in articles or books intended for professional audiences, yet at the same time preserve and present the significance of archaeological investigations for all.

ABOUT THE AUTHOR

Kenneth Lewis grew up in a military family, living in New England, the Southeast, the Pacific Northwest, and Germany. His experiences exposed him to the vast natural and cultural panorama of two continents and helped develop an abiding interest in understanding the past. A fascination with the relationship between complex societies and their material remains and the impact of change arose early, growing out of his exploration of Iron Age, Roman, and Medieval remains in Germany at a time not that far removed from the cataclysmic events of the mid-twentieth century. His interests led him to anthropology and to a focus in historical archaeology.

Lewis completed his BA and MA degrees at the University of Florida in the late 1960s and, following a two-year hiatus in the U.S. Army, he entered graduate school at the University of Oklahoma. The early 1970s saw the emergence of historical archaeology from a descriptive, particularistic undertaking to a discipline that sought to explain past social change. Intrigued by ethnographic work on contemporary colonization, he saw the processes associated with frontier change as a fundamental element shaping the American past. The Oklahoma Symposia on Comparative Frontier Studies drew the attention of scholars from many disciplines to the study of colonization and provided an opportunity to explore the frontier as an archaeological phenomenon.

After completing his Ph.D. dissertation in 1974, he served as a staff archaeologist at the Institute of Archaeology at the University of South Carolina. During this time Lewis carried out investigations at the sites of a number of seventeenth-, eighteenth-, and nineteenth-century settlements in that state, including Camden. His work emphasized the role of urban and rural settlements in South Carolina's development and culminated in his book, *The American Frontier: An Archaeological Study of Settlement Pattern and Process.*

Lewis came to Michigan State University in 1984 and is currently Professor of Anthropology. Colonization remains the focus of his research. His recently completed *West to Far Michigan: Settling the Lower Peninsula, 1815–1860* examines its role in creating the landscape of the Midwest. He maintains a research interest in the Southeast and continues to conduct fieldwork at Camden. He has produced numerous monographs, book chapters, and articles derived from the results of these investigations.

ABOUT THIS CASE STUDY

Most students who take beginning archaeology classes are under the spell of the romance of explorations and excavations in steamy jungles or in sandy deserts. Of course, such exotic settings are appealing for a variety of reasons, but there is also archaeology in our own backyards, and this is the case of *Camden: Historical Archaeology in the South Carolina Backcountry,* by Kenneth E. Lewis. Such research has a very different appeal than that offered by the far away and unfamiliar settings of the Maya or Egypt but it is appealing nonetheless.

Historical archaeology in the United States has always had its appeal and its followers. Notable names include Ivor Noël Hume and the research he conducted in Tidewater Virginia and at Williamsburg as well as James Deetz and his pioneering research at Plimoth Plantation, Massachusetts. The field, in general, was energized by interest and precious funding resources as the bicentennial of the Declaration of Independence, in 1976, drew near, and it hasn't slowed down since. Increasingly, Americans are coming to appreciate the archaeology of the era from the first Euro-American settlements to the present day and there are a number of subdisciplines within historical archaeology as a whole, as well, such as the archaeology of industrial sites, the archaeology of colonial missions, and the like. There is even an organization, The Society for Historical Archaeology, separate from the other societies that support mostly prehistoric archaeology (The Society for American Archaeology) and Old World archaeology (The Archaeological Institute of America). While all of these are signs of the vigorous health of historical archaeology in the United States, they also point out the somewhat separate spheres of archaeology and archaeologists.

Technically it is the existence of documents that defines what history is, and it is documents that make all of the difference between historical archaeology and the archaeology of prehistory. The number and nature of documents may vary. For some places and eras, documentary sources are scant and we can only rely on general descriptions of people, places, and things. In other cases, as is the situation for Camden, documentary sources are numerous and we not only know the general historical circumstances in which sites were created and objects discarded or left but sometimes very specific information, such as the names of the owners of houses and the lengths of times their dwellings were occupied. These kinds of historical records offer different opportunities for researchers and also different challenges than those faced by archaeologists working at sites and for cultures and time periods for which no written records exist.

In this book Kenneth Lewis offers a true "case study" in the best sense of the term. He provides the reader with the larger theoretical framework in which his research was carried out, namely, issues regarding the colonization process. He then moves, however, to show the wealth of historical information we have for the specific proofs of colonization of Camden, citing details of initial settlement, economic conditions, and changes through time in the nature of settlement and the shift in the frontier of the colonizing process. The reader is thus able to see how the details of the historical record can be augmented, enriched, and even challenged by what the archaeological spade reveals. It is this tension between what history has written, what the archaeologist uncovers, and how different modes of interpretation may supplement or contradict one another that makes historical archaeology, and this case study, so fascinating.

Historical archaeology, perhaps more than any other discipline, continually demonstrates that "history" is not just a collection of facts. Rather, it is a story about the past that is constructed with bits and pieces—a personal diary, a military map, broken pottery, brick rubble—in the present, with specific questions in mind, shaped by contemporary points of view and understandings. This case study will thus offer the beginning student, as well as more advanced investigators, opportunities to examine "big" questions of culture change that can be related to even larger historical and anthropological issues as well as "small" issues of dirt archaeology. It is a pleasure to welcome it to the Case Studies in Archaeology series.

Jeffrey Quilter, Series Editor

Preface

How can archaeology teach us anything new about a colonial settlement already well known through historical sources? This is the problem that confronted me when I began my involvement with Camden, South Carolina, a town whose roots extend from the mid-eighteenth century to the present. In working out an answer to this question, I faced one of the central dilemmas in historical archaeology. How does the study of material things inform us about the past in a way that is different from written accounts, pictorial images, oral histories, and other types of information?

By themselves, material objects may seem to be poor and often confusing sources of information. The meaning of artifacts cast off in the past is often unclear, and researchers often see them as having a secondary importance. We can identify familiar relics excavated from the ground or locate and trace the outlines of buildings, forts, and other recognizable architectural features we already know exist. But beyond describing such things, an examination of material remains can yield much more information. Because we deal with objects whose nature and arrangement were the results of actions by past people, archaeologists can observe how they carried out the activities that were a part of their daily lives. Activities such as preparing food, building houses, conducting warfare, and carrying out trade all leave material evidence of their occurrence. We have the opportunity to study behavior directly by examining its material residue.

The composition and arrangement of the archaeological record are shaped by the activities that created it and can provide information as useful as that contained in historical sources. To learn about past peoples, archaeologists seek to discover patterns in the material record and link them to the kinds of human activities that produced them. For example, because churches and houses were designed for different purposes, the layout of each kind of structure will usually identify its function. Similarly, the distribution of pits where people discarded their trash can divulge whether or not cooking or manufacturing once took place nearby. Because the activities of daily life can reveal many things about the society in which they occurred, archaeology holds the key to exploring all sorts of wider questions. Archaeology has been an important means of gathering information about society in colonial America and the processes that shaped its development, and it has been crucial to understanding the emergence of the southern frontier.

This case study examines how archaeologists have used material evidence to understand the growth of a particular settlement that played an influential role in the backcountry of South Carolina. Camden came into being in the mid-eighteenth century as British settlement moved inland from the Atlantic seaboard and immigrants adapted to conditions encountered on the edge of expansion. As one of the few substantial settlements in the province's interior, Camden became a hub of trade, a court town, a regional market, and the focal point for many other activities covering a wide area. It even served briefly as a British military base during the bitter southern campaign of the American Revolution, and after the devastation of war it arose again to become an agricultural center in the emerging plantation economy. As the focal point of activity in the backcountry, Camden shaped larger economic, social, and political institutions and left behind a material legacy of the influences that formed the settlement and shaped the region.

But why is it necessary to rely on the archaeological record to investigate Camden? We already know much about the town's past. Contemporary visitors and residents left us a substantial written record that tells of dramatic events and prominent personalities associated with the town and gives us an overview of its history. But while the documents tell much about Camden's past, they are also incomplete and sometimes biased toward particular points of view. People don't record everything and do not always recall it accurately. As a historical archaeologist, I have investigated Camden's material record for nearly three decades to address questions that documents failed to answer. The structures early residents built and inhabited, the artifacts they used, and the refuse they discarded have all revealed information about their lives and the development of their community. In this case study, I examine how my work and that carried out by other archaeologists produced a body of material data that allowed us to explore a number of questions concerning various aspects of Camden's past that could not otherwise have been addressed.

My archaeological inquiry centered around Camden's role as a central frontier settlement. A number of factors influenced the town's development, and these factors shaped the strategy I followed to examine its past. In the chapters that follow, I will introduce Camden and place it in the historical context of colonization. Next, I will explain how I settled on a strategy designed to examine which critical aspects of Camden's development were likely to be reflected in the patterning of the settlement's material remains. Because the historical changes accompanying frontier colonization affected the entire community at one level and its individual residents at another, the research strategy had to be able to address different scales of analysis. As a result, I explored settlement-wide changes by examining material patterning over the whole town site, but investigated particular changes associated with smaller social groups within the more restricted context of the buildings or areas within which they lived and worked. This approach allowed me to use Camden's material record to observe the impact of change at multiple levels within the community. Its flexibility was helpful in answering a wide variety of questions ranging from Camden's role as a trading center, to the nature of its businesses, to the wealth and ethnic diversity of its residents.

My research at Camden has been facilitated by the concern of its citizens and their efforts to protect, preserve, investigate, and interpret the site of this unique colonial town. Unlike most of the central settlements that arose with European expansion into the interior of the American Southeast, Camden does not lie beneath a modern city. Abandoned early in the nineteenth century, the early town site was never reoccupied, and has lain largely undisturbed by later development. The site's accessibility and the relatively intact state of its material remains have made it an ideal focus for archaeological research. Although no structures or aboveground evidence is visible, the remains of buildings and activities still lie intact beneath the surface. Vestiges of the earlier landscape are also reflected in the modern city plan, the layout of which has helped determined the boundaries of the colonial town and locating features within it. All of these factors make Camden an ideal site for archaeological research.

Preservation efforts have grown out of the interest and support of local individuals and organizations who worked to acquire and maintain the site of Camden, and who recognized the role of archaeological research in interpreting its contents. The Camden District Heritage Foundation, founded by Richard and Margaret Lloyd in 1967, provided the impetus for preserving the town site and has been instrumental in raising funds to support the historical park, called Historic Camden, and conduct research there. Two years later, the state legislature created the Camden Historical Commission as a local administrative entity to operate and develop the site, which later became an affiliated unit of the National Park Service. In 2000, the commission and the foundation merged to form the Historic Camden Foundation, which currently administers the historical park.

Over the years the Camden Historical Commission has sponsored a number of archaeological research projects at Camden, support for which has come from a number of sources. The early work, which focused on the military fortifications, the powder magazine, and the Kershaw House, was funded by the Camden District Heritage Foundation and carried out by archaeologists employed by this organization. Subsequently, the South Carolina Institute of Archaeology and Anthropology conducted extensive sampling excavations in the town and further investigations at the Kershaw House. This research was supported by grants from the Coastal Plains Regional Commission and the National American Bicentennial Committee. The Camden District Heritage Foundation also contributed to these projects. A matching survey and planning grant from the U.S. Department of the Interior, Heritage Conservation and Recreation Service, administered by the South Carolina Department of Archives and History under provisions of the National Historic Preservation Act of 1966 supported the examination of the jail site, and the brewhouse excavations were conducted as a field school by the Department of Anthropology of the University of South Carolina. The Camden Historical Commission sponsored investigations conducted within the town from 1996 to 1998. These were funded in part by a congressional appropriation to Historic Camden, administered by the National Park Service, as well as by grants from the John T. Stevens Foundation, the Belk-Simpson Foundation, the South Carolina Archaeological Research Trust, John Bonner, and an anonymous Camden donor.

Many people and organizations have contributed to the success of the archaeological work at Camden. Historic Camden has been the sponsoring agency for all of the research, and the directors with whom I have worked exhibited great foresight in recognizing the importance of archaeology in developing this important site. Both Hope Cooper, under whose directorship my work in the 1974–1977 and 1981 took place, and Joanna Craig, director of Historic Camden in the 1990s, were instrumental in securing support for the major projects and, together with their staffs, provided assistance throughout the investigations and were of inestimable help in coordinating the support of other agencies. Shirley Ransom, who assisted Hope Cooper and Stephen Smith, also worked tirelessly to ensure the success the success of our endeavors. I also wish to thank former director Stephen Smith for his encouragement of the research. I have always enjoyed the support of the Camden Historical Commission and the Camden

District Heritage Foundation, whose members always expressed great interest in our work.

None of the field projects could have been completed without the help of the City of Camden, whose various departments supplied heavy equipment to assist excavations, arranged for water to screen artifacts, back-filled excavation units, and provided a boom truck to allow high angle photography of the site. Several Camden businesses also contributed to the various projects over the years. They include Tetterton and Riddick, registered land surveyors; Burns Hardware; Camden Machine Works; Camden Gas and Oil; Camden Tractor Sales; and the Dilmar Oil Company. A number of individuals contributed to the research, including Niles Blackburn, Bruce Mayer, and Joe Henderson. Additional support came from the South Carolina Institute of Archaeology and Anthropology (SCIAA), through which I carried out investigations at Camden in the 1970s. From the beginning, the institute maintained an active interest in the archaeo-logical work at Camden, and Robert L. Stephenson, its director from 1968 until 1984, was particularly supportive of my work there. His successor Bruce Rippeteau continued SCIAA's commitment to archaeology at Camden by gener-ously providing specialized field equipment for the projects conducted in the 1990s. The analyses in this study required access to records of all previous work at Camden, a task greatly facilitated by the hard work and concern of SCIAA collections manager Sharon Pekrul. The Consortium for Archaeological Research at Michigan State University provided laboratory space for the analysis of materials collected in these investigations.

Perhaps the most critical people to an archaeological project are those who labored in the field. The regular crew members on the various Camden projects I supervised included Frank Babbitt, Geraldine Belvin, Travis Bianchi, Dale Borders, Bob Burtman, Cort Calk, Jacqueline Carter, John Caylor, Tommy Dallas, Paige Luttrell Edwards, Elizabeth Farkas, Andrew Farry, John Frierson, Sam Higgins, Shelly Hite, Heathley Johnson, Frank Jordan, Linda Light, Carl Merry, Kevin Nichols, Elizabeth Paysinger, Sharon Pekrul, Eric Perkins, John Prescott, Leslie Riegler, Carol Sanford, Ken Sassaman, Harriet Smith, Bobby Southerlin, Louise Steffens, Kristen Stevens, Laura-Ann Summerall, Fred Swain, Sean Taylor, Ricks Vaughn, Barbara Wilde, and Lois Zemp. I would also like to acknowledge the assistance of Kristen Bowles, Niles and Ingrid Blackburn, Fritz Briggs, Debbie Clanton, Joanna Craig, Jim Hall, Cindy Hatfield, Jennifer Lee, Frank Moran, Melissa Outlaw, Michael Outlaw, Jonathan Parks, Bruce Penner, Don Siems, Holly Silvig, Bill Vartorella, and Hally Winthenbury for their participation in the fieldwork. The success of an archaeo-logical project owes much to the enterprise of the field supervisors, whose efforts and insights often go unmentioned and unappreciated. Without the assis-tance of Michael O. Hartley and Frank Krist, the results of the 1974–1975 and the 1996–1997 projects would have been greatly diminished and I thank them both for their efforts. Analyses of the archaeological data are critical to identify-ing, interpreting, and understanding the material record, and I would like to acknowledge Jacqueline Carter, Frank Krist, Leslie Riegler, Andy Farry, Kevin Nichols, and W. Thomas Langhorne, Jr. for their assistance. Managing the vast amount of data for the various Camden projects was greatly facilitated by the central computerized database created by Frank Krist and Andy Farry.

Information derived from Thom Langhorne's spatial analyses of settlement patterning at the Kershaw House and settlement spread in the town has also been important to the interpretation of Camden's archaeological record.

My research at Camden has relied on the input and assistance of many others not directly involved in the fieldwork. The archival research so necessary to the archaeological research could not have been completed without the efforts of Jo Ann McCormick and Carolyn B. Lewis, and Darby Erd produced the excellent illustrations of the Kershaw House. Over the years I have benefitted from conversations with a number of South Carolina scholars whose knowledge and insights often helped me see what I might otherwise have overlooked. They include David Anderson, Mark J. Brooks, Richard D. Brooks, Richard F. Carrillo, David Colin Crass, R. P. Stephen Davis, Jr., Leland G. Ferguson, John H. House, Susan Jackson, Charles Joyner, Chris Judge, Charles F. Kovacik, H. Roy Merrens, Robert D. Mitchell, James D. Scurry, Carl Steen, Robert N. Strickland, Steven D. Smith, George Terry, Gail Wagner, John J. Winberry, Peter Wood, and Martha Zierden.

Stanley South has been a continuing influence on my work at Camden and elsewhere. As perhaps the most profound innovator in historical archaeology in the 1970s and certainly its greatest proponent, Stan's encouragement gave me the confidence to explore change on a broad scale and to use new methods to discover and examine the processes that shaped Camden and the backcountry. Central to his approach to historical archaeology has been an emphasis on a sound methodology and an insistence that conclusions about the past be based on clear and demonstrable links between patterning in the material record and the behavior that produced it. The construction of bridging arguments tying the nature of Camden's evolution to the form, content, and distribution of its archaeological remains were crucial to examining the historical processes that shaped South Carolina's backcountry and lie at the center of this study. The rigor with which these statements were developed and employed owes much to the logical soundness of Stan's approach and it is on its strength that the conclusions of this case study rest.

The direction of my work at Camden grew out of an interest in frontier studies that began earlier in graduate school. The late Steve Thompson's research in both modern and historical colonization provided a basis for examining processes of colonization archaeologically, and his interest and guidance helped me refine the models of change used in my subsequent work. Delineating the material manifestations of colonization rests on the use of archaeological methodology grounded in theory and capable of explaining the larger behavioral context of objects, and I acknowledge my debt to Rich Pailes for helping me understand that archaeology must be more than culture history.

Although this study emphasizes the analysis of the archaeological record, the interpretation of Camden's material remains and the regional milieu in which they accumulated would have been impossible without the historical context assembled from archival records. I wish to acknowledge the assistance of the staff members at the various repositories where I conducted documentary research relating to the Camden projects. These are the South Carolina Archives and the South Caroliniana Library of the University of South Carolina, in Columbia; the Camden Archives and the offices of the Clerk of Court and

Probate Judge of Kershaw County, in Camden; the South Carolina Historical Society, in Charleston; the Southern Historical Collections of the University of North Carolina, at Chapel Hill; the Wisconsin Historical Society, in Madison; the Clements Library of the University of Michigan, in Ann Arbor; and the James A. Rogers Library of Francis Marion University, at Florence, SC.

Finally, I would like to thank those who have been involved directly in the production of this book. Jeffrey Quilter, series editor of the Case Studies in Archaeology, critiqued the original manuscript and offered many helpful suggestions for improving the book. Turning a manuscript into a book is never an easy or painless task and I thank those responsible for helping me through this process. I am particularly indebted to Carolyn B. Lewis for proofreading the entire manuscript and for long discussions that helped refine the content and coherence of the arguments presented in it. The clarity of the text also owes much to her meticulous attention to the details of grammar and construction. I also wish to thank Margaret Holman, Frank Babbitt, Linda France Stine, Joseph Chartkoff, and Joanna Craig for reading and commenting on portions of the manuscript. At Wadsworth, senior acquisitions editor Lin Marshall encouraged me to develop this project and helped move it forward. I also wish to thank anthropology editorial assistant Kelly McMahon and project manager Christine Sosa. I appreciate Mary Deeg and the staff at Buuji, Inc. for their efforts.

1/Camden, a Community in the South Carolina Backcountry

INTRODUCTION

In 1850, Sarah Thompson Alexander began a memoir of her life in Camden, South Carolina. The town where she resided had experienced an eventful past, and much had changed during her lifetime, but nothing stood out more than the fate of the early settlement. "Should anyone curious in matters of antiquity set out to find the Camden of Revolutionary memory," she wrote, "they would be badly disappointed, for not a vestige now remains of that once memorable city; even the ancient city of Nineveh has been found and many relics discovered, but of Camden naught remains . . ." (Alexander 1850). Camden's residents had abandoned the original site so rapidly and completely that within a few decades almost no recognizable material remnants bespoke its existence. Colonial Camden suffered the fate of many past settlements that were simply vacated as conditions changed and drew its residents elsewhere. The fact that early Camden's disappearance was not associated with unique, dramatic events, such as the sack of Nineveh or Pompeii's fiery destruction by a volcano, did not diminish its importance. On the contrary, the more mundane fate it shared with many other colonial settlements has made the town especially useful for studying widespread developments that occurred throughout the southern backcountry. As an early settlement in South Carolina's interior, Camden provides a unique opportunity to investigate the region's past and the forces that shaped it (Figure 1.1).

Today the old settlement has long faded from living memory, but Camden's historical significance and the unique character of its site have made the town a center for archaeological research in the South Carolina backcountry. In the 1960s, historical archaeologists began the painstaking task of rediscovering the colonial town and analyzing its remains. The roles of Camden as a center of trade and commerce, a seat of justice, and a fortified garrison in the American Revolution had long fascinated historians, and the town offered an opportunity to explore the nature of these important developments firsthand. Camden's particular history also produced ideal conditions for archaeological study. Less than

Figure 1.1 Map of modern South Carolina showing Camden and other cities.

a lifetime passed between the arrival of the first colonists and the abandonment of the old town site. Although this period was hardly uneventful, its relative brevity produced an archaeological site with the remains of a single, short-term occupation. At its close, the town site was avoided by later settlement and its contents lay intact, uncontaminated, and substantially undisturbed by the forces of nature and human activities. Such sites are rare and the richness of their contents makes them well worth examining. Although the site of Camden is visually unassuming, the investigation of its material record proved to have implications far beyond its own boundaries (Figure 1.2).

I became involved with archaeology at Camden in the 1970s when I joined the staff of the Institute of Archaeology and Anthropology at the University of South Carolina, and my commitment to the site has continued until the present. Camden appealed to me from the beginning, even before I saw the site for the first time, because of the opportunity it offered to explore both the history of the South Carolina backcountry and the nature of the processes that created it. I had become interested in frontier colonization as a graduate student. I discovered that scholars from many disciplines had explored this phenomenon as a contemporary process as well as a historical development, and I was concerned that the results of their work had profound implications for historical archaeology in the United States. Comparative studies of colonization had identified critical variables associated with the expansion of complex industrial societies and linked

Figure 1.2 Aerial view of the site of Camden from the southwest. In this photograph, taken in late 1974, the colonial town site lies in the cleared area and its northeastern corner is partially covered by the auditorium and athletic fields. The modern city is visible immediately to the north.

these factors to the form and function of settlements, their order of appearance, and their distribution on the land. The colonization process described the creation of distinctive settlement types that could be defined in time and space. It seemed logical to assume that each of these types might have left characteristic material remains that could also be observed archaeologically. I anticipated that characteristics of colonization would be recognizable in the form, layout, and contents of key settlements. My dissertation research in eastern Virginia, settled in the seventeenth century, led me to this conclusion, and convinced me that archaeological evidence could play a central role in identifying this process. I felt that Camden would be an ideal location to employ such data to determine how colonization shaped settlement in the backcountry.

This study relates how historical archaeologists have carried out excavations at Camden and employed the results to investigate its role in the colonization of the South Carolina backcountry. This well-preserved site yielded the residue of activities that shed light on settlement function and change over time and made it an ideal laboratory in which to study the processes of change that shaped its development and the history of the larger region. During my three decades of archaeological work at Camden, I have carried out field research and used the results of others to answer questions regarding patterning and processes associated with colonization and the growth of commercial economies in frontier regions. The unique nature of this settlement and the material record left behind by its inhabitants have provided a rich source of data with which to observe these phenomena and address a variety of questions relating to this fascinating settlement and its remarkable past.

Conducting research at Camden demanded an approach capable of assessing the town's changing role as the region in which it lay evolved from a frontier in the 1750s to a stable agricultural area in the closing years of the eighteenth century. In the six decades that it occupied its original site, the town responded to broad developments in the South Carolina backcountry, changes that derived from the nature of agricultural expansion in the age of European overseas colonization. I believed that observing Camden's evolution required a model that was regional in scope, yet able to recognize the form and variation at the level of individual settlements.

A *model* is a scheme devised to explain some aspect of the real world. It is a representation of reality intended to simplify its complexity and clarify the relationships among phenomena under consideration. A model of colonization, for example, would attempt to identify the elements most significant to this process, describe their relationships with one another, and recognize the causes that underlie their occurrence. Archaeologists use models to organize the elements of some phenomena, such as colonization, in order to understand their structure and its change over time, and how these elements are manifested in the material record.

Archaeologists have long used models to organize and interpret the past, and by the 1970s model building and testing had become an important tool in analyzing the material phenomena they studied. Researchers used models to examine the behavior of people in the prehistoric past and explain change in complex societies. Advocates of the "New Archaeology," which stressed the importance of theory-guided methodology, espoused the employment of such models to discover and explain the material patterns they observed. Among historical archaeologists, Stanley South (1977) urged others in this field to use the information available in archival documents to create models to explain such patterning on colonial American sites. To support his assertion, he modeled historic ceramic use and demonstrated the relationship between the relative occurrence of known types and the midpoint and range of a site's occupation. He further contended that models had explanatory power, citing their use in linking ideology and decorative motifs on grave markers and exploring relationships between variation in ceramic use and the complexities of social structure on antebellum plantations. Camden was a large and complex site, shaped by the forces of global change, and I felt that its archaeological record could only be understood in the context of the settlement's role in the larger world. The key to interpreting the meaning of Camden's material remains was creating a model capable of describing the processes responsible for its existence.

Camden emerged as a result of British agricultural colonization in South Carolina and grew as the region evolved. In order to account for Camden's development, a model would have to describe the process of change associated with colonization in South Carolina and link this process to the nature of the settlements it produced. Such a model not only had to portray the types of settlements associated with agricultural colonization, how they were distributed, and how they formed parts of larger systems, but it would also have to explain *why* the settlements assumed these characteristics. Constructing a model that recognized Camden as a distinctive element of a larger changing settlement system became a crucial part of my research. I will explain how I derived the model and why it is an appropriate tool for examining both archaeological and documentary evidence.

THE PROCESS OF COLONIZATION

A model capable of examining Camden's role in the historical development of South Carolina's backcountry had first to account for the nature of colonial society and how it evolved. Underlying such a model is the assumption that these changes involve common adaptations by complex societies to conditions encountered at the edge of settlement, where social, economic, and political institutions are incomplete, aboriginal peoples are encountered, and impediments to establishing a subsistence base must be overcome. These adaptations affect the organization of colonial societies and guide their maturation over time, and may be characterized collectively as a general process of change.

The process of agricultural colonization describes the creation of a new society through the organized transplantation of immigrants and addresses those variables that bear most directly on this development. For this reason, its focus is on the colonizers and the evolution of the society that stems from their intrusion. Because the circumstances of colonization vary, factors unique to the time and place of settlement may affect the course of the process or even its outcome; however, the universal adaptations involved in agricultural expansion are so closely tied to its success that they are likely to underlie the overall development of most colonial regions. I anticipated that the nature of colonization in South Carolina would have followed the general trend characterizing such regions, but I also had to be aware of how these adaptations would be manifested in this particular area. The colonization process would explain why the region developed the way that it did; however, identifying the occurrence of this change required a model that specified the form such evidence would take.

To investigate the development of Camden, I had to employ a model that linked this settlement to the larger process that created it. Colonization in South Carolina was shaped by the expansion of Europe, and the social system that emerged from this phenomenon has been characterized as a *world system*. It comprised an economy whose extent reached beyond the control of any single nation and was marked by a capitalist mode of production, which attempted to increase productivity through the reorganization of labor under increasingly unified management and the introduction of more efficient manufacturing technology. Capitalist production flourished in an environment that allowed entrepreneurs a vast freedom to operate outside one state's domain in order to obtain necessary resources. Increasing production spurred the creation of new markets, which encouraged the expansion of trade into new areas. The structure of this system divided the world geographically. In the core states at its center, strong state mechanisms and a national culture encouraged the formation of capital and protected the system's economic disparities. In the peripheral areas at its boundaries, however, indigenous institutions were weak or nonexistent and the production of essential goods was less well rewarded, placing them in an inferior position to the core states. This structure created an unequal exchange relationship, characterized by the movement of cheaper raw materials from the *periphery* to the *core* in exchange for more expensive manufactures and services in the opposite direction (Gould 1972; Wallerstein 1974; Braudel 1984). South Carolina's role as a periphery of Great Britain defined its role in the world system, a position that helped me model the emergence of this region and settlements in it.

The economic position of frontier regions on the periphery of the world system sets the course of their historical development. The nature and organization of production, which strongly influences how the areas are settled and evolve over time, also affects this process. The requirements of production determine the degree of the colony's insularity, as expressed by the number of links connecting it with the homeland. Insularity influences the level of trade, communication, and other types of interaction between the two regions, and the nature of these ties affects the degree of change experienced by the colonial society. Fewer and more tenuous links to the homeland increase the region's relative isolation and force a greater degree of change as an adaptive response to this situation (Steffen 1980).

The economies of agricultural colonies depend the least on specialized production for export and exhibit the greatest insularity. Unlike those devoted to shipping valuable high-demand raw commodities to core markets, such areas lack strong ties to homeland merchants, corporations, banks, and other institutions whose economic and political control work to direct production and restrict indigenous growth. Instead, permanent settlers practicing more diversified agriculture create an internally focused economy that promotes regional exchange and the rise of internal colonial markets as well as the growth of separate social and political institutions to manage and administrate affairs in the new country. The isolation that leads colonists to develop local resources also encourages the reinvestment of surpluses locally instead of returning wealth to the homeland. The rise of colonial elites surrounded by wealth gained from the fruits of their enterprise strengthens perceptions that the colony's business is centered there rather than in the homeland and that its residents' stake lies in their region's future. As a result, the interests of colonists often diverge from those of the core nation and create pressure for greater autonomy. The new economic orientation inherent in agricultural frontiers fosters the potential for change and independent development, which manifests itself in the nature of colonial settlement and the distinctive form of its patterning (Baldwin 1956; Gray 1976).

Agricultural frontiers experience profound change that creates a base for commercial production. As a new population settles the land and alters it to suit the needs of production, Native peoples are displaced, environments are modified, and a new infrastructure of processing, transportation, and communication arises to accommodate the demands of expanding trade. Farmers usually do not immigrate to escape the economy in which they have participated, but rather attempt to improve their position in it. Because they seek to replicate familiar economic structures, the regions they settle move toward full participation in commercial export exchange. Their evolution continues from first settlement through their becoming integral parts of the larger economy.

The process of *insular frontier colonization* creates a distinctive patterning of settlement. One aspect of this patterning is the arrangement of settlements on the land, a phenomenon closely related to the region's role as a producer of raw agricultural commodities. Such an endeavor encourages dispersed settlement, but transporting produce within and out of the region, promoting immigration and trade, and administering the region also require that a network of trade and communications link colonists. Because the colony's interests remain directed toward the homeland, this network usually takes on a dendritic form, connecting isolated clusters of interior settlements to an entrepôt that serves as the gateway to the region. Changes in transport efficiency are closely tied to colonial development as the structure of the transportation network evolves to promote more efficient regional and export trade among settlements that become more evenly distributed across the region over time. A complex network of routes connecting growing internal markets comes to dominate the region, reflecting its transition to full participation in the larger economy (Taffee, Morrill, and Gould 1963; Peet 1970–1971).

The size, form, and content of settlements constitute a second aspect of their patterning. These characteristics are influenced by the structure of the frontier economy and the manner in which it organizes and distributes activities in the colony. Because colonial production is initially in the hands of scattered immigrant farmers, these regions possess a low population density. Homesteads are distributed between fewer and smaller settlements than in stable settled areas. As a result, the integrative functions spread among a number of communities in the homeland are concentrated in a small number of settlements. Insular frontiers are characterized by an abbreviated settlement hierarchy centered around central places, called *frontier towns,* which possess important economic, social, and political institutions and serve as intermediate points connecting the entrepôt with smaller nucleated, semi-nucleated, and dispersed settlements in the hinterland. The uneven complexity of settlements in this hierarchy forms a colonization gradient, ranging from frontier towns through smaller places possessing progressively lesser functions (Casagrande, Thompson, and Young 1964). The gradient also reflects the structure of the trade and communications network and the central position of the frontier town. Although changing demographics and increasing economic complexity redistribute functions and alter the structure of settlement over time, frontier towns remain important places in the post-frontier era.

MODELING FRONTIER CHANGE

The process of insular colonization may be used as a basis for constructing a model of frontier change. This model examines the phenomena associated with the development of agricultural frontiers and expresses them in the form of several characteristics that may be used as an accurate predictive framework to explore the nature of this process in regions where it is likely to have occurred. Because the model's characteristics deal with organizational aspects of society that affected entire regions as well as the individual settlements within them, they form a set of hypotheses through which we may examine data at different levels. Recognizing the link between phenomena on different scales is important in the study of Camden as a settlement whose development was influenced by a larger process. The model may be organized around three broad characteristics (Lewis 1984a).

The first is the maintenance of a distinctive relationship between the colony and homeland. Because they remain dependent on the parent state for support and as a market for their produce, colonies retain strong economic, social, and political ties despite their insularity. Indeed, colonists often copy homeland cultural institutions and attempt to reproduce aspects of the society from which they came. Nonetheless, the initial adaptation to new environments, alien societies, and conditions of remoteness affects the pervasiveness of these ties and the manner in which the relationship is expressed.

Second, the unique organization of the colonial economy affects the distribution of activities and the nature of the settlements where they are conducted. An agricultural colonial region should possess the settlement types described in the colonization gradient and they should be arranged within a trade and communications network centered on an entrepôt linking the region to the parent state. As interior foci of economic, social, and political activities on the frontier, frontier towns play a central role on the frontier. Differing in composition from other settlements, they should be readily recognizable.

Finally, because colonies are transitional by nature, they are characterized by rapid and profound change. An expanding frontier economy, accompanied by the growth of regional social and political institutions, brings about changes in the function of settlements and alters the network linking them together. These changes should be observed at the regional level by changes in the structure and distribution of settlement, and at the settlement level by changes in their size, form, and composition.

EXPLORING COLONIZATION AT CAMDEN

Because the process described by the model of insular frontier colonization affected both the development of a region as well as its component parts, it could be examined at different *scales*. The vast geographical scope of colonization in the entire South Carolina backcountry made the implementation of a regional scale archaeological project difficult. Observing its material manifestations would involve an extraordinary and expensive effort. An archaeologist simply could not adequately survey the entire interior of South Carolina and dig up enough sites to examine colonization on a regional scale. One could, however, conduct excavations and record pertinent features associated with a settlement that played a key role in this process and whose form and content were shaped by the larger forces of insular colonization. As a central component of the backcountry frontier, Camden participated in this process and evolved with the growth of the region. I believed that Camden's role as a focus of regional change would be reflected in the nature of its archaeological record and that an examination of the colonial town site could be employed to demonstrate the occurrence of insular frontier colonization in the backcountry. The challenge arose in determining how to observe the operation of a regional process on the scale of an individual settlement.

The solution to this problem lay in understanding the manner in which the elements of the wider process affected the social unit represented by a central place. To what extent was Camden a microcosm of the backcountry and the forces that shaped it? The key to defining the link between the region and its components was the anthropological concept of *community*. Definitions of community stress the association between people and institutions and links them to the material world in geographical and social space (Arensberg 1961; Cusick 1995). As a center of activity on the frontier, Camden constituted the hub of a wider community that served as the basic unit of organization and transmission for the intrusive society and its culture. Although confined spatially to the boundaries of a settlement, Camden's institutions extended outward to encompass the much broader surrounding area occupied by the members of its community. As regional phenomena, these institutions were shaped by the forces of insular colonization and should embody the characteristics of the frontier model. The settlement in which these institutions were centered would have experienced the structural changes undergone by the area it served. In its role as a central settlement in the emerging South Carolina interior, I reasoned, Camden would provide a context in which to examine the process of insular frontier change in the backcountry. By tracing Camden's evolution over time, I believed that it would be possible to examine the wider processes that affected the settlement and transition of this region.

Observing the occurrence of insular colonization in the material record at Camden required a methodology capable of recognizing the characteristics of the process outlined in the model. Its success rested on establishing strong links between archaeological content and patterning and the behavior that produced them. These ties depended on compelling bridging arguments that, in turn, relied on analogies. Analogies are based on the premise that if two classes of phenomena are alike in some respects, they will be similar in others, and this line of reasoning is used to investigate the identity or function of unknown items by comparing them to those whose use is documented ethnographically or historically. In settlements occupied by literate societies, written documentation provides an advantage for drawing analogies at several levels. Historical documents, like ethnographic knowledge, may be employed at a practical level to identify objects and places, at a specific level to understand the function of artifacts and assemblages, and at a general level to examine broader events or processes. The wealth of contemporary written material relating to South Carolina provided the information necessary to identify the location of Camden and other settlements. Documents were also employed extensively to chronicle the historical trends in the backcountry that placed the study in context. Perhaps the most important use of the written record in understanding Camden's role as a frontier center, however, lay in its ability to create analogies linking the material record with activities that created it, activities associated with Camden's function as a frontier center.

The investigation of Camden, as a historical settlement, has involved the examination, assessment, and analysis of numerous documentary sources of information. These consist largely of primary sources: letters, diaries, accounts, reports, official records, and other documents produced at the time of the events and activities described, which were often written by those who took part in or who had firsthand knowledge of them. In this study, I have omitted reference to such sources, not because they are unimportant or insignificant, but because their inclusion would be awkward in a book focused on archaeological methodology. Citations appearing in the following chapters refer to pertinent secondary sources. Compiled by authors after the events described, they contain commentaries and interpretations based on a broader use of comparative data. Full citations for the primary sources and discussions of their contents may be found in these works. Those interested in exploring the historical sources should consult these secondary sources.

As a source of analogies for insular frontier change, historical documents permitted clarifying the function of the settlement through its layout and content.

They provided the comparative data necessary to translate the characteristics of the model into expectations for the material record. These expectations, in turn, predicted archaeological patterning linked to the occurrence of the colonization process on a settlement scale. Such patterning might be exhibited in architecture and activities, in their spatial arrangement, and the change of both over time. I anticipated that patterning in the material record would identify Camden's role as a frontier center and help examine insular colonization at the settlement scale. The results of archaeological analyses of data at the settlement level would not exhaust the potential of the material record at Camden; however, the information they provided only opened the door to a more in-depth investigation of this phenomenon.

In addition to observing the operation of a regional process at the scale of a settlement, archaeology can provide a basis for examining its impact within the settlement as well. Just as Camden comprised the core of a wider community, it contained numerous *households* wherein the activities of the community's members were carried out. Consisting of groups of individuals who regularly live or work together, households are the foundation of human societies. Households contain their most basic social and economic institutions, and the facilities occupied by households define functional spaces that form the fundamental units of a settlement. Studying households in Camden made it possible to do more than identify the activities that defined settlement function. It offered the opportunity of examining the adaptations of settlers, traders, merchants, craftspeople, soldiers, and others to conditions encountered on the backcountry frontier. Household archaeology at Camden concentrated on how frontier colonization impacted the groups of people who made up backcountry communities and held the potential to explore the ramifications of this process on the scale of individual behavior.

For nearly 40 years Camden has been a subject for archaeological research, the results of which have helped address both its own past and the nature of colonization in South Carolina's backcountry. Directed by a variety of goals, historical archaeologists have examined much of the site once occupied by the colonial town, explored related sites in the vicinity, and uncovered a tremendous amount of material evidence relating to this past settlement. These data have created an incomparable base from which to examine the form and content of Camden and its change over time. The analysis of the archaeological record was not intended to corroborate the occurrence of insular frontier change in the South Carolina backcountry nor to reveal Camden's importance in the development of this region. As the historical summary in Chapter 2 will show, these facts have already been established. Rather, I intended to demonstrate that, because of the town's central role in the evolution of the South Carolina backcountry, *Camden was influenced by the processes that shaped the larger region and should reflect these processes in microcosm.* Historical archaeologists have employed material data from Camden to examine insular frontier change on the scale of an individual settlement and used archaeological evidence to explore the process further on the level of particular households. This study will show how they designed their research to accomplish these tasks.

2/The Historical Context of Colonization in South Carolina

INTRODUCTION

Camden arose in the milieu of British colonization in South Carolina and must be seen in light of this larger development. Founded in 1670, the early colony remained confined largely to the lower coastal plain where colonists found conditions conducive to establishing a commercial export economy increasingly based on using slave labor for the large-scale production of rice. Although its European population was confined geographically, the colony's influence extended well into the interior. Trade for deerskins and slaves, together with intermittent warfare with and among aboriginal peoples, altered the native landscape and opened South Carolina's backcountry to settlement. These conditions encouraged interior colonization, but the frontier diverged sharply from the economy of the plantation coast and its historical trajectory took a markedly different course. The region's development followed a pattern associated with insular frontier colonization, a process that characterized agricultural expansion carried out under conditions of isolation and limited exchange. To understand the rise of the backcountry and the role of Camden, we must first examine the historical context in which it emerged.

THE ECONOMIC BACKDROP TO EXPANSION

By the third decade of the eighteenth century, the vast majority of South Carolina's European and African population lived in scattered settlements along the province's Atlantic seaboard. Here plantations arose along the region's wide coastal rivers and came to dominate settlement in the region. Driven by the great wealth promised by the increased demand for rice, planters moved rapidly toward specialized commercial production of this commodity, employing enslaved labor and increasingly more complex technologies to better exploit the lowcountry's hydraulic resources. The resulting growth in plantation agriculture also encouraged planters to occupy the best lands, a practice that created a landscape of dispersed settlements and one that restricted the range of economic opportunities for European immigrants to

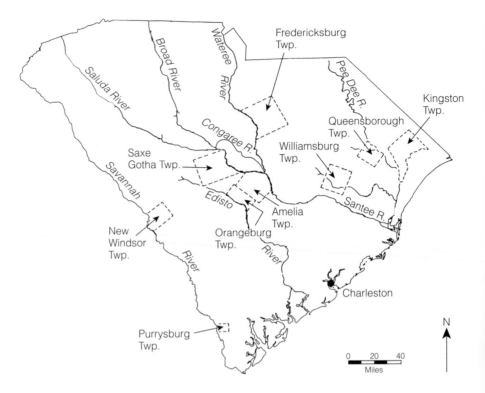

Figure 2.1 South Carolina in the eighteenth century, showing principal settlements and the townships established in 1731. This plan attempted to distribute European settlers across the entire backcountry by situating them in townships along all of the major river systems of the interior. Source: Petty (1943).

South Carolina. The growth and extensive scale of plantation production limited their presence in the agricultural economy of the lowcountry, while encouraging the proliferation of a captive black population (Clowse 1971; Coclanis 1989).

The wealth generated by the plantation economy passed through the entrepôt of Charleston (Figure 2.1). Export commodities and imported goods passed through its warehouses on their way to and from the ports of Europe and the Caribbean. As a major port on the Atlantic highway, Charleston was the center of trade and attracted merchants and the lawyers, shipbuilders, mechanics, and others who served them. It was also the entryway for immigrants and the portal through which travelers passed on their way in and out of the colony. The provincial seat of government lay there as well as that of the established church. The settlement grew rapidly as a focus of economic, political, and religious activities and acquired the retail shops, small manufacturing and repair facilities, inns, taverns, markets, and other services of an urban center. Eighteenth-century Charleston was South Carolina's chief city, easily eclipsing the smaller coastal ports of Georgetown and Beaufort as the center of the colony's wealth and the hub of its internal and external commercial activity (Rogers 1969).

An incredibly wealthy region, the South Carolina lowcountry possessed an economy that was founded with the expectation of export production and that grew in response to the expansion of international markets. By the early years of the eighteenth century, colonists began to amass capital and credit sufficient to curtail initial production based on land-extensive activities such as livestock herding, naval stores, lumber, deerskins, and foodstuffs to concentrate on growing rice for export (Gray 1933; Clowse 1971). A large-scale intensive form of agriculture, rice growing required high initial investment and managerial skill and attracted those possessing the wherewithal to provide both (Greene 1987). Planters invested in increasing numbers of slaves whose exploitation minimized production costs and maximized output of labor-intensive agriculture, the profits from which were enhanced by changing economic conditions. Rising commodity prices, the development of an internal riverine transport system that facilitated the movement of goods, increasing size of overseas markets, improvements in the communication of marketing information, a mortgage market that provided extensive credit, and a provincial fiscal policy that fostered the growth of an export-oriented staple economy all served to focus production in the lowcountry around lucrative specialized crops. As a result, the plantation economy of coastal South Carolina expanded rapidly and allowed the accumulation of tremendous wealth (McCusker and Menard 1985; Coclanis 1989). This booming lowcountry economy created a stable colonial presence in South Carolina, yet the narrow environmental requirements of rice growing restricted settlement to the major coastal rivers and left large portions of the region unoccupied, particularly the area north of the Santee (Petty 1943). Commercial agriculture constrained the geographical range of the colony and its weakness limited Britain's strategic influence on the southern Atlantic coast.

Although agricultural settlement of the lowcountry involved only a portion of the territory claimed by Great Britain, the impact of its development reached far beyond the boundaries of rice production. South Carolina's position relative to lands claimed by Spain to the south and France to the west placed the province in a vulnerable position, yet one strategic to British interests in North America. The situation was complicated further by the proximity of the country's aboriginal inhabitants, whose presence served both the economic and political interests of the province. Over a century of contact with European-introduced diseases had decimated coastal groups by 1670. Thus weakened, Native societies offered little resistance to the appropriation of their lands and resources, and their condition facilitated colonial expansion. Access to the interior allowed colonists to participate in an increasingly lucrative exchange with more distant Native peoples, and trade in deerskins soon became a major source of wealth. This activity also led to alliances that extended British influence into the territories that separated them from competing European colonial powers. Indian allies served as British surrogates in warfare to undermine the ambitions of France and Spain in North America. These conflicts served dual purposes. Indian captives became a valuable commodity for sale to planters constantly in need of labor. At the same time, the disruption of groups allied with rival European states in the Southeast accomplished the political end of destabilizing the security of their colonies. The defeat of a massive 1715 Indian uprising known as the Yamassee War sealed the fate of coastal peoples, accelerated the appropriation of Native lands, and opened the interior to extensive trade (Corkran 1970; Edgar 2000; Gallay 2002). The outcome of colonists' early experiences with Native peoples had important implications for South Carolina's subsequent growth. It provided a knowledge of the interior and its resources, increased the dependence of its aboriginal residents on colonial suppliers, eliminated the immediate threat posed by expansion, and provided a precedent for acquiring aboriginal lands. All of these set the stage for British settlement of the backcountry. Only a pretext was absent.

INTO THE BACKCOUNTRY

In 1730 Robert Johnson arrived as South Carolina's new royal governor with instructions from the Board of Trade to carry out a bold scheme to settle the interior. The board, which oversaw colonial affairs in America, sought to protect the increasingly valuable plantation colony by strengthening the British presence on the frontier. Fearing attack by the Spanish and French or their Indian allies, the interior settlements would provide a militia to defend the colony. The European immigrants recruited to populate these frontier settlements also helped balance the increasingly large population of African slaves concentrated in the lowcountry. To attract new settlers, the province offered them land grants based on household size and subsidies to relocate to one of several interior tracts. Situated along major interior drainages from the Savannah River in the south to the Pee Dee River near the North Carolina border, a number of townships were laid out with the intent of distributing small clusters of agricultural colonists across the entire length of the backcountry (Petty 1943; Weir 1983). South Carolina surveyed eight townships during the next decade and later added three more on the upper Savannah (Figure 2.1). The townships lay largely within the inner coastal plain, a well-drained, forested region whose loamy soils were perceived to be good agricultural land. These tracts served as magnets to immigrants, and pioneer settlement closely followed their distribution (Lewis 1984a; Kovacik and Winberry 1987).

The economic context of backcountry settlement differed substantially from that of the coastal region. Distance from the entrepôt of Charleston and the absence of an effective infrastructure for transportation and communications mitigated large-scale market production of agricultural commodities and promoted settlement by small farmers (Baldwin 1956). Such a region, offering few opportunities to amass capital rapidly and only limited possibilities for early return on investment, failed to attract commercial planters. The area, however, offered opportunities to those of limited means who were willing to defer entry into commercial production. Immigrants to the South Carolina interior, like those occupying other frontier regions on the eastern seaboard, did not seek isolation from the larger world economy. Most saw the resources of the frontier as a means to improve their material well-being and came there to take advantage of them. Lacking the start-up capital available to commercial producers, pioneers realized that they could improve their economic situation only by creating capital out of the land (Cronon 1983). Consequently, they concentrated on improving real assets in anticipation of eventually obtaining access to commercial markets, at which time they would realize the value of their investment. In the meantime, pioneer households worked to establish farms and small plantations and adopted a strategy of diversified production for rural exchange through regional markets (Nobles 1989; Kulikoff 1993).

The relative isolation of the backcountry frontier affected more than its economy. Distance and poor accessibility also prevented the establishment of larger national social, political, and religious institutions and encouraged pervasive social change. Regional administration and the organization of pioneer society depended less on the imposition of outside authority than on the rise of viable regional institutions shaped by the colonists' cultural traditions. In their absence, the household arose as the basic unit of organization. Households engaged in a variety of activities to exploit different resources to sustain themselves and exchange for other products. Most appear to have come with the intent of becoming farmers, but others turned to the exploitation of animal resources. Backcountry frontier communities included households engaged in hunting, herding, and raising a variety of cultigens (Meriwether 1940; Otto 1986). In the absence of external market demand, production was controlled by need rather than price, and distribution involved direct exchange of goods and services without an accumulation of wealth. Households engaged in unspecialized production possessed an organization flexible enough to adapt to the shifting needs of a developing region (Shammas 1982).

Households also served as initial political and religious institutions. Prior to 1769 the backcountry was without an effective administrative structure. Government offices and the court systems were centralized in Charleston, leaving local administration in the hands of justices of the peace, who lacked jurisdiction in criminal cases. Although churches and the militia helped maintain civil order among backcountry residents, they could not deal with the increased criminal activity that arose in response to the inequalities that accompanied agricultural expansion. Organized by elite households on the frontier, the Regulator Movement developed spontaneously as a grassroots organization to police the region and advocate the creation of necessary legal and administrative institutions (Brown 1963; Klein 1990). Despite its official establishment in South Carolina, the Church of England also failed to become a dominant force in backcountry religious life. Weak central ecclesiastical control, together with an official policy aimed at attracting Protestants regardless of their denomination, encouraged religious factionalism and the formation of charismatic churches in the interior. Churches played a central role in the lives of those living in a region lacking institutions of social integration, and their activities were commonly conducted in private homes by itinerant or lay leaders. Households comprised the basis for frontier churches and formed the backbone of the Presbyterian and Baptist denominations, which rose to dominate religious life in the backcountry (Brinsfield 1983).

Insular colonization shaped the nature of settlement in South Carolina's interior. The region's isolation gave rise to household-based institutions from which economic, social, and political organization in the backcountry emerged. They provided the means of integrating immigrants in an area of low population density into communities that consolidated the British presence on the frontier. Although these early communities represent an adaptation to the conditions encountered during the time of initial settlement, they also became the foundation for later development. Frontier communities are important to our understanding of the region's past because they are the baseline from which to measure all subsequent change. Historical sources can provide evidence about the organization of early communities, particularly with regard to the way in which it affected the patterning of settlement.

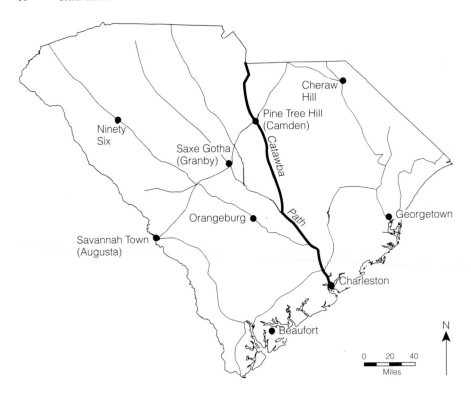

Figure 2.2 A network of principal roads stretched into South Carolina's interior by 1780. It provided communication between the frontier settlements and linked them to the entrepôt of Charleston. Source: Faden (1780).

How did these institutions shape the backcountry landscape? The opening of lands in the 11 new townships spread immigrants across the central interior of South Carolina. Protestant colonists from Britain, Germany, Switzerland, and France took up lands and soon extended their occupation well beyond the original township boundaries. Over time, an initial tendency to settle along the interior river valleys evolved into a more uniform distribution. The success of this widely dispersed agricultural settlement rested heavily on the creation of a viable frontier economy. Dependent on regional exchange to obtain the necessities of life, settlers developed networks of internal trade and communications. Such networks focused on small settlements such as Cheraw Hill on the Pee Dee, Saxe Gotha on the Congaree, Orangeburg on the Edisto, Ninety Six on the Saluda, Savannah Town on the river by the same name near present-day Augusta, and Pine Tree Hill on the Wateree (Figure 2.2). Branching out from these settlements, roads and paths provided farmers, hunters, herders, and traders access within the backcountry and, through the centers, linked area residents with the entrepôt. Large interior rivers and streams allowed further movement by the interior's new residents. Lacking direct water routes into the interior, Charleston became the hub for a dendritic system of major roads. Radiating outward from the entrepôt, these roads followed routes that originated with the Indian trade and served as arteries for immigration as well as for continuing exchange and communication with Native peoples of the interior. The patterning of early pioneer settlement reflected the importance of routes of movement. Analyses of the distributions of mills, militia muster locations, churches, settlement sites, and cemeteries have revealed that, although widely dispersed, settlement exhibited a strong tendency toward clustering that remained until mid-century. This distinctive patterning represented an adaptation to conditions encountered during the initial phase of settlement. Although emerging from transitory conditions, South Carolina's frontier landscape established a base for all subsequent settlement in the backcountry. It is to this landscape we must turn to understand colonial development in the Wateree Valley (Meriwether 1940; Lewis 1984a; Edgar 2000).

THE WATEREE VALLEY AND PINE TREE HILL

Pioneer settlement in the Wateree Valley followed routes of entry and access into the backcountry and achieved the greatest density around one key location. Land records indicate that early grantees favored locations along the river as well as those near the Catawba Path, a route connecting Charleston with the Catawba settlements. Pine Tree Hill arose on this road, at a point near the head of navigation on the Wateree (Figure 2.3). Samuel Wyly, the colonial agent to the

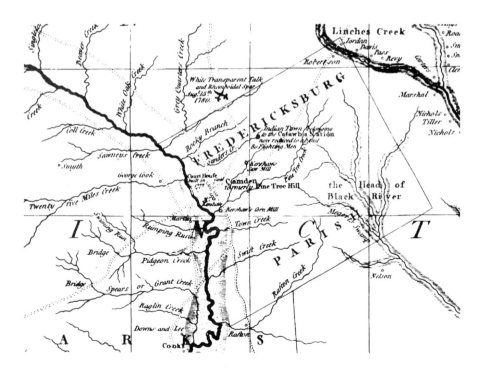

Figure 2.3 Pine Tree Hill/Camden in Fredericksburg Township in 1780. Situated at the head of navigation on the Wateree River, Camden also lay at the center of an overland network of roads connecting it to Charleston and other interior points. Source: Faden (1780).

Figure 2.4 The Wateree River near Pine Tree Hill. The view is down river looking towards Friends Neck, named for the region's early Quaker settlers.

Catawbas, established a store there in the early 1750s and it became a center for the deerskin trade. A dramatic upsurge in settlement occurred with the arrival of a group of Irish Quakers, who took up lands near Pine Tree Hill and erected their meeting house there. The location became the focus of social and religious activity for this rural community. Wyly soon erected grist- and sawmills nearby to accommodate the local demand for processing grain and lumber. These facilities drew pioneer farmers to Pine Tree Hill, which began to expand its economic role as a place of exchange (Figure 2.4). Although its market was regional in scope, the presence of early mills there made Pine Tree Hill a center for the redistribution of corn, wheat, barley flax, and garden crops; the sale of imported finished goods; and for tanning and the production of leather goods. Its central location and accessibility via water and overland routes enhanced the settlement's position as a strategic point for various other activities and made it an ideal location for further growth (Kirkland and Kennedy 1905; Meriwether 1940).

Pine Tree Hill's central position in the regional economy of the backcountry allowed it to take on the role of a "frontier town," the central settlement found in the interior of emerging agricultural regions. Frontier towns are necessary for the success of colonization because they provide the primary foci for economic, social, and political activity within the newly occupied areas. As the central points through which immigrant traffic and imports flow, these settlements become the places that collect and disseminate regional information as well as that passing between the colony and the homeland. Frontier towns position themselves well to attract formal institutions such as courts, jails, churches, customs warehouses, schools, stores, and other centralizing activities and become the largest settlements in the area of colonization (Casagrande, Thompson, and Young 1964). Pine Tree Hill became a frontier town in the years immediately preceding the American Revolution as outside forces began to restructure production and draw the Wateree Valley into the larger economy and replace the informal arrangements of the frontier period.

Rapid economic growth in the 1750s set the stage for increasing agricultural production in the backcountry, and a growing export market for wheat offered an opportunity to participate in the larger colonial economy. Frontier farmers were encouraged to cultivate this crop as a staple by a rise in the demand for foodstuffs in the British West Indies and a persistent need for imported flour in the South Carolina lowcountry (Ernst and Merrens 1973; McCusker and Menard 1985). Two developments, however, had to occur before they could take advantage of this commercial market. First, market agriculture rested on an increase in the scale of backcountry production. This, in turn, depended on the introduction of sufficient capital and organization. Entry into commercial production also depended on the availability of a means of transportation adequate to accommodate the increased volume of long-distance traffic. When these conditions were met in the early 1760s, the accompanying changes altered the function of Pine Tree Hill dramatically and enhanced its role as a frontier town. Camden's rise as a regional export center would also be reflected in the settlement's size, form, and composition.

CAMDEN AND THE EMERGENCE
OF A TRANSITIONAL ECONOMY

In 1758 Joseph Kershaw arrived at Pine Tree Hill as the representative of the Charleston mercantile partnership of Ancrum, Lance, and Loocock. Their decision to send an agent into the backcountry rested on the growing perception among lowcountry merchants that the interior possessed a largely untapped market for the finished goods they imported and constituted a vast source of raw commodities. Wanting to expand their business, they planned to establish facilities to collect and process wheat in the interior so that they could ship milled flour to their storehouses in Charleston. Long engaged in export trade, the firm possessed the capital and resources to invest in backcountry commercial production. Pine Tree Hill's location and access to routes of travel suited the interests of these outside investors who sought a strategic site for their activities. Their determination to place their facilities there initiated the economic transformation of the Wateree Valley.

Ancrum, Lance, and Loocock established a base of operations at Pine Tree Hill. After acquiring Wyly's store and mills, they built additional facilities to expand grain production and storage. The firm exported flour to the entrepôt as early as 1760 and their business grew rapidly in the following decade. Joseph Kershaw, together with his brother Ely and John Chesnut, became partners and managed business in the backcountry. As resident managers of a reorganized firm known as Kershaw and Company, they increased the volume of business by extending the network of stores to Cheraw on the upper Pee Dee drainage and

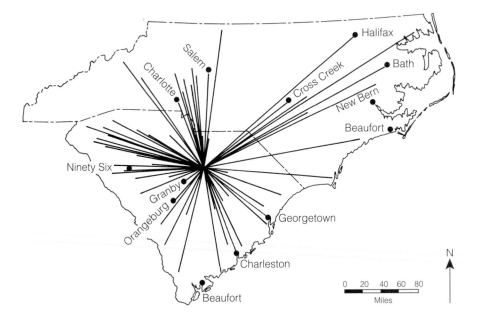

Figure 2.5 The geographical extent of trade conducted by Joseph Kershaw and his associates during the 1770s. Store account books revealed their widespread business in the backcountry. Source: Schulz (1976).

Granby on the Congaree. During the next decade, their economic influence spread over a wide portion of the interior, encompassing a hinterland with a radius of 60 miles from Pine Tree Hill, with lesser activity occurring at nearly twice that distance (Figure 2.5). Kershaw and Company also promoted the development of the area through extensive speculative land dealings, particularly in the vicinity of Pine Tree Hill. The settlement's central role in regional trade attracted additional activities. By the early 1770s the town included stores, taverns, a bakery, a brewery, a distillery, and a brickyard, and was home to a tailor, two blacksmiths, three merchants, a potter, and a lawyer. The company's business prospered and Joseph Kershaw became Pine Tree Hill's wealthiest resident. In addition to his mills and store, his ownership of a tobacco warehouse and indigo works allowed him to capture control of two additional emerging frontier exports. Kershaw's large Georgian mansion, "his great white house," newly constructed on a hill east of town, symbolized his success as well as the town's growing ties with the greater British colonial world (Figure 2.6). The dissolution of Kershaw and Company in 1774 provided capital for the former partners to invest in this growing array of activities; however, the distribution of its assets also benefited a wider group of merchants and entrepreneurs, who sought to take advantage of the opportunities offered by the growing commercial economy (Kirkland and Kennedy 1905; Schulz 1976).

Expanding trade required a transportation system adequate to ship bulk products directly to the entrepôt, and colonists made efforts to open both overland and water routes to the Wateree Valley. The Catawba Path offered the most

Historic Camden Revolutionary War Site

Figure 2.6 Joseph Kershaw's Camden mansion as it looked in the 1840s. The view is looking north with the antebellum town in the distance.

direct route, and this road was improved for wagon traffic as far as Pine Tree Hill by 1755 and extended north to the Waxhaws within five years. By the 1770s, roads also provided lateral connections to other points in the backcountry (Figure 2.7). The Wateree River also linked Pine Tree Hill with a large portion of the interior and, with major obstacles removed, offered direct access to the sea. Its outlet lay far from Charleston, however, mitigating its effective use as a transportation route. The additional cost of transferring cargo to coastal vessels for its final movement to this port discouraged a high volume of river traffic during the eighteenth century (Meriwether 1940). Neither overland nor water transport offered the Wateree Valley ideal access to entrepôt markets, but the value of merchandise carried on the interior roads was adequate to justify the cost of transportation during the 1760s. Together with the building of an enlarged processing infrastructure, the creation of an overland road network supported the economic emergence of the backcountry and the development of Pine Tree Hill as its principal settlement.

Capital investment and improvements in transportation enmeshed the inhabitants of Pine Tree Hill more tightly within the fabric of the larger economy in British North America and enveloped the frontier settlement more closely within its political milieu as well. The town's growing importance in South Carolina did not go unnoticed by those who recognized the advantages of employing ideological symbolism to associate their settlement with larger currents of change within the empire. In 1768 the settlement became Camden, apparently at the urging of its leading merchant, Joseph Kershaw. Named in honor of Charles Pratt (Baron Camden), a defender of colonial rights against unrepresented taxation, the change

Figure 2.7 Transportation by wagon in the backcountry. The drawing depicts the Catawba Path where it crossed Sanders Creek just north of Camden. This important overland route provided interior settlements with access to this growing frontier town and connected it directly with the port of Charleston. Source: Lossing (1860).

linked the settlement, or at least its emerging commercial class, with the political interests of elites elsewhere in the province (Kirkland and Kennedy 1905).

The emergence of Pine Tree Hill as a center of trade in the 1760s marked the rise of formal economic institutions in an area once dominated by household exchange. Similarly, the settlement's political integration within the province also brought about formalization in other aspects of frontier society. The Regulator Movement, which had arisen in response to the absence of official mechanisms to control increasing criminal behavior in the interior, provided the impetus for the provincial government to create a number of backcountry judicial districts. Each of these regions encompassed a portion of the province and placed courthouses and jails and the officials who maintained them at central locations in the frontier. Their presence not only facilitated the apprehension and punishment of malefactors, but also greatly shortened the time and eased the difficulty involved in carrying out land transactions, legal procedures, and other actions requiring government sanction. The Circuit Court Act of 1769 established Camden as the seat of the Camden Judicial District, an extensive area stretching from the center of the province to its northern boundary. Camden's growing role as an administrative center attracted other urban activities as well. In 1774 biannual fairs were established by law at Camden, and regular sites were set aside for these and regular markets. Residents constructed several churches there prior to the American Revolution, by which time Camden had become a substantial settlement housing the centralizing institutions for a substantial portion of the backcountry (Lewis 1998).

At the time of its emergence as an urban center, Camden was a small cluster of structures that stretched along the Catawba Path and extended outward along several intersecting roads. Its buildings and lots were arranged according to a

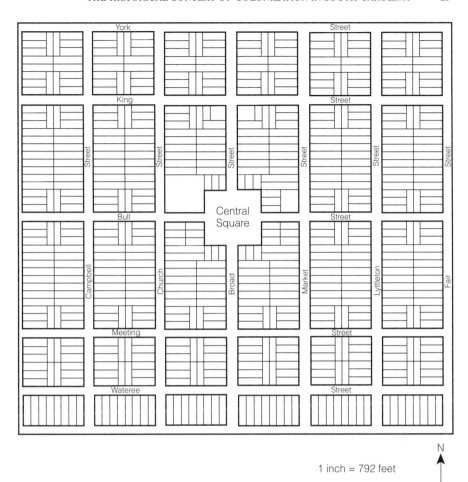

Figure 2.8 Plan of Camden surveyed in 1771. The Catawba Path passed through the center of town as Broad Street and the central square marked the northern boundary of the 1780 settlement. Source: Cooper (1839).

formal gridiron plan surveyed in 1771 (Figure 2.8). Intended to facilitate the orderly development of the town site, the plan divided Camden into a number of rectangular blocks, each containing deep, narrow lots. A central square lay at the confluence of two major roads. Camden's design had previously been employed by planners of other cities in British colonial America, including Charleston and Philadelphia. Although its principal elements originated in Europe, colonials found the ability of the gridiron plan to accommodate rapid settlement by large numbers of people well suited to conditions encountered in fast-growing American cities (Reps 1965). Hoping for an upsurge in growth as the frontier era came to an end, Camden's proprietors adopted an arrangement suitable for a central place in the backcountry. In emulation of the entrepôt, they not only copied its design but duplicated the names of Charleston's major streets. Situated along these avenues, all of the principal state institutions were placed in direct line with the central square. The courthouse and jail lay to the north on Broad Street, while Bull Street led eastward to the market and fair grounds and westward to the Anglican Church tract. Each institution represented a distinctive centralizing entity, and their juxtaposition to Camden's square symbolized the town's new role as a focus of political, economic, and religious authority, activities that unmistakably identified its role as a key settlement on the developing post-frontier landscape (Lewis 1998).

By the 1770s, the changes responsible for Camden's growth had begun to transform the backcountry. A growing export-oriented economy based on specialized crops affected both the scale and organization of agricultural production. Plantation farming increased agricultural output and lowered per unit costs of production, but it also altered the nature of rural society by promoting a hierarchical order based on wealth and race. Capital generated by new commercial endeavors facilitated investment in land, technology, and enslaved labor. The introduction and growth of a large enslaved population of African descent dramatically changed the social demography of the interior, just as the introduction of a new settlement form associated with large-scale specialized production began to restructure agriculture in the region (Klein 1990). As plantation farming assumed a more important role in the backcountry, it brought profound changes to the cultural landscape of the Wateree Valley.

THE INTERIM OF WAR

Camden's rise as a central place ensured its future growth as the economy of the backcountry matured. As a focus of social and political activity lying in the center of an extensive transportation network, the town also became a magnet for other forces that shaped the region. In the last quarter of the eighteenth century, 13 of Britain's North American colonies formally separated from the mother country at the close of a lengthy and often bitter war for independence. Perhaps nowhere was this conflict more pervasive and its effect farther reaching than in the Carolinas. Here rival loyalist and rebel factions vied for dominance for nearly five years, after which invasion and occupation by a British army exacerbated simmering animosities into a vicious civil war that devastated the backcountry and made South Carolina's interior a major seat of conflict in the southern colonies (Buchanan 1997; Edgar 2001). Although the American Revolution did not obliterate Camden's significance as a regional center, it nonetheless impacted the town and its inhabitants dramatically and left an indelible mark on the settlement's physical characteristics.

The American Revolution in South Carolina emphasized differences that separated the established commercial rice economy of the lowcountry and an interior still in a state of transition in the 1770s. Disagreement between the planter elites, who dominated the provincial assembly, and the royal government arose over taxation and control of funds, issues that remained largely irrelevant to most inhabitants of the backcountry. Political relations deteriorated in the early years of the decade, crippling the British administration and supplanting it with a provincial government. The power of the planter elite allowed the rebels to effectively control the coastal region; however, their influence in the backcountry was less certain. Still largely disenfranchised by a colonial government that often ignored their interests, most residents of the interior did not unquestioningly follow a cause with whose adherents they felt little connection. Influenced by a variety of motives, backcountry settlers' loyalties fell on both sides of this issue. Not surprisingly, the rising class of inland merchants and planters, whose fortunes were most closely tied to the developing export economy, most consistently sided with the rebel interests of the lowcountry (Klein 1990; Edgar 2001).

Among these frontier elites were the Kershaw brothers and John Chesnut. Joseph Kershaw actively participated in a committee sent by the Provincial Congress to counter the influence of prominent backcountry loyalists and erected a magazine at Camden to store munitions for provincial forces. He organized and led a militia unit, in which his brother Ely and Chesnut both served, in the ensuing campaigns to secure the region from Loyalist interests. Their participation in the defense of Charleston against an invading British army in 1780 led to their capture on the city's surrender. The Kershaw brothers were exiled to Bermuda and Chesnut's parole confined him to his Camden plantation. Despite their circumstances and the traumatic military occupation of Camden during the following year, Joseph Kershaw and John Chesnut survived and reestablished their business activities after the war. Their economic and political leadership proved crucial to completing the transition to commercial agriculture in the Wateree Valley, and Camden rose again from the devastating effects of the war. Despite the postwar recovery, the experience of 1780–1781 left an indelible imprint on both the settlement and its residents.

Camden's strategic position in the interior transportation system ensured that it would play an important role in British plans to control the province (Figure 2.9). In a campaign intended to open a second front by occupying the southern colonies, the army captured the ports of Charleston and Savannah and moved inland to establish a chain of strong points at central inland locations. Several interior settlements became bases for securing the province, pacifying its inhabitants, and supporting an invasion of the neighboring provinces. As a gateway to the upper Pee Dee drainage and central North Carolina, Camden became the base for launching the northern expedition. Following its occupation, the town became a fortified garrison. Military units replaced its civilian residents and its buildings were converted to military use. A palisade surrounding the settlement and a protective ring of redoubts made Camden an impregnable post, and its garrison successfully withstood two attacks by American armies during the coming year. Despite these victories, the British position in South Carolina became increasingly untenable. The military presence in the backcountry, intended as a magnet for loyalist support, inflamed earlier animosities and polarized its residents. Rebel opposition galvanized around partisan leaders, and the region became engulfed in open civil war characterized by revenge and retribution on both sides. British strength in South Carolina waned with the removal of a major portion of the army to invade North Carolina and Virginia and the decline of loyalist support. Although still too weak to openly challenge British forces on a traditional battlefield, the Americans adopted the unconventional methods of guerrilla warfare to successfully vanquish smaller forces and inflict irreplaceable losses even when defeated. Unable to maintain control of the backcountry,

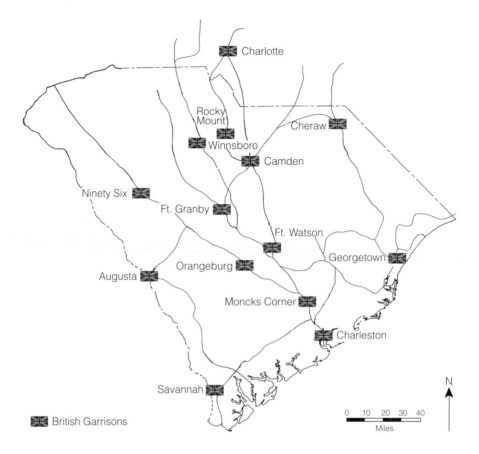

Figure 2.9 Major British garrisons in South Carolina, 1780–1781. Camden's central location in the road network of the backcountry gave it a strategic role in supporting military operations in the region. Source: Lewis (1984a).

British forces abandoned their interior posts and withdrew to Charleston in the spring of 1781. On leaving Camden, they destroyed their baggage, stores, and defensive works, as well as the jail, nearby mills, and some of the buildings in the town (Weigley 1970; Buchanan 1997; Edgar 2001).

A contemporary American military map provides our only image of eighteenth-century Camden. It reveals a town consisting of about 20 structures arranged along Broad Street and several perpendicular side streets (Figure 2.10). Seven orderly clusters of smaller structures, whose arrangement suggests the huts erected for quarters during the military occupation, paralleled their orientation. All were surrounded by a rectangular palisade that constituted the main defensive work. Six redoubts, each protected by a ditch and abatis, encircled the settlement. One, containing the jail, lay to the north along the Catawba Path. A palisade enclosed Joseph Kershaw's mansion to the east of the settlement, and in Camden's southeastern corner, the magazine was enclosed by a wall and ditch. South of town, two structures surrounded by a palisade were situated along Catawba Path. Although not drawn to a consistent scale, features on this

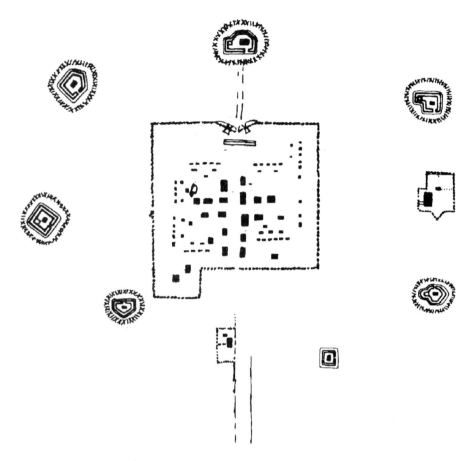

Figure 2.10 The fortified settlement of Camden in 1781. The jail was surrounded by the northernmost redoubt and Joseph Kershaw's mansion lay within the palisaded enclosure east of the settlement. A separate fortification protected the powder magazine southeast of town. The layout of larger buildings defined the course of Broad Street as well as an unnamed cross street leading toward the Kershaw House. The location of the brewery in southwestern Camden necessitated an extension of the town palisade to protect this structure. Source: Nathanael Greene Papers (1781).

map could be compared with earlier town plats and other written descriptions to identify the locations of particular structures and activities associated with Pine Tree Hill and Camden.

RECOVERY, CHANGE, AND ABANDONMENT

In spite of the destruction and dislocation caused by the Revolutionary War and the poor economic conditions associated with the depression that followed, Camden recovered relatively rapidly and regained its position as a focus of interior commerce. The last two decades of the century also witnessed the rebuilding and expansion of flour milling as the town assumed its former prominence as an agricultural processing center. Additional produce including tobacco, indigo, beef, pork, and lumber passed through Camden, and small industries such as boat building, brick making, tanning, and brewing arose there. Camden's retail business developed when a number of merchants located there and at least two taverns were in operation. Craftspeople, including a watchmaker, a printer, a saddler, a silversmith, a tin worker, boot and shoemakers, a hatmaker, and a blacksmith set up businesses there, and a lawyer and two doctors opened offices in the postwar settlement. In 1800 Camden remained the largest and most important settlement in the South Carolina backcountry (Drayton 1802; Kirkland and Kennedy 1926; Schulz 1972).

Several important changes contributed to Camden's postwar growth. Of particular importance were improvements in water transportation that facilitated export trade. The Santee canal was completed in 1800. By linking the Santee River, into which the Wateree flowed, and the Cooper, which entered Charleston harbor, the canal permitted cargoes from the interior to be shipped by boat directly to South Carolina's principal port. The early years of the nineteenth century also witnessed an expansion in the size and scale of commercial agriculture with the introduction of cotton as a viable crop. Easily processed with the recently introduced Whitney gin, cotton increased the profitability of farming and encouraged the growth of plantation agriculture. It rapidly became South Carolina's leading export staple and began to supplant earlier commercial crops. As the state's principal interior market, Camden had become an important collecting and shipping point for cotton by 1820 (Mills 1826; MacGill 1917; Kirkland and Kennedy 1926).

The growth of South Carolina's commercial agricultural economy that bolstered Camden's success also brought with it the seeds of decline. The canals and other river improvements that opened new avenues of trade to the interior increased the importance of those settlements centrally located in the riverine network. The new state capital of Columbia, situated at the confluence of the Broad and Saluda Rivers, was particularly well positioned to capture the trade of the central interior. The completion of a state turnpike through Columbia further enhanced the capital's importance as a transportation hub by the 1820s, and the water power provided by the recently completed Columbia Canal encouraged industrial development there. As Columbia's star rose, Camden's expansion slowed dramatically and the settlement assumed the role of smaller regional trading center, one of several in the South Carolina backcountry (Moore 1993; Edgar 2000).

Camden's postwar development brought dramatic changes to the early settlement in the closing years of the eighteenth century. Although residents reoccupied the original town site south of Bull Street, its proximity to the swamplands along Pine Tree Creek increased perceptions of its unhealthiness and many newcomers chose to settle farther north. New construction began to avoid the old town altogether, and by 1810 Camden's business district was situated around the old courthouse square. By the 1820s, only Joseph Kershaw's old mansion marked the location of the old town. Its site had become agricultural fields, under which the material remains of the early settlement survived relatively undisturbed for the next century and a half.

3/The Development
of Archaeological Research
at Camden

INTRODUCTION

When I began my research at Camden in 1974, I had the advantage of drawing on the work of several other archaeologists who had previously conducted excavations there. Although their efforts had not been directed at questions of colonization, they nevertheless contributed to the analyses on which this study is based. The archaeologists who carried out the earlier work were interested in a number of different questions that shaped the research designs they employed. Their designs guided the location of their excavations as well as the techniques used to gather evidence, which, in turn, affected both the data produced and the conclusions they derived. Regardless of their orientation, the results of the earlier archaeology added to existing knowledge of the early settlement and generated information that helped design the investigations that followed. My work at Camden drew on and incorporated the conclusions of the earlier investigations, and a review of their results helps provide a context for later archaeological work.

THE IMPORTANCE OF THE AMERICAN REVOLUTION

As one of the original 13 states, South Carolina has a long and eventful history and maintains strong ties with its past. Connections between historic events and the present are direct and strong and have played a key role in defining the state's character. It may be argued that the seminal historical experience in its development is the American Revolution, out of which came national independence and a legacy of suffering and triumph over superior odds. Since the middle of the nineteenth century, historic preservationists in the United States have focused their attention on sites associated with the Revolution, and this tradition often involved archaeological investigation designed to reveal material evidence of structures, earthworks, and other features related to these places. Indeed, supplementing such specific research became a major focus of the emerging field of historical archaeology (King, Hickman, and Berg 1977; Orser and Fagan 1995).

Figure 3.1 The American Revolution continues to play an important role in the celebration of Camden's past. The historical park frequently hosts events commemorating battles and other military activities in the backcountry. Here costumed reenactors have erected a camp at the historical park. The site of colonial town lies to the west.

Camden's role in the Revolutionary War piqued the interest of historians and preservationists, who turned to archaeology to provide tangible evidence of the town's role in this critical period.

The American Revolution has long dominated the consciousness of those familiar with Camden's history (Figure 3.1). When local historians Thomas J. Kirkland and Robert M. Kennedy compiled their monumental history of Camden in 1905, the war and its aftermath absorbed three-quarters of its more than 400 pages. Unlike other sites associated with the conflict, however, Camden had no recognizable features to link it with its past. No monuments marked the location of the fortified garrison that had played so important a role in this struggle. Anxious to rectify this situation, residents sought to acquire and investigate the site of the early settlement. In 1967 Richard and Margaret Lloyd provided funding to establish the Camden District Heritage Foundation, a nonprofit organization committed to raising funds to acquire and preserve the town site and support research there. The state legislature created the Camden Historical Commission in 1969 to develop and operate the historic property, called Historic Camden (Calmes 1968a; Santee-Wateree Regional Planning Council 1972).

The initial interest in Camden's role in the American Revolution guided the early archaeological work there. This research took the form of a series of large and small projects aimed at discovering and exploring architectural features associated with the town's fortifications. This work focused on the powder magazine constructed by Joseph Kershaw, the Kershaw House palisade, and the palisade and redoubts surrounding the town. Because all of them were constructed within a settlement that preceded their existence, these wartime features were part of a

site that encompassed much more than the fortifications themselves. The archaeology carried out to explore the Camden fortifications also unearthed structures,
artifacts, and other material evidence associated with the early town and its
inhabitants. Indeed, this early work not only helped establish Camden's form and
boundaries, but also contributed material data that proved useful in interpreting
the nature of the settlement's occupation before and after the war.

THE CAMDEN FORTIFICATIONS

The earliest excavations at Camden centered on the discovery of Joseph
Kershaw's powder magazine, a 1777 structure closely associated with the war
and Camden's most prominent patriot (Figure 3.2). Guided by a 1796 plat and
twentieth-century aerial photographs, a local historian, Reverend Millard
H. Osborne, explored a portion of the southeastern part of the town site in 1963
and 1964. His discovery of fill and features containing brick rubble led to further
investigations at this locality. In the summer of 1965 Elizabeth Ralph of the
Applied Science Center for Archaeology at the University of Pennsylvania conducted proton magnetometer surveys at Camden. Her discovery of several anom-
alies in this vicinity suggested the presence of additional subsurface structural
features. In an effort to evaluate these findings, William E. Edwards, Director of
the South Carolina Department of Archaeology, conducted test excavations that
yielded additional structural debris (Ralph and Börstling 1965; Calmes 1968a).
The newly created Camden District Heritage Foundation set about the task of

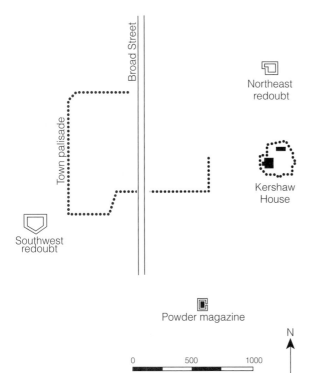

*Figure 3.2 British
fortifications at
Camden revealed by
archaeological
investigations.
Source: Lewis (1977).*

systematically investigating this site. Alan Calmes, who served as its research director, initiated large-scale excavations at the powder magazine in the late summer of 1967. Using the brick features discovered earlier as a guide, he and his crew removed the layer of plowed soil in the surrounding area and exposed the foundation trenches of the walls, the floor of the structure, and the surrounding defensive ditch. Both its architecture as well as the presence of black powder, munitions, and other eighteenth-century artifacts at the bottom of the ditch clearly identified the function of the building. Calmes noted that the orientation of the magazine was 2 degrees west of north, exactly the same alignment as the town grid surveyed in 1771. Built as part of the settlement well before the British occupation of South Carolina, the powder magazine was carefully laid out in accordance with Camden's urban plan. With its discovery, archaeologists could now estimate the positions of other features on the military map and expand their investigations of the fortifications (Calmes 1968b).

The location of the magazine allowed Calmes to calculate the position of other fortifications situated on the eastern side of Camden. The first fortification feature examined was the palisade surrounding Joseph Kershaw's mansion (Figure 3.2). Because the large house remained standing until 1865, its location on Lyttleton Street was well known and brick rubble unearthed by agricultural activity provided researchers a point from which to begin a search. The 1965 soil resistivity survey discovered a promising area that Calmes explored three years later. His trenches revealed the foundations of the structure as well as the line of the palisade wall in front of the Kershaw House. Following a short hiatus, Robert N. Strickland continued archaeological investigations at the Kershaw House under the sponsorship of the Camden District Heritage Foundation. In 1970, he expanded the earlier excavations in order to ascertain the size of the fortified area. His efforts exposed the line of the palisade wall and revealed a more complex plan than that shown on the 1781 map (Figure 3.3). A well-designed structure, the Kershaw House palisade employed irregular angles to take advantage of the site's uneven terrain and included two triangular bastions to provide enfilading fire, along its longest walls (Strickland 1971).

A second fortification, the northeast redoubt, lay directly north of the Kershaw House and consisted of a magazine enclosed by an L-shaped wall and ditch (Figure 3.2). Alan Calmes estimated its distance from the Kershaw House and in 1968 excavated a north-south trench in search of architectural features in the subsoil. Just southeast of the corner of modern Bull and Lyttleton Streets, he discovered a defensive ditch together with evidence for a wall and firing steps and expanded his excavations to expose the defensive ditch. Although Calmes's work revealed that much of this fortification lay beneath modern roadways and perhaps had been destroyed during their construction, it clearly defined the northeastern point of the town fortifications and raised hopes that other defensive structures might be found. The following year Robert Strickland expanded Calmes's excavations, exposing the entire area of the fortification and the remainder of the ditch surrounding it. His work revealed the plan of the fortification and indicated that it was abandoned immediately after the military occupation. His findings confirmed documentary accounts of the rapid destruction of the "British works" immediately following the departure of the occupying troops (Strickland 1971).

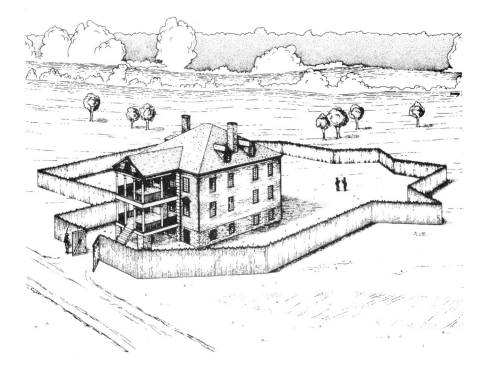

Figure 3.3 Conjectural bird's-eye view of the Kershaw House and the palisade that was erected to fortify it during the British military occupation of Camden in 1780–1781. Illustration by Darby Erd courtesy South Carolina Institute of Archaeology and Anthropology, University of South Carolina.

Following his discovery of the northeast redoubt, Alan Calmes turned his attention to the remaining town fortifications. Because the 1781 military map of Camden showed the placement of all the redoubts relative to the palisade surrounding the town, he concluded that locating the wall would be the key to finding the sites of these structures. He searched for the wall footing in several separate locations, intersecting its southeastern corner, its northwestern corner, and the southern portion of its western line. Modern construction covered the northeastern portion of the wall and made it inaccessible for archaeology. Nevertheless, his excavations indicated that the plan of the palisade conformed to that shown on the military map with the addition of a diagonal section in its northwestern corner (Figure 3.2). In locating this defensive work, Calmes's excavations revealed Camden's boundaries in 1780 and delimited the spatial extent of the colonial town.

In 1970, Robert Strickland examined a portion of the town palisade in greater detail. After locating the southeastern corner of this feature, he exposed a large portion of the palisade trench in which post molds bore evidence of its construction. As Strickland's crew exposed the stratigraphy along a 440-foot length of the south wall, he observed a remarkable change in the topography of this portion of the colonial town. The uneven thickness of the fill and the irregular depth of the trench indicated that the eighteenth-century ground level was higher at both Broad Street and Market Street. It also showed that a depression approximately

6 feet below the present surface lay between them. At its lowest point he found a large, rectangular pit containing several British "Brown Bess" muskets, bayonets, balls, gunflints, and gun parts. The pit's location and the presence of water-born fill implied that its contents had been quickly discarded, presumably as the army jettisoned excess stores when it rapidly abandoned Camden. But the presence of dramatic topographic variation within the town had greater significance because the wet conditions associated with it are likely to have deterred occupation of this portion of the settlement. This consideration had important implications for later investigations of the town site (Strickland 1971).

Calmes's success in locating the powder magazine, the Kershaw House, and the northeast redoubt led him to search for the remaining four redoubts shown on the military map. The northernmost redoubt surrounding the jail lay well north of the palisaded town. On private property, the site was occupied by modern buildings, the presence of which made it inaccessible for archaeological exploration in 1968. Unable to examine this site, Calmes began his search for fortifications elsewhere. With great difficulty he explored a heavily overgrown area south of the Kershaw House site for the southeast redoubt without success. The suspected redoubt site was covered by debris from a more recent city dump, where subsequent earthmoving activity had disturbed the original surface and destroyed evidence of earlier occupations. Next Calmes attempted to find the three redoubts lying on the west side of Camden. Again using the military map as a guide, his crew excavated a network of trenches in the likely locations of these fortifications. Although he found no evidence for those situated west and northwest of the town, his excavations revealed portions of the ditch surrounding the southwest redoubt (Figure 3.2). Situated near the early town cemetery, this structure was not examined further (Calmes 1968b).

Calmes's and Strickland's archaeological investigations of the Camden fortifications were successful in several ways. First, they accomplished their goal of discovering structures and artifacts associated with the Revolutionary War and provided evidence useful in developing interpretive exhibits relating to this portion of the town's history. Although the design of this research was narrowly focused on examining a short, albeit dramatic, episode of Camden's development, the archaeology had useful implications for later studies of social change. Because the existing settlement of Camden became a military garrison in 1780, its size and form dictated the layout of the works erected to defend it. In discovering their locations, these investigations delineated the spatial boundaries of the prewar colonial town and revealed that later settlement had not expanded eastward, westward, or southward. They also demonstrated that material remains of the early settlement remained largely undisturbed. These findings assisted me in determining the feasibility of archaeological investigations within the town and aided the design and implementation of my work. One other aspect of the early research would also play an important role in later analyses.

THE KERSHAW HOUSE

The Kershaw House had been enclosed by an element of the 1781 fortifications and it became a second focus of the early archaeology at Camden. Alan Calmes's discovery of the house foundations in 1968 revealed the remains of

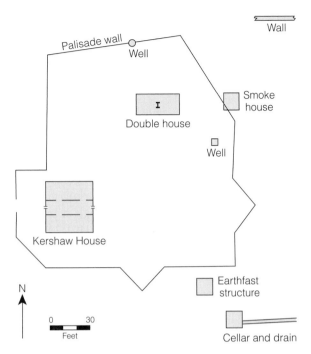

Figure 3.4 Structures and architectural features discovered by Calmes's and Strickland's archaeological investigations conducted at the Kershaw House from 1968 to 1973. Source: Lewis (1977).

a large rectangular building with a central hallway, front portico, and rear porch. Its orientation of 2 degrees west of north matched that of the powder magazine and conformed to the city street plan of 1771. The similar alignment of these two structures implied that orientation would be an important factor in identifying buildings constructed in the late 1770s. Guided by the results of Calmes's work, Robert Strickland began an extensive investigation of the area surrounding the Kershaw House in 1971. During the first excavation season, he examined the yard area inside the palisade. Assuming that archaeological materials contained in the plowed zone covering the site no longer retained their original context, he removed and discarded this layer in order to expose subsurface features likely to contain undisturbed cultural deposits. This project unearthed many structural features that comprised the Kershaw House complex (Figure 3.4). These features included a building with a central fireplace hearth, a square structure on a brick foundation, a small earthfast building, and two wells. The great number of pits and postholes Strickland found could not be excavated during the current field project, and he completed this task as part of the following two years' work. The 1972 investigations extended well outside the palisaded area. In searching for evidence of a wider Revolutionary War occupation in this area, he examined much of the high ground on which the Kershaw House rested. This massive endeavor found only additional structural remains associated with the house complex, a brick wall northeast of the house and a brick cellar and associated drainage trench lying just outside the southeast corner of the palisade. Strickland devoted the 1973 field season to excavating these structures and the unexamined features from the 1971 project (Strickland 1976).

   In four field seasons, Robert Strickland and his crews completed an immense archaeological undertaking at the Kershaw House site, the results of which provided the administrators of Historic Camden crucial information to begin developing the old town site as a historical park. This project, together with Alan Calmes's work six years earlier, concluded the first phase of archaeology at Camden. The two archaeologists' combined endeavors served as a basis for reconstructions and interpretive exhibits intended to orient visitors to the Revolutionary War occupation of Camden and help them visualize and comprehend its military aspects. A focus on architecturally oriented interpretation limited to a singular phase of Camden's past, however, restricted the scope of their research. Intended to understand the military fortifications of 1780–1781, the early archaeological work employed excavation techniques and analyses of material evidence intended to discover, identify, and describe these features. Although successful in achieving these goals, this research ignored other aspects about Camden's past and its results left many questions about its history unanswered. The events of the wartime occupation had a dramatic impact on the town and its inhabitants, but they were only a brief interlude in its larger historical development. Questions about the equally profound processes that gave rise to the colonial settlement and shaped its growth were also well worth examining through an analysis of Camden's material remains. To address the settlement's role on the backcountry frontier, however, required that one develop a research design directed at this topic specifically. Although such a design would require new excavations aimed at acquiring additional data, it might also demand a reexamination of evidence gathered in the early fieldwork.

SETTLEMENT ARCHAEOLOGY AT CAMDEN: DEFINING THE SETTLEMENT IN TIME AND SPACE

In the fall of 1974 archaeological investigations moved into the town site of Camden for the first time. This shift in emphasis grew out of a desire to examine the development of the eighteenth-century settlement that had briefly served as a British garrison. Camden's importance in backcountry trade and communications precipitated its role as a military strong point and led directly to its postwar growth as a regional center. Recognizing that knowledge of the town's contents and appearance and its transformation over time were crucial to understanding its past and interpreting its role as a garrison settlement, the Camden Historical Commission initiated a series of agreements with the Institute of Archaeology and Anthropology at the University of South Carolina to conduct archaeological work aimed at exploring Camden's interior. As a member of the institute's staff, I became involved with archaeology at Camden and directed subsequent projects there. It quickly became obvious to me that the previous findings would contribute much to the task of exploring the town site.

   Calmes's and Strickland's overwhelming concern with military fortifications heavily influenced the nature of the data they collected. Although their work helped me understand this facet of the settlement's past, their research focus led them to avoid investigating areas associated with the civil community and discouraged their analysis of features and materials not immediately associated with the defensive works. Knowledge of Camden's fortifications, however, did shed light on the town's location and extent. The discovery of the fortifications had been guided by documents that showed their proximity to the town and the distribution of buildings within it. Once the positions of the fortifications had been ascertained, it became possible to gauge the layout of the town site relative to Camden's street plan. Especially significant in this regard was the detection and delineation of the town palisade. This defensive wall encompassed the built-up area of the colonial period and marked the boundaries of the 1781 settlement. Because this urban zone is not likely to have expanded until well after the Revolution, I reasoned that the palisade line could serve to effectively demarcate the area of future archaeological study.

A second contribution to the study of the settlement was the collection of artifacts generated by the extensive excavations at the Kershaw House site. The fortifications surrounding this outlying town structure represented a small, and relatively brief, component of the settlement in this portion of Camden but were extensive in nature and required exploration of a wide area. As a result, the archaeology did much more than simply document these military features. Four seasons of excavations had uncovered a great deal of material evidence, both architectural and archaeological, associated with life and activities at the Kershaw House. Its remains represented a nonmilitary occupation likely to have spanned nearly nine decades. Because the Kershaw House site offered archaeologists an opportunity to examine a major component of the early town over a substantial period, it held great potential for addressing questions of Camden's development.

Archaeological investigations intended to explore colonial Camden and its evolving community would rely on a research design capable of examining the colonial town on a scale small enough to observe the community as a whole while permitting the incorporation of larger-scale investigations aimed at exploring components within the community. Such a study required new excavations largely within the town site itself and could also use appropriate material evidence contributed by the earlier fieldwork. The previous excavations became a part of the continuing work at Camden by indicating promising areas for future excavations and supplying data relating to a major component of the settlement. Integrating the results of the preceding projects did not always come easily. Each had been carried out with specific goals in mind, objectives that governed the methodology employed and influenced the nature of the data recovered. In order to successfully incorporate these older data with those to be gathered in the new projects, I would have to formulate an *archaeological research design* flexible enough to integrate information pertaining to the whole settlement with those associated with its individual components.

The research design for Camden, like all research designs, would provide the means to explore specific questions about the settlement's past through an examination of material remains. To accomplish this, it had to specify both the categories of evidence needed to observe past organization and change and the methods by which such evidence would be recovered and analyzed. The nature of the design determined how new evidence and that acquired previously would be examined to answer the critical questions. The implementation of settlement archaeology at Camden also rested on the ability of the research design to incorporate the multiple levels of observation possible on a large and complex site.

A successful design for Camden needed to allow an investigator to (1) identify and define precise research questions that linked processes of change and other pertinent variables to the settlement and its development over time, (2) understand the appropriate scales on which to observe activities and other phenomena associated with each question, and (3) determine the manner in which the occurrence of these phenomena are likely to be expressed in the content and patterning of archaeological evidence. Implementing a research design in a systematic manner also meant that it be in place before the project began. In the fall of 1974, all of these requirements had to be considered in constructing a workable research design for Camden.

DEVELOPING A DESIGN FOR SYSTEMATIC RESEARCH

The site of colonial Camden presented great promise for archaeological research because it contained the remains of a settlement that played a central role in the colonization of the South Carolina backcountry. An investigation of the site offered the opportunity to *examine insular frontier colonization from the perspective of an individual settlement and to observe how this process was reflected in its size, form, and content.* Addressing Camden's role as a frontier town was central to formulating an archaeological research design for the site. In order to answer questions about function and change, I needed to know if I had the kind of material evidence capable of supplying this information. The condition of the site held the key to its research potential. It was obvious that remains of the town had survived, but before proceeding further, I had to find out if they were intact enough to provide the evidence I needed. If the remains of Camden were sufficiently complete and relatively undisturbed, they might reveal crucial clues to the nature of the early settlement.

Before examining the site, I had to determine the spatial limits of its eighteenth-century occupation. When I began work on the town site in 1974, identifying these boundaries became the first step in assessing the state of the archaeological remains. Documents proved very helpful. They revealed that the town followed the orientation of the 1771 survey plat but remained largely confined to the relatively compact area surrounded by the British palisade. The line of this wall seemed to be the most accurate indicator of the town limits, and I decided to employ it as the boundary of the study area. For purposes of managing the excavations, the enclosed area was divided into three subareas based on the manner in which it was segmented by modern city streets, all of which followed courses laid out in the eighteenth century (Figure 3.5). That portion of the site lying west of Broad Street and north of Meeting Street became Area A. Area B encompassed the southern extension of the town below Meeting Street and Area C consisted of the area east of Broad Street. Areas A and B had been cultivated in the past and were presently covered in grass. A plant nursery had recently vacated a portion of Area B. In contrast, Area C was partially covered by modern construction. A baseball field, a football stadium, and an enclosed arena covered a large part of the area and curtailed archaeological work on this portion of the old town site. With the exception of the built-up portion of Area C, much of the early town site was accessible and could be delineated by tracing the course of the palisade.

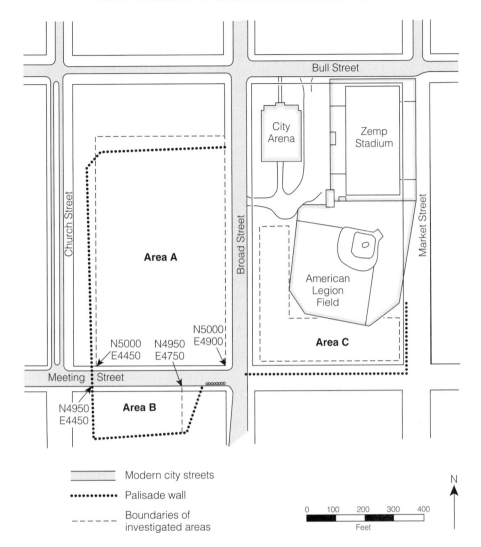

Figure 3.5 Map of the Camden site showing the areas examined in the 1974–1975 archaeological sampling. The areas examined enclosed all accessible portions of the 1780 town, the boundaries of which were defined by the British palisade wall that surrounded the settlement. Camden's current property lines followed those established in the 1771 survey and all roads lay within their eighteenth-century rights-of-way. Modern construction in the eastern portion of the colonial town site limited the extent of the archaeological investigations. Source: Lewis (1976).

The 1781 map of Camden also identified three additional outlying areas of settlement: the fortified Kershaw House to the east of town, the jail to the north, and two buildings situated farther south along the road from Charleston. Unfortunately the last two areas lay under modern construction and were inaccessible for investigation, but the site of the Kershaw House had already been located and completely excavated. Previous archaeology had identified the boundaries of this outlying settlement area and revealed the existence of many intact architectural and activity-related features that were likely to reveal information about this distinctive element of the settlement.

Locating the town boundary by tracing the palisade line was a relatively straightforward process in Areas A and C. Using Calmes's and Strickland's measurements as a guide, my crew and I excavated a number of narrow additional exploratory trenches to reestablish the course of the wall in Area A. Strickland's reconstructed palisade in the southeast corner of the town wall marked the town boundary in Area C. Because earlier excavations had detected only the west line of the palisade only in Area B, it became necessary to excavate several exploratory trenches to ascertain the remainder of this fortification. The 1781 map indicated that the palisade extended southward in the southwest corner of Camden to surround two buildings, and I anticipated that its southern face would again turn northward to join the line of the wall uncovered earlier by Strickland's excavations. In spite of ground disturbance from the recent nursery and erosion, we located both the southern and eastern palisade lines and found that the latter turned northward diagonally, rather than at a right angle as shown on the map. With all the palisade lines delineated, we established the boundaries of the settlement and the size of the area to be investigated. With this information I could develop a plan to systematically explore the colonial town site.

Although I now knew the extent of the eighteenth-century occupation, the surface of the ground provided no clues to its form or content. Past cultivation had removed all traces of previous occupations, and earlier exploratory trenches revealed that parts of the site had also been modified by natural forces and human activities. The next phase of the archaeology would have to be capable of examining the entire town area to identify the location and distribution of buildings and activities as well as other documented and undocumented phenomena. It also had to address the site's physical condition and its potential for yielding intact archaeological remains.

EXPLORING THE TOWN SITE:
THE DOCUMENTARY RECORD

As a settlement occupied by a literate society, Camden possessed a literary record produced by its inhabitants, visitors, and those who had business or administrative duties there. These documents provided many details about people and activities. Because they were written by persons who were familiar with the town, however, they are often unclear in specifying where activities occurred or where particular places were located. Because most records refer to people rather than places, my ability to identify where different activities took place in Camden depended on learning who owned various parcels of land in the town through time. The inhabitants of eighteenth-century British America produced many types of historical records relating to real and personal property. The province granted land to individuals who subsequently conveyed it by sale, gift, or inheritance. Deeds, often accompanied by plats, describe their holdings and locate them in space. Plats, such as that subdividing the town of Camden in 1771, provide a detailed look at individual settlements. Wills, inventories, and

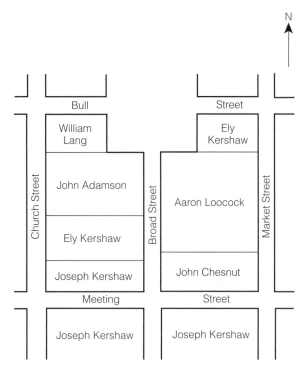

N

Figure 3.6 Ownership of lands in Camden on the eve of the Revolution. At this time nearly all of the property in the settlement remained in the hands of the Kershaw brothers and their business associates. Compiled from deed records.

other probate records also refer to land, and property almost always figures in the accounts of legal proceedings contained in pleadings and judgments. Losses of property during the American Revolution produced accounts in which loyalists sought compensation for property lost and rebels attempted to recover war expenses. Military records, including maps, often mention real estate and portray its distribution on the land. In addition to these official documents, the accounts contained in diaries, ledgers, letters, and other personal papers provide information about individuals and their activities. Together they gave us a glimpse of the eighteenth-century settlement, the nature of its households, and the activities of the people who comprised them.

Documents allowed me to accurately trace the history of land ownership in Camden, but they yielded much less information about the actual placement of people and activities in the colonial town. The 1781 town lay within a large parcel granted to William Ancrum in 1758 and in the 1760s became part of a vast holding of 2,498 acres held by the partnership of William Ancrum, Aaron Loocock, Ely and Joseph Kershaw, and John Chesnut. They undertook the survey of Camden in 1771 (Figure 2.8) and, after the partnership's dissolution three years later, put the tract up for sale with their other properties. Prior to the Revolution, the lands in the area actually settled in 1781 were held in large parcels by four of the partners and John Adamson, another merchant (Figure 3.6). These were broken down into smaller units only after the middle of the subsequent decade. By the 1790s, smaller properties began to emerge on the old town site, although contemporary descriptions of Camden reveal that few residents remained in that area just after the turn of the century.

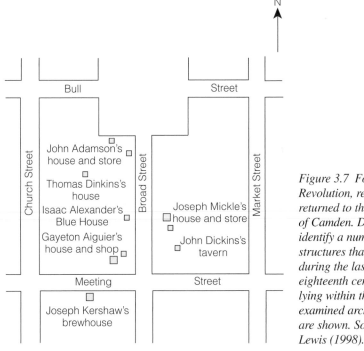

Figure 3.7 Following the Revolution, residents returned to the old town site of Camden. Documents identify a number of structures that were occupied during the last decade of the eighteenth century. Those lying within the area examined archaeologically are shown. Source: Lewis (1998).

Other documentary accounts mentioned structures belonging to the persons who owned land in the settled area of the Revolutionary War period; however, this evidence was insufficient to identify their precise, or even approximate, locations or tie them with the buildings shown on the 1781 military map. Indeed, the sketch's uneven proportions and other errors made it difficult to use as a guide to eighteenth-century architecture. Documentary sources stated that the Kershaw brothers and John Adamson all operated stores in Camden and that Joseph Kershaw had constructed a "brewhouse" on his property south of Meeting Street, but their exact locations remained uncertain. Presumably they and others also lived in the town. Additional residents who did not own property may have operated businesses out of other buildings that lay within the British palisade of 1780, but documents provided few clues as to their identities or the activities that occurred there.

The postwar occupation of Camden complicated matters even further. Properties in the area of the old palisaded town were reoccupied and subdivided and many new owners appeared. Contemporary observers and legal records mentioned both residences and businesses, but they placed none in specific locations and did not always indicate whether or not owners reused older structures (Figure 3.7). John Adamson's house and store were situated on his property on the west side of Broad Street. Farther south lay Thomas Dinkins's house and the home of Dr. Isaac Alexander. The shop and residence of Gayeton Aiguier, a tin worker and recent refugee from Saint-Domingue, occupied the old Chesnut and Kershaw tracts in the southern portion of the block. And the old Kershaw brewhouse apparently still stood on the block known as the "brewhouse square."

Buildings on the east side of Broad included Joseph Mickle's house and store and John Dinkins's tavern, which contemporary observers recalled was the social center of the old town. Although residents returned to claim their properties, the old town site remained sparsely settled. Hard economic times and a slow recovery from wartime devastation in the backcountry retarded growth in Camden, but a growing perception of the unhealthiness of the low terrace on which much of the town sat also directed much of the new expansion toward the higher ground to the north. By the end of the eighteenth century, houses and businesses surrounded the old square at the intersection of Broad and Bull Streets and continued in the direction of the courthouse and jail. Gradually residents abandoned the area of the 1780 settlement, and soon the old Kershaw House, now alone on the hill, looked down on a vacant site (Kirkland and Kennedy 1905; Lewis 1998).

DESIGNING A PLAN FOR ARCHAEOLOGICAL RESEARCH

A successful investigation of Camden's role as a frontier center required a research methodology capable of addressing development within the town on different scales. Although the broad process of insular frontier colonization shaped the community as a whole, it affected the people and activities that comprised them differentially. We may examine this process at either level; however, the questions asked must be appropriate to the scale of the context investigated. Similarly, when we investigate the material manifestations of colonization, we should be careful to coordinate the questions with the scale of the archaeological context under consideration. If one wishes to investigate subsistence, craft specialization, exchange, or some other aspect of adaptation within households, archaeological investigations confined to a specific structure or group of structures are probably appropriate. If, on the other hand, one is dealing with the evolution of social or economic systems in the larger community, then excavations must be designed to examine the material record representing the entire settlement. Because the scale of my questions is linked to that of the archaeological context explored, the research must be designed to identify contexts of the appropriate scale. I was interested in investigating frontier adaptations on both community and household scales in Camden but realized that the large size of the site would dictate the order in which these questions could be addressed.

Asking questions of the archaeological record requires that the unit of inquiry first be defined. At Camden, the position of the palisade wall revealed the boundaries of the settlement and demarcated the space within which community activities took place. In 1974 the enclosed settlement was the smallest archaeological unit that could be defined at the town site. Although documentary records provided clear evidence of land ownership within the palisaded town and identified its residents and the nature of their activities, details of the settlement's layout remained uncertain. Before I could examine individual households, I needed to locate them and identify their spatial extent. Archaeological research at Camden had to begin by studying the settlement as a whole. Only after smaller elements within the town were discovered and delineated could they be inspected and their contents analyzed together with data already gathered at the Kershaw House to examine questions pertaining to household adaptations.

A desire to answer questions regarding Camden's role as a frontier central place, coupled with the necessity of treating the settlement as a whole to delineate smaller material contexts, required a multistage field methodology that provided an overview of the entire site while retaining the ability to focus on particular aspects of it. This methodology employed a number of logically related steps involving the progressively more intensive investigation of increasingly restricted portions of the total site area. I intended that each step provide data capable of answering broader questions relating to behavior as well as identifying archaeological contexts within which to explore questions relating to activity on a larger scale (Redman 1973).

The first stage of this research would provide the first glimpse of the remains of the colonial settlement. The methods employed had to be capable of examining the entire site in order to determine its potential for further research. I was particularly concerned about the condition of the material remains of the town itself. If I could not identify objects and recognize their patterning in the ground, then I would be unable to obtain information about Camden's layout and content, and it would be impossible to define smaller archaeological units such as buildings or yards. First, I had to verify the assumptions that the plow zone covering the accessible portions of site was intact and the underlying layer of soil was undisturbed. The initial examination of the town site had to disclose whether the site was in good enough condition to warrant further work. I had to employ a methodology that would accomplish this evaluation while at the same time permit me to observe site-wide archaeological patterning capable of revealing Camden's size, form, and composition as well as changes in each of these characteristics over time. I believed that these attributes would mirror the town's role as a central place and reveal the influence of insular frontier colonization on its development.

The design of the discovery phase of archaeology at Camden had to accommodate several conditions posed by the nature of the site. First, it was relatively large. The accessible area encompassed by the palisade comprised nearly 13 acres. Recalling that the .06 acre around the Kershaw House involved more than four years of fieldwork, I quickly realized that total excavation would be a tremendous, lengthy undertaking and prohibitively expensive. Another way had to be found. The physical structure of the site itself presented a second factor that influenced the design of the fieldwork. Exploratory trenches dug to locate the palisade wall and excavations at the Kershaw House and elsewhere indicated a shallow site with most of its cultural remains contained in the layer of plowed soil lying directly beneath the sod. Because structural foundations and subterranean features did not appear to constitute a substantial part of Camden's material remains, I felt that an investigation of the settlement would have to depend largely on an analysis of plow zone materials. The ability of plow zone data to reflect archaeological patterning rested on the assumption that, although their vertical context and association with features had been disturbed by cultivation, the plow zone artifacts were unlikely to have shifted far horizontally and that broad patterning in their distribution would not have been greatly affected. If, as I believed, plow zone excavations could derive meaningful patterning, then a large shallow site like this could yield much information if this material could be recovered and examined. But first I had to devise a field strategy that permitted an extensive examination of the site within a reasonable time frame. In fact, budget and time constraints would play a major role in shaping the initial phase of archaeology at Camden.

The investigation of the town site employed a technique that satisfied both these conditions by gathering a *representative sample* of the material remains deposited within the palisaded settlement. The inspiration for using this technique came from the work of prehistoric archaeologists, who had recently carried out promising research on the efficacy of employing probabilistic sampling as a means of discovering sites and ascertaining their content. Because the data obtained would be examined statistically, they were to be taken from randomly selected sample units. Random selection offered the advantage of providing each unit within the sample area the same chance of being chosen and eliminates the potential bias inherent in a sample based on arbitrary measurements. Archaeologists who had employed sampling successfully on large sites advocated *stratified unaligned systematic sampling* as the best method for examining artifact patterning because it prevented the clustering of sample units and assured that no part of the site was left unexamined (Redman and Watson 1970; Mueller 1974). Using this technique, the site is divided into a series of large units based on the coordinates of the site grid. Within each of these squares one unit of a smaller size is randomly chosen. The sizes of the units involved determine the percentage of the site area sampled. Naturally, the greater the size of the sample, the more reliable are the results; however, the difficulty in enlarging the magnitude of such a sample increases with the size of the site. For this reason, the proportionate size of the sample usually becomes smaller as the area examined becomes larger. The most reliable picture of the total population can be attained by using the smallest-sized squares practical because their use permits the maximum area to be covered for a given amount of effort.

Because sampling attempts to obtain an adequate representation of a universe of data without examining its entirety, proponents of sampling recognized the importance of the research problem at hand and stressed that the *size* of the sample be adequate to gather data capable of addressing the hypotheses to be examined. Archaeologists had begun to use sampling to explore sites with the intent of detecting the nature and distribution of activities, assuming that these could provide clues to settlement function. Employing samples approaching 11 percent, they had explored sites smaller than Camden and successfully observed variation in the patterning of specific activities carried out in relatively limited spaces (Redman and Watson 1970; Watson, LeBlanc, and Redman 1971). In the initial examination of Camden, I sought evidence of activities associated with the town's role as a frontier economic and social center. At this point in the research, I thought that data capable of providing this information might be obtained by identifying and defining the spatial extent of structures and key activities through the distribution of diagnostic categories of artifacts. I hoped to discern the general layout settlement, identify centralizing functions, and perhaps even observe their change over time by choosing broadly defined activities that were likely to have generated a relatively dense output of artifacts and by recording the dispersion of architectural debris.

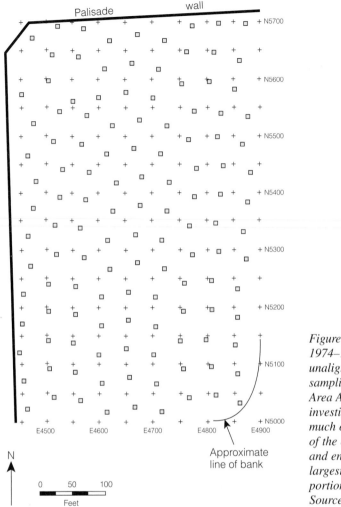

Figure 3.8 Map of the
1974–1975 stratified
unaligned systematic
sampling excavations in
Area A at Camden. These
investigations examined
much of the western half
of the early settlement
and encompassed the
largest undisturbed
portion of the town site.
Source: Lewis (1976).

Because the initial investigations at Camden required only a relatively small sample of the total site area, they were intended only to identify general areas of interest rather than to precisely define activity boundaries or locate all building foundations. It was critical, however, to spread the sample units across the site densely enough to discover broad artifact patterns. The exact sample size was also affected by budget constraints that placed limits on the length of the field operation. Given the amount of time available, the physical condition of the site, and the average length of time it would take to excavate a sample pit of adequate size, I estimated the number of sample units it would be possible to dig. Dividing this number into the total area, I determined that the crew could excavate about 1 percent of the site. I could accomplish this by dividing the site into 50 by 50 foot units, within each of which a smaller 5 by 5 foot sample unit was placed (Figure 3.8). This plan involved a much smaller sample size than advocates of sampling methodology recommended, but data from other eighteenth-century

British colonial communities suggested that the structures and activity areas in Camden were large enough to be detected by the distribution of my excavation units. Employing such a small sample was risky, but the distribution of sample units seemed tight enough to intersect the artifact patterns formed by the debris of typical colonial buildings and the activities associated with their accompanying yards. And, as important, the units were sufficiently large to provide a measurable sample of their contents.

My decision to use the English foot as a unit of measure at Camden contrasted with the practice of most prehistoric archaeologists, who rely on the internationally accepted metric system of measurement. However, historical archaeologists working in British American sites find the foot a convenient unit because it corresponds to that used to lay out the settlements they examine. Camden, like other colonial towns, was platted on a grid measured in English feet. Measurements in feet defined the course of streets and the boundaries of the blocks they bordered as well as the limits of individual properties within the blocks. Surveyors measured all property lines in feet and builders laid out foundations in these units. Given its pervasive use in eighteenth-century British settlements, the English foot is the logical unit to employ when investigating their remains.

Utilizing stratified systematic unaligned sampling over an area the size of Camden made it necessary to coordinate points over a wide area. To facilitate this, I established a site grid with a datum point placed at an arbitrary location south and west of the town. This technique permitted all locations on the site to be measured north and west of a single datum. A recent survey of the Camden District Heritage Foundation properties allowed me the additional advantage of tying this grid to the eighteenth-century property boundaries. The survey reestablished the street corners laid out in the original 1771 town plat and from these points, I could reconstruct the locations of early property boundaries and associate them with material patterns revealed by the archaeology (Lewis 1976).

THE SAMPLING EXCAVATIONS: THE CONDITION OF THE SITE

The sampling excavations at Camden took place in the fall of 1974 and over the spring and summer of the following year (Figure 3.9). Because one goal of this work was to ascertain the condition of the site, the first step was to examine the stratigraphy over the entire occupied area. I already knew from the exploratory trenches dug in search of the palisade line and from Robert Strickland's earlier stratigraphic profile cut on the west side of Broad Street that the western portion of Camden was characterized by a plow zone of gray sandy loam overlying a sequence of naturally occurring sandy clays. Strickland's previous excavations east of Broad Street, however, had uncovered a more complex situation there. His discovery of a buried wartime pit feature adjacent to the palisade wall suggested that a portion of the eighteenth-century surface here had been overlain by subsequent erosion and now rested well below the present surface. My crew began the sampling excavations in Area C hoping to clarify this situation. What we discovered had both encouraging and discouraging implications for the success of the project.

Figure 3.9 Excavating a sample unit at Camden in 1975. Fred Swain shovels dirt into the mechanical sifter where Jacqueline Carter and Michael O. Hartley retrieve artifacts.

The sampling units east of Broad Street quickly revealed just how much the surface here had been altered. Pits dug in the southwestern part of the area and those at its extreme eastern end encountered the sandy clay subsoil directly below the modern sod, indicating that all of the overlying soil had been removed. In units excavated nearer the center of the area, on the other hand, the subsoil lay up to 6 feet below the present surface beneath a strata composed of various soils. These contrasting sequences implied that the east and west portions of the southeast town had been stripped away while the center lay intact under more post–eighteenth-century fill. Searching for an explanation, my crew excavated several stratigraphic trenches crosscutting the area from east to west and north to south. The trenches allowed us to follow the edge of the outcropping subsoil and map the soil profile across the entire area. The resulting profiles confirmed my suspicions that the higher elevations at the peripheries along the eastern and western margins had been graded off, apparently to level the ground at the south end of the baseball field. The intermediate area formed a natural depression that had been gradually filled by erosional deposits and subsequently topped by a layer of modern clay to stabilize the outfield wall of the ballpark. At the base of the erosional fill, a humus layer that marked the original surface remained undisturbed and features on it appeared intact. In short, this area presented the two extremes anticipated at Camden. The buried portion contained the best preserved remains on the site, but no trace of the early settlement existed on those areas where construction had removed the upper layers of soil.

The southwestern extension of the town west of Broad Street encompassed a sloping surface that had suffered from erosion and disturbance from nursery planting activities. Nevertheless, much of the top layer of soil remained intact and contained a large number of artifacts, and traces of subsurface features extended into the underlying subsoil. Although damaged, this portion of Camden appeared to contain substantial deposits of archaeological evidence, the spatial patterning of which was unlikely to have been markedly altered. These patterns would be useful in analyzing the nature and distribution of activities in the fortified area around the brewhouse square.

This area enclosed much of the western half of Camden. Sampling excavations revealed that a plow zone of varying color extended over its entire surface and contained a considerable amount of cultural material. The occurrence of many intact subsurface features indicated that agricultural displacement was limited to the upper layer. The fact that debris from buried structural features tended to be concentrated in the overlying soil immediately adjacent to them suggested that plowing had not significantly shifted the original deposition of artifacts and argued strongly that the spatial patterning of artifacts remained unchanged over this large portion of the site. In the northeast corner of this area, presumably in the vicinity of the palisade wall's northern gate, the plow zone became noticeably thicker and covered a humus zone lying just above the subsoil. Its similarity to the buried humus east of Broad Street implied that it was part of the same early surface and was likely to contain undisturbed evidence of the town's eighteenth-century occupation.

Information gathered from the sampling investigations relative to the site's condition confirmed earlier observations that the plow zone covering most of the area enclosed by the palisade contained a sizeable archaeological deposit generated by the eighteenth-century settlement of Camden. Although some portions of the site seemed to have sustained more damage than others, only a small part of the area east of Broad Street had actually been destroyed by modern construction activity. In contrast, several parts of the site were buried by later accumulation of soil, preserving intact colonial surfaces where early archaeological deposits were likely to have remained unmixed. Subsurface features appeared in all areas of the site and their nature and distribution promised another source of information regarding activities in the settlement. Based on the results of the sampling excavations, I concluded that the site of Camden contained sufficient intact archaeological material to discern patterning that would provide information about the size, form, and composition of the colonial town.

HYPOTHESES FOR IDENTITY, FUNCTION, AND CHANGE

I hoped to use the results of the sampling excavations to demonstrate that the archaeological deposits in the town of Camden exhibited patterning shaped by past activities and the distinctive function of the settlement. In order to use this material data to investigate Camden's role as a central place on the backcountry frontier, I first had to develop a series of *hypotheses* that specified what sort of material remains would be capable of reflecting the different aspects of Camden's role as a central settlement in the South Carolina backcountry. The hypotheses would also spell out what form that evidence was likely to take. Like all archaeological hypotheses, those for Camden were derived from a model and linked its behavioral characteristics to their manifestations in the ground. The extent to which the hypotheses were supported by material data would determine the model's appropriateness to the situation at hand.

I designed the hypotheses employed in this study to determine how well the process of insular frontier colonization modeled in the previous chapter would account for the form and nature of Camden's development. In other words, by comparing the growth of this backcountry center to the characteristics of the model, I hoped to ascertain the degree to which Camden's evolution was a consequence of the changes associated with insular frontier colonization. These hypotheses were not intended to identify the nature of this settlement. We already possessed sufficient documentation to know this. Rather, they were meant to provide confirmation that the form of Camden's historical development derived from the distinctive nature of a particular process. As a form of data separate from the written documentation, the archaeological record could reveal new knowledge about the settlement's form and function. Because Camden's documentary record was far from complete, this independent line of evidence promised to be an important source of information, providing a fuller picture of Camden's role on the South Carolina frontier.

The hypotheses for Camden's role as a frontier town involved two separate levels of analysis. The hypotheses themselves were tied to the social, economic, and political nature of the community and were related to its size, form, and composition. The behavioral characteristics they described *then* served as the basis for archaeological expectations testable through an analysis of material data. Analogies drawn from period historical sources and comparative ethnographic literature relating to colonization figured prominently in constructing the hypotheses describing the layout, nature, and distribution of past activities. Once I had framed these hypotheses, I could use historical and archaeological information pertaining to the function of material objects and their utilization in various activities to predict how the activities described in the hypotheses might be reflected in the archaeological record. But first the hypotheses had to be formulated.

For convenience, I grouped the hypotheses for investigating the nature of the colonial community at Camden into three categories each of which encompassed a separate aspect of its role as a central place in the South Carolina backcountry. These categories included (1) its *relationship with the outside world,* (2) its *function* as a frontier center, and (3) its *evolution* over time. The first group was intended to examine the settlement's position as an entity on the periphery of the European world economy, while the second group would explore the elements of form and function that distinguished its role. Finally, the third group attempted to document the manner in which Camden mirrored larger regional changes.

Camden's Relationship with the Larger Colonial World

Participation in the larger world economy enmeshed the periphery in a close exchange relationship with the core. As suppliers of raw materials and recipients of finished goods, colonial settlements depended on the manufactures of Europe. More specifically, because the control of trade lay in the domain of the colonizing nation, the goods imported were usually the products of that state. The rapid expansion of Great Britain's commercial economy in the eighteenth century not only increased the production of English goods but also incorporated the production of other countries that had fallen within its sphere of trade. As overseas trade expanded, foreign goods increasingly took a position alongside the exports of the parent state (Darby 1973; McCusker and Menard 1985). Both these trends affected Britain's colonial trade and should be expressed by the consumption patterns of residents in backcountry settlements such as Camden.

The tendency of agricultural colonization to rely on local and regional economic institutions, however, would have affected the degree to which British products dominated trade in the backcountry. Supply shortages, transportation difficulties, and an inability to pay for imported goods generally gave rise to regional economies that circulated colonial products made by immigrants as well as Native peoples. Usually distinctive in appearance, their occurrence was widespread and these goods became an integral part of the material culture of the frontier. I anticipated that such distinctive items would have played an important role in the early settlement of Camden and developed two non–mutually exclusive hypotheses regarding artifact use in Camden.

1. Material goods employed by its residents will be primarily of British manufacture but should also incorporate items acquired as a result of that country's extensive trade. These artifacts should comprise the greatest portion in the archaeological record.
2. Items used in Camden should also include regionally made products of colonial or aboriginal manufacture or both. These American products should constitute a much smaller part of the artifacts recovered.

Camden's Function as a Frontier Central Place

Documentary evidence had indicated that Camden possessed institutions characteristic of frontier towns, a class of settlement that played a central role in the development of agricultural regions. I believed that Camden's distinctive role influenced the nature and patterning of its inhabitants' activities and that evidence would be discernible in the material record. Because settlement function affected the town in its entirety as well as its constituent components, I reasoned that evidence should be observable on two scales, that of the entire site and that of activity areas within it. I intended the initial phase of archaeological research at Camden, however, to examine the settlement on the basis of a small representative sample, and such evidence was incapable of revealing the composition of activities occurring in limited space. Consequently, this work focused on the settlement as a unit rather than on its individual parts and attempted to recognize patterns linked to its function within the larger colonial region.

As a center of economic, political, and social activity on the South Carolina backcountry frontier, Camden is likely to have held a status comparable in many ways to certain other settlements in contemporary Great Britain and its possessions. Camden's location on the periphery of British colonial expansion, however, caused it to assume characteristics unlike those of settlements in the homeland. Its central role on the frontier required it to maintain certain functions such as being the site of fairs and markets as well as a center for courts and other administrative activities. At the same time, the settlement had to adapt to conditions of dispersed settlement and attenuated trade and communication. Such adjustments restructured the community's integrating institutions, which, in turn, altered its form.

To examine the nature of these adaptations, I had first to establish a baseline for change. This baseline required identifying the type of settlements in the urban hierarchy of contemporary Europe that possessed functions comparable to frontier towns. Because the central role of frontier towns made them the only interior settlements that depended on inter- as well as intra-regional exchange, they could be compared to European settlements of similar function. The urban settlements most closely fitting this description were market towns. In addition to their role in exchange, market towns exhibited greater specialization in production, offered a greater variety of employment, and offered a greater range of goods than settlements ranking lower on the urban scale. In addition, market towns possessed integrating political and social functions not found in lower-ranking settlements and the influence of these institutions extended over a wide area (Blouet 1972; Grove 1972).

Although sharing their basic functions with European towns, frontier towns differed strikingly with regard to size and form. The insignificant appearance of these settlements was related to the nature of frontier expansion, which spread population rapidly over a large area and resulted in a widely dispersed pattern of settlement and low population density. In Europe, urban centers arose in settled areas, and growth in population density was closely tied to economic complexity and status within the urban hierarchy. Growth was associated with an increase in the level of social and economic activity, and size became a reflection of function (Fox 1973). Because a frontier town came into existence very rapidly, it did not arise solely to integrate existing settlements. It also tied them into the network of a complex and often far-reaching interregional economic system by coordinating social, economic, and political activities in a newly occupied country. Immigrants established a frontier town as an economic center without its first passing through a number of intermediate stages of growth and without its having taken on the roles and the forms of less complex settlement types. Frontier towns were not older population centers that assumed more complex urban functions, and they generally remained smaller than European market towns.

It may be best to view a frontier town as part of a larger, dispersed social entity. Each served as a site of region-wide integrating institutions. The concept of community is useful in dealing with a settlement of this type because it stresses function rather than form and sees a society in an organizational rather than spatial sense. Thus, a community may include more than a contiguous settlement, and its form may vary according to the adaptive mode of the particular society. Camden, as a frontier town, seemed to represent the focal point of a dispersed community whose limits were not easy to define, although they encompassed primary subsistence production and included residents who lived outside the immediate nucleated settlement. If Camden were the center of such a community, I reasoned, one might expect to observe certain alterations in the settlement pattern and the distribution of activities at the site. The distinctive nature of frontier towns generated four hypotheses regarding Camden's form and composition.

3. Because most activities in the town are likely to have been associated with Camden's function as a center of trade and communications, buildings housing

these activities would have had access to transportation routes. As a result, the bulk of the settlement would have been concentrated along the major route connecting it with the outside world.

4. Because the large, localized supporting population normally associated with market towns in Europe were absent in frontier towns, I anticipated that the total number of structures in Camden would be fewer.

5. The lack of a large supporting population meant that fewer structures in the town were being utilized solely as dwellings. In contrast, a substantial portion of Camden's buildings would have been the sites of nondomestic endeavors associated with trade, administrative, and other public affairs. Their functions involved transferring and storing goods and commodities, small-scale manufacturing and maintenance, and political and social activities associated with the periodic gathering of people for collective purposes such as trials, markets, and socializing.

6. Finally, Camden's central role relative to the dispersed settlements of the backcountry made it the residence of individuals who oversaw the distribution and collection of goods and produce passing to and from Charleston. Although perhaps not possessing the wealth of their counterparts in the entrepôt or Great Britain, individuals involved in commercial activities enjoyed relatively high status compared to others on the frontier, including those living in town. Such status provided greater access to available resources and some individuals, such as Joseph Kershaw, displayed their wealth through architecture. Although other frontier merchants did not follow his example, they and other prominent individuals were likely to have exhibited their status in other ways, and I felt that material evidence of it would be discernible in Camden.

Time, Space, and Change in Camden

Rapid and dramatic change is an inevitable accompaniment of agricultural frontier colonization, and it characterized settlement in the Wateree Valley during the second half of the eighteenth century. Documentary evidence indicated that British settlers first occupied the site of Camden in the 1750s and began to abandon the old town site for adjacent higher ground to the north around 1820. It was reasonable to assume that an analysis of the artifacts deposited during the occupation would reveal both the presence of the colonial community and the changes that occurred as it evolved over time. Written sources also revealed that the town had been occupied by the British Army for nearly a year and served as a strong point in the backcountry. Previous archaeological work had identified the fortifications built by the military, but neither the nature of the army's presence nor its impact on the settlement had ever been investigated. To examine the temporal aspects of the town's past, I developed three more hypotheses.

7. I expected that an analysis of time-sensitive material evidence from the site of Camden would indicate that it was occupied from about 1760 to around 1820.

8. Similarly, the spatial distribution of such artifacts was likely to show the layout and configuration of the town over time and provide evidence for its size, form, and eventual northerly movement in the direction of the modern town.

9. Because the Revolutionary War occupation of Camden focused on the town itself, this episode must have impacted the settlement, and I anticipated the presence of the British military would be visible in the archaeological record.

The sampling excavations at Camden provided material data sufficient to evaluate the nine hypotheses relating to Camden's role in the development of the backcountry frontier. These investigations explored all accessible portions of the colonial town site and recovered over 29,000 artifacts from 126 units distributed across its surface. Although cultivation had disturbed the site, I could observe clear variation in the spatial patterning of these materials. The presence of this patterning, together with the existence of intact architectural remains and other types of subsurface features lying below the plow zone, gave me confidence that I possessed the evidence necessary to explore questions about Camden's past. In order to address the hypotheses, however, I had to anticipate how each would be manifested in the archaeological record. Analyzing the material implications of each hypothesis required an examination of explicit expectations, and this task formed the next phase of research.

4/Examining the Results
of the Sampling Excavations
Exploring Hypotheses for
Identity, Function, and Change

INTRODUCTION

The sampling excavations at Camden sought to provide important information about the nature of the colonial town and its evolution through time. Because I was interested in investigating Camden's role as a central component on the frontier, this work was designed to provide material evidence representative of the settlement as a whole. My inquiry, at this stage, was aimed at the collective experience of the town and not at the varied experiences of its individual inhabitants. This strategy required that I ask general questions addressing phenomena on the scale of the community rather than on that of the households that comprised it. I set forth these questions as nine hypotheses constructed on the basis of comparative information. Each hypothesis predicted that if Camden developed in the manner I expected, the settlement would have exhibited certain broad characteristics of size, form, and content. Because these characteristics left their mark on the archaeological record, each should be recognizable if I could ascertain the material form it would take. To address the issue of material form, I developed clearly defined sets of expectations for each hypothesis. These anticipated patterns provided the means by which to explore Camden's past through an analysis of its material remains.

HYPOTHESIS 1: CAMDEN'S ECONOMIC
TIES TO GREAT BRITAIN

The first hypothesis presumed the predominance of goods produced in the parent state or acquired through its control of trade. Great Britain's rise as a commercial power was reflected in changes in the composition and destination of its export trade. The nation's growing mercantilist orientation encouraged social and political realignments that favored economic centralization. This, in turn, accelerated the expansion of home industries and the incorporation of economic "colonies" within Britain's sphere of trade. The eighteenth century witnessed rapid industrial growth that increased the volume of production as well as the rate of innovation in manufacturing. An expansion of overseas trade with its colonies provided an enlarged market for British goods as well as the increasing quantities of foreign commodities re-exported by British suppliers (Darby 1973; Wallerstein 1980). I assumed that evidence of these developments would be found in the archaeological record at Camden.

To measure industrial change and the structure of exchange, I employed a class of artifact whose physical characteristics were capable of revealing the nature of both. Ceramics were especially useful in this regard; their composition and method of manufacture lend them to wide variation in form and finish, and their fragile nature ensures their rapid passage into the archaeological record as a continuous deposition throughout a site's occupation. Documentary and archaeological studies had shown that most European colonies used the distinctive ceramics manufactured in their parent state even after the colonies achieved independence. During the time of Camden's occupation, Britain's ceramic industry underwent a technological transformation that brought rapid innovation and increasing industrialization. British manufactures changed dramatically during this period as new wares replaced older ones in rapid succession. I expected this diversity to be present in the archaeological record (Clow and Clow 1958).

Direct links to the homeland and an exclusion of foreign trade generally discouraged the use of other nations' products unless the mother country had come to dominate their trade. For instance, Great Britain's commercial growth in the eighteenth century resulted not only in its capturing the lucrative oriental porcelains trade and expanding the re-exportation of German and Flemish stonewares. British merchants exported both in quantity to North America, where they comprised a small but recognizable portion of the ceramic remains on colonial sites (Noël Hume 1970).

When laboratory analysts cleaned and sorted the nearly 13,000 ceramic artifacts recovered in the sampling excavations, their examination revealed the predicted occurrence of British wares. The 32 separate types found represent the range of ceramics in use during the second half of the eighteenth century and included heavy utility wares as well as fine table wares and decorative pieces. The appearance of functionally similar types that succeeded one another, such as white salt-glazed stonewares, creamwares, and pearlwares, indicated the continued dominance of British ceramics over time. Fragments of oriental porcelains and Westerwald stonewares from the Rhineland attested to the re-exportation of foreign wares within the British empire; however, the smaller than normal quantity of porcelains seemed to reflect the relatively low level of American trade with Asian ports following the Revolution. The war's disruption of the traditional ties between colonists and British ceramic producers resulted in the importation of wares from other European nations. France, which became actively allied with Britain's rebellious colonies, shipped Rouen faïence to America briefly in the late 1770s and 1780s (Noël Hume 1970). This type of pottery was also found at Camden. The overwhelming presence of British ceramics together with the re-exported wares indicated clearly that Camden participated in the global economy as the colony of Europe's leading power, yet at the same time, the ceramics bore witness to the political conflict that continually altered the economy's structure (Lewis 1976).

HYPOTHESIS 2: A REGIONAL MARKET IN SOUTH CAROLINA

As part of a region undergoing colonization, the South Carolina backcountry remained lightly settled and suffered from poorly developed lines of trade and communications. The regional market ensuing from these conditions generated a number of products to supply local needs. Ceramics were one such item, and because they possessed recognizable traits and were durable enough to have survived as part of the archaeological record, they became the focus of our search for evidence of regional marketing activities. I hypothesized that Camden, as a center of trade in the backcountry, would contain distinctive forms of ceramics that played a major role in internal colonial exchange.

Regional trade involved exchange among European immigrants and between the newcomers and resident aboriginal people. At the time Pine Tree Hill arose, the remnants of a number of displaced groups, who became known collectively as the Catawba Nation, occupied the Wateree Valley. Like many Native peoples, they adapted to the colonial presence through the exchange of traditional manufactures. An unglazed, highly burnished pottery, called "River Burnished" ware by archaeologists, formed part of this extensive trade, and these ceramics have been found on the sites of eighteenth-century colonial settlements in many parts of South Carolina and at the sites of the Catawba towns where they were manufactured (Baker 1972). The Catawba wares included plates, cups, bowls, jars, and pans, some of which were decorated with black or red painting (Figure 4.1). Evidence that Catawba potters manufactured their wares for trade may be seen

Figure 4.1 River Burnished ware vessel from South Carolina.

in their efforts to imitate imported ceramics. Their placement of footrings on bowls and octagonal rims on plates both recall English forms (Ferguson 1989; Davis and Riggs 2003). Camden's proximity to the settlements of the Catawba Nation enhanced the likelihood that River Burnished wares would have found their way into the hands of European immigrants.

As expected, the sampling excavations at Camden yielded a substantial number of River Burnished ware fragments, which comprised 3 percent of the total ceramics recovered. These broken pieces were found distributed across much of the sample area, implying the wide use of Catawba wares in the colonial town. Although they were too small to allow the reconstruction of complete vessels, their shapes indicated the presence of bowls, pans, and perhaps other rounded containers. The presence of River Burnished ceramics in the archaeological record attested to regular trade between Camden's residents and the potters of the Catawba Nation, and their quantity implied that colonists employed Catawba ceramics regularly in their daily lives (Lewis 1976).

Colonial manufactures also played a vital role in the regional economy, and again ceramics provided proof of regional exchange. Potters representing two separate European traditions produced wares during the eighteenth century. The Moravian colony of Wachovia in central North Carolina established the first ceramic industry. Organized around a covenant, its settlements were administered by the Moravian church through a number of formal institutions. Although socially distinct, the colony was not economically isolated, and its members engaged in a number of ventures to attract earnings from its neighbors in the surrounding region. Pottery manufacturing was one of these enterprises. At Bethabara, master potter Gottfried Aust made ceramics in the style of the European earthenware tradition in which he had been trained, and these distinctive wares began to enter the regional market of the backcountry in 1756 (Thorp 1989; Rauschenberg 1991). During the third quarter of the eighteenth century, Aust and his apprentices produced a wide variety of often colorful, wheel-thrown, slipped and unslipped vessels ranging from milk pots and pans to jars, plates, mugs, egg cups, and even smoking pipes (Figure 4.2). His wares found great demand in North and South Carolina and were carried as far west as the Watauga settlements in present-day Tennessee (Bivins 1973; South 1999).

A second ceramic industry based on the manufacture of British fine earthenware was centered in South and later North Carolina. Its appearance was the result of the migration of a single individual to South Carolina from the pottery-making district of Stoke-on-Trent. Documents revealed that John Bartlam, a master potter from Staffordshire, left England in 1763 in an effort to escape debt and better his lot in America by manufacturing the latest style of molded fine earthenware. His flight incurred the wrath of Josiah Wedgwood, the powerful ceramic innovator and industrialist, who did not hesitate to use his influence to protect the British ceramic industry by thwarting any who sought to take the secrets of fine ceramic production outside of the country.

Despite Wedgwood's opposition, Bartlam succeeded in establishing a factory at Cain Hoy on the Wando River in South Carolina by 1765. In 1770, with the assistance of the provincial legislature and private interests who sought to encourage local pottery manufacture, Bartlam moved his operation to

Stanley South

Figure 4.2 Moravian tradition ceramics from Bethabara, North Carolina.

Charleston, but within two years he relocated to Camden. There his production reached its peak and over the next eight years his wares reached a wide market in the backcountry. Although the Revolution brought Bartlam's production in South Carolina to an end by 1780, his apprentice William Ellis introduced the techniques involved in fine earthenware manufacturing to the Moravian settlements in North Carolina. They replaced the earlier Moravian ceramic tradition and continued to be made into the nineteenth century (Rauschenberg 1991). Known to archaeologists collectively as "Carolina creamware" or "Carolina earthenware," Bartlam's ceramics emulated the style and variety of their British counterparts. Produced by his innovative potters, they imitated contemporary English wares and included a wide number of forms including plates, cups, jars, and other vessels, which exhibited a number of impressed patterns

Stanley South

Figure 4.3 English-tradition ceramics from North Carolina. Although not made in John Bartlam's Camden kilns, these vessels closely resemble his wares. They were produced by Rudolph Christ under the tutelage of William Ellis, Bartlam's apprentice, who had recently left Camden to work at the Moravian settlements.

and a variety of glazes (Figure 4.3). This fine earthenware, the greatest quantity of which originated in Camden, was traded extensively in both Carolinas (South 1993).

Camden's role as a center of trade would have brought Moravian ceramics through the settlement, although the extent of their use there was uncertain. As a center of Carolina creamware production, the settlement was likely to have seen both the exchange and use of these ceramics, activities that ensured that they accumulated in the material record. The sampling excavations yielded both kinds of ceramics as anticipated, but the quantity of each was markedly different. Comprising 5 percent of the total of more than 5,000 ceramic artifacts, Carolina creamware emerged as a minor ware at Camden. Because it was only manufactured for a few years, the presence of such a large quantity implied that it was used extensively during that time. In contrast, only a few Moravian ceramic fragments appeared in the archaeological record. Their existence clearly indicated the use of this early trade ware, yet an insubstantial presence of Moravian pottery also suggested a low volume of trade (Lewis 1976).

HYPOTHESIS 3: SETTLEMENT PATTERNING AND TRANSPORTATION

The third hypothesis was related to the layout of settlement in Camden and predicted that buildings would be situated to permit access to the major transportation route linking the settlement with the outside world. This road was Broad Street, the segment of the Catawba Path that ran through the town in a

north-south direction. The 1781 military map showed that contemporary structures lay either on this road or near it along two other thoroughfares that intersected it at right angles (Figure 2.10). This plan was similar to that of smaller
European medieval settlements that were laid out along transportation routes to
take advantage of trade. The need for its inhabitants to maintain close proximity to each other limited the length to which such settlements might grow. As a
town expanded lengthwise, cross streets would appear to provide access to the
main thoroughfare. Generally, structures on the side streets did not extend far
to either side of it (Roberts 1973).

Although the 1781 map indicated that Camden conformed to this pattern, it
depicted the town at only one moment in its history. Therefore, it would have
omitted buildings constructed and demolished before that time and could not have
portrayed those erected after the war. Because the engineer created the map to
illustrate Camden's military features, he probably included the many temporary
structures erected during the short British occupation. In a military camp, the layout of structures reflects the organization of the garrison it contains, and its patterning could well distort that of the civilian community. The map's limitations
made it necessary to rely on the archaeological record to discover the layout
of the settlement over the entire time of its existence. I expected material evidence collected in the sampling to indicate the locations of all substantial buildings and their distribution to reveal a permanent settlement oriented to its
principal thoroughfare.

To examine structural patterning at Camden, I observed the differential presence of architectural materials across the site. This class of artifacts comprises
such items as brick, nails, window glass, and other articles associated with construction. These artifacts routinely accumulated in the ground after the destruction of a building and may be relied on to furnish evidence of its existence. The
distribution of architectural artifacts was examined by displaying their spatial
distributions using SYMAP, an early computer program designed to generate
contour maps depicting their relative occurrence. The maps divulged a number
of artifact clusters that allowed the locations of a number of structures on both
sides of Broad Street to be identified (Figure 4.4).

The distribution of the architectural concentrations revealed the arrangement
of buildings in eighteenth-century Camden. The material evidence showed a
total of 15 buildings in the contiguous settlement. One cluster lay at the north end
of the settlement near the southern edge of the public square. John Adamson's
house and store lay here at the close of the eighteenth century. Concentrations
just to the south seemed to represent Ely Kershaw's store on the west side of
Broad Street and the postwar "Blue House," owned by Dr. Alexander. On the east
side of the road, concentrations marked the remains of Joseph Mickle's house
and store and John Dinkins's tavern. In the center of the western block, a
concentration set back from Broad Street corresponded to the location of
Thomas Dinkins's house, while several clusters were likely to designate multiple structures associated with Joseph Kershaw's and, later, Gayeton Aiguier's
presence at the southern end of the block. A large architectural concentration
in the brewhouse square south of Meeting Street bore evidence of this large
industrial structure. With the exception of the postwar structures at the northern
end of town, the distribution of buildings was similar to that shown on the

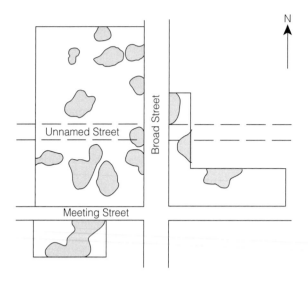

Figure 4.4 Structure locations indicated by the results of the 1974–1975 sampling investigations at Camden. Architectural artifact distributions produced by SYMAP formed spatially distinct concentrations that corresponded to areas identified on the basis of documentary evidence and revealed a layout conforming to that shown on the 1781 military map. This patterning reflects the orientation of the town to its major route of trade. Source: Lewis (1976).

1781 military map. Structures paralleled Broad Street and extended along an unnamed east-west thoroughfare suggested by the arrangement of buildings. Just as indicated on the map, the course of this road led directly to the Kershaw House east of town.

Material evidence obtained in the sampling excavations clearly demonstrated the paramount importance of access to transportation throughout the eighteenth century. The distribution of artifacts, together with graphic and written documentation, showed that early inhabitants found it useful and desirable to cluster settlement along the town's major thoroughfares despite that by doing so they modified the town's official plan and ignored the placement of public institutions outside the contiguous settlement.

HYPOTHESIS 4: SETTLEMENT SIZE

I assumed that, lacking the large supporting population of contemporary European market towns, frontier centers such as Camden would have been noticeably smaller in size than their counterparts in Great Britain. Because no population figures were available for Camden, I would have to calculate its size based on the number of buildings in the town. This figure might be computed on the basis of documentary and archaeological evidence and compared to the number of structures found in contemporary British settlements. Historical written and graphic sources provided information about market town size in Great Britain. These data indicated that such settlements varied greatly depending on the scale and extent of their trade and related activities. Those that supported periodic markets seemed to be the most similar to Camden and had populations ranging from 800 to several thousand. I arrived at a rough upper estimate of the number of structures in such settlements by first assuming that most structures housed at least a single family and then dividing these numbers by 4.75, the estimated mean family size of eighteenth-century British households (Laslett 1972). The result suggested that small market centers included anywhere from 168 to 632 houses, and this range compared favorably with published figures for such settlements by contemporary observers (Eden 1973). I used the lower end of this range to compare British market centers with Camden.

An examination of the 1781 military map of Camden provided a figure for the town at this point in its development. A building count showed that the palisaded area enclosed 21 structures with Kershaw's mansion and another outlying building lying apart from the concentrated settlement (Figure 2.10). I compared this to the number of architectural clusters identified by the archaeological sampling (Figure 4.4). The results of the sampling indicated that at least 15 structures had existed in the portion of the town examined over the entire time of the town's occupation. Because these excavations had not explored a substantial part of the town's eastern side, I would have to estimate the number of missing buildings in this part of Camden.

I used the distribution of structures on the 1781 map as a guide to their arrangement over time. It showed that they were just about evenly dispersed on both sides of Broad Street, a pattern likely to have prevailed later. A similarity in the arrangement and number of mapped buildings and archaeological structural clusters on the west side of Broad Street north of Meeting Street also implied a continuity in settlement patterning. These observations led me to conclude that I could estimate the total number of structures in the town by doubling the 11 clusters on the west side of the street. This calculation implied that 22 buildings lay north of Meeting Street. The addition of the structural concentration on the brewhouse square brought the total within the contiguous settlement to 23, two more than indicated by the map. Even counting the two outlying structures, the total of 25 the size of Camden fell well below that of contemporary British settlements of comparable function.

HYPOTHESIS 5: THE ROLE OF SPECIALIZED ACTIVITIES

Camden's role as a focus of frontier urban functions brought a wide range of specialized activities to the settlement. Documents disclosed the identity of many of Camden's structures, such as Dr. Alexander's Blue House, John Adamson's house and store, and Dinkins's tavern. Documents also named several others built before 1780. Stores belonging to Ely Kershaw and Joseph Kershaw as well as Gayeton Aiguier's tin-working shop all lay near the southern end of the western side of town, and on the south side of Wateree Street, sat two buildings comprising Joseph Kershaw's brewhouse. On the north end of the east side of Broad Street, John Mickle's house and store were situated on the unsampled portion of the site just below the public square. Only three of these eleven known buildings were likely to have been dwellings, and one of these probably served as a medical office as well. Although this high ratio of specialized to domestic activities seemed to reflect a prevalence of structures devoted to the former at Camden, a reliance on them alone ignored other buildings shown on the 1781 map and left the functions of half of the town's edifices unidentified. Documentary evidence illustrated the diverse nature of activities at Camden, but left the function of many parts of the settlement uncertain. To address the distribution of activities, I again turned to the material record.

In order to examine activity patterning over the sampled portion of the settlement, I first had to spatially define activity areas associated with structural concentrations and then compare the contents of such areas with regard to their function. The areas were based on my knowledge of the role of yards adjacent to most structures in eighteenth-century British America. Yards served as work areas and contained outbuildings, such as privies, wells, sheds, workshops, barns, and warehouses, where activities were carried out and tools and materials stored. They also became the primary refuse dumps where garbage littered the surface or was disposed of in pits (Noël Hume 1969). Archaeological evidence of such heavy use areas often took the form of postholes, pits, and other intrusions associated with construction, modification, and burial of waste. I identified structure-based activity areas by plotting the estimated distributions of these features generated by SYMAP relative to the structural debris and used the results to divide the site into 10 units for purposes of analysis (Figure 4.5).

At first glance, one might expect that specialized activities would be represented archaeologically by diagnostic items related to their function. Sometimes this is true, as in pottery making, where kiln wasters are discarded nearby in large numbers, or blacksmithing, which generates a large amount of waste material. On the other hand, most activities produce a much smaller by-product and leave remains that are sometimes far from obvious. For example, store keeping leaves notoriously little debris. In light of these limitations and the fact that I was basing my analysis on a very small sample, I decided to employ very broad data categories to distinguish activities at Camden.

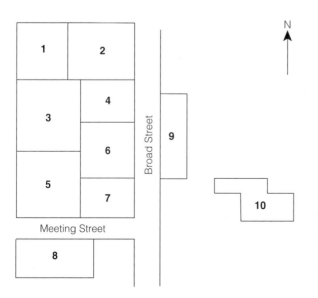

Figure 4.5 Structure-based activity areas at Camden derived from the distributions of architectural material, portable artifacts, and subsurface features discovered in the 1974–1975 sampling excavations. Source: Lewis (1976).

First, I defined a category of subsistence artifacts associated with household domestic activities, such as the production, preparation, consumption, and distribution of subsistence products. Second, I assumed that commercial and industrial activities would have employed artifacts linked to manufacture, repair, modification, storage, and shipment of goods. Because these technological artifacts occur much less frequently in the archaeological record and would not form quantities of discard comparable to subsistence artifacts, it would be difficult to compare them statistically. I knew, however, that a great number of artifacts such as architectural materials and personal articles were used in both domestic and specialized contexts and that these usually formed a substantial amount of discarded material. I assumed this common assemblage of subsistence-technological artifacts would remain more or less constant regardless of the activity performed. The relative size of the subsistence category, on the other hand, would likely vary with the extent to which the area was devoted to domestic activities. Areas used for specialized activities, even if those activities left little material trace, would be characterized by the smallest frequency of subsistence artifacts. Areas where domestic and specialized activities overlapped such as in a store occupied by the store owner's household might exhibit a larger proportion of subsistence artifacts. Finally, artifacts in this category were expected to dominate domestic areas. I anticipated that the relative size of these data categories, rather than the presence of discrete sets of data, would reveal functional diversity at Camden.

A comparison of the activity areas showed significant variation in the nature of their archaeological deposits and allowed me to separate those likely to have been dwellings from those used for other activities. When I compared the frequencies of subsistence and subsistence-technological artifacts in each of the areas, the latter clustered in three groups. The first group exhibited the highest percentage of domestic artifacts and implied that Areas 2, 3, and 6 once contained nonspecialized household occupations, all of which took place after the Revolutionary War. John Adamson's house and store lay in Area 2 at the north end of the block. Farther south, the Blue House was probably situated on Broad Street in Area 6. The structure in Area 3 was situated far back in the center of the block and may have represented Thomas Dinkins's house. The second cluster of areas held a somewhat lower frequency of subsistence artifacts and included Areas 1, 4, 7, 9, and 10. The 1781 map pictures structures in all of these locations except Area 1. Its identity, as well as that of the edifice in Area 10, could not be determined. But the other three areas could be tied to the remains of known buildings. The remains of Joseph Kershaw's stores and the Aiguier tin-working shop were probably in Area 7. Farther northward, Area 4 included land owned by Ely Kershaw and may include portions of his store. Across Broad Street, Area 9 very likely represented Dinkins's tavern. The third cluster consisted of two areas that yielded a relatively low frequency of subsistence artifacts. These were Area 5 well west of Broad Street and Area 8 lying south of Meeting Street. Structures in the first area may have been located along the unnamed street shown on the 1781 map. I was more certain, however, about the identity of those in Area 8. Lying on the brewhouse square, they appeared very likely to have been the remains of this early industrial complex.

Although the size of the sample recovered in the initial stage of excavations limited the degree to which I could identify the nature of past activities at Camden, the material record produced evidence of the diverse nature I anticipated in a frontier central place. The town's single manufacturing activity stood out clearly from those buildings known to have housed stores and a tavern. At the other end of the spectrum, the three areas identified as domestic could all be linked to residences. The fact that this last group all dated from the later years of Camden's occupation was significant because it indicated that the earlier settlement likely lacked structures used solely as dwellings. The colonial town would seem to have consisted of buildings of mixed use but always containing a non-domestic function related to Camden's role as a market center.

HYPOTHESIS 6: STATUS AND WEALTH

Camden's central position in the backcountry economy ensured its rise as a hub of trade and made it a magnet for social and political activity on the frontier. Its role fostered the development of integrating institutions, the presence of which attracted people who were instrumental in the region's development. The town became the temporary or even permanent residence of many traders and merchants as well as others involved in the marketing of produce and distribution of imported goods. Camden's roles as judicial center and transportation node also brought judges, politicians, travelers, and other persons of high status to town on a regular basis. All of them would have exhibited their wealth in various ways. In complex, stratified societies, status is associated with the unequal distribution of scarce goods and services, and I believed that evidence of such differential allocation would be observable in the archaeological record.

Identifying the material manifestations of high status is often straightforward but may also be elusive. Architectural style can identify the status of a building's occupants, and the Kershaw House, excavated earlier, certainly indicated the presence of colonial Camden's leading merchant. But discerning architectural style was beyond the capability of the sampling scheme. Designed to discover patterning through an analysis of individual artifacts, my investigations had to rely on the occurrence of portable objects deposited by those who possessed or used them. Unfortunately for the archaeologist, some aspects of high status are not detectable in the material record. Many items such as fine clothing leave little trace and are represented only by buttons, buckles, and other resilient components. Other expressions of high status such as patterns of speech leave no evidence at all. In addition, high status items were valuable and did not usually pass into the archaeological record deliberately. Unlike broken ceramics, this kind of artifact did not become common refuse subject to discard. Instead, they were carefully looked after and often repaired or refurbished. They became archaeological specimens only when lost. The likelihood of an object's loss increases the smaller and more portable it is, the more often it is used, and the greater the capability of the surface onto which it falls to conceal it (Schiffer 1976). Because my sample came from a plowed site, I could not evaluate the nature of the surface but could identify structural locations where the likelihood of loss would have been higher. And, through the use of historical analogy, I could expect the kinds of artifacts that would have accumulated as a result of inadvertent deposition.

I predicted that the high status artifacts most likely to be found at Camden would fall into the category of small, portable objects that were subject to frequent use. Such personal items especially included those associated with dress. In the last half of the eighteenth century, a great disparity characterized British dress. In general, persons of higher status wore elaborate costumes adorned with large numbers of fasteners made of precious metals in contrast to the much simpler dress of lower status commoners. Ordinary buttons, for example, were made of a variety of materials including lead, bone, pewter, brass, glass, and wood; however, those worn by the wealthy are more likely to have been of silver, silver or gold plate, or pearl (Steel and Trout 1904). Although an anticipated low rate of loss for valuable items together with the small size of the archaeological sample collected decreased the likelihood of recovering a large number of high status artifacts, I suspected that some of these objects would be present and their distribution would provide evidence that such persons resided in or at least passed through Camden, and identify the particular parts of the town associated with their activities.

The sampling excavations revealed that Camden's population included a high status component and indicated that their activities were concentrated in two areas. As anticipated, the excavations found only a small number of diagnostic artifacts; however, their distribution was highly concentrated in the town site. They consisted of four high status personal items. Area 2, at the northern end of town yielded a silver-plated brass button with an engraved floral design and a silver cane tip with the initials "RH" engraved on its head. The cane tip was worn and the hole through which the pin passed to secure it to the shaft was torn, implying that it became dislodged from the cane and was lost. Farther south in Area 6, an initialed brass button and a silver-plated brass button marked this as a second high status area.

The distribution of the high status artifacts also correlated well with areas likely to have been associated with persons of high status in Camden. Area 6 included lands owned by Ely Kershaw, whose stores were situated there. His estate later transferred this property to his partner John Chesnut, who with the Kershaw brothers, was a member of Camden's resident social and political elite. Both Ely Kershaw and Chesnut certainly spent time on this tract and either might have lost these small, portable items during their visits. Dr. Isaac Alexander, who lived on the southern part of this property at the end of the century, may also have contributed these artifacts. Although not possessing the wealth of Kershaw or Chesnut, he was a prominent physician and a member of the social elite. In contrast to the multiple occupations of Area 6, the lands farther north in Area 2 appear to have been built on only after the Revolution. Prominent merchant John Adamson located his store and residence there and his presence could have accounted for the high status personal items recovered from this area. The "RH" engraved cane tip may have belonged to Rubin Harrison, who purchased lots directly across Broad Street in 1800 (Kirkland and Kennedy 1905).

The uneven distribution of high status items recovered in the sampling excavations provided evidence for the settlement's role as a focus for central integrating institutions in the backcountry and the participation of particular individuals in activities central to this development. Because of the low frequency of high status artifacts, I felt that the second part of this conclusion had to remain tentative. The patterns they revealed, however, were certainly worth noting in the analysis of the settlement as a whole, and their accuracy could be tested further with the results of more intensive archaeological work at Camden.

HYPOTHESIS 7: THE TEMPORAL RANGE OF CAMDEN'S OCCUPATION

Contemporary documents indicated that the settlement of colonial Camden emerged about 1760 and was abandoned by 1820. During this 60-year period, people occupying the town engaged in activities that continually generated a material record of their presence. Because Camden grew from the small settlement of Pine Tree Hill and was deserted as its residents relocated northward in the early nineteenth century, the town site was not occupied with the same intensity throughout its existence. Its occupation was likely to have grown, reached a peak, and then declined. Archaeologists believe that the size of the material record produced by the inhabitants of a settlement follows a similar unimodal curve reflecting changes in the volume of deposition over the time of its occupation. This assumption has an important implication for determining the temporal position of past settlements. It permits dates to be derived from a comparison of the ranges of individual artifact types and their frequency of occurrence. Techniques for dating are especially useful when applied to historic sites because of the accuracy with which the ranges may be fixed. I felt that employing a technique based on a class of exactly dated artifacts would provide a true date for Camden's occupation.

Historical archaeologists have relied on ceramics to calculate the dates for eighteenth-century British sites for several reasons. First, innovations in the manufacture of these artifacts during this time produced a wide variety of types, the morphological characteristics of which are readily discernible even on small specimens. Second, the rate of innovation occurred so rapidly that the types often had relatively short use ranges and are very useful time markers. Third, consumers rapidly adopted the new ceramic types, making their manufacturing and use dates virtually identical. Finally, documentation relating to the production and marketing of ceramics is complete enough that historical archaeologists have been able to accurately calculate the use ranges for each type. Following established procedures, I compared the ranges of the ceramic types from Camden to ascertain the beginning and ending dates of its occupation. I began by establishing temporal brackets between which the site's occupation was likely to have fallen. The placement of the brackets represented the points where half of the types came into or passed out of use. A comparison of the 27 ceramic types recovered at Camden indicated brackets of 1765 and 1820, dates that closely matched the beginning and ending dates inferred from documentary sources (South 1977).

To determine the accuracy of these dates, I employed Stanley South's (1977) mean ceramic dating formula to compute a median date for the site's use. This method compares the median date for the range of each ceramic type and the type's frequency of occurrence to arrive at a mean date for the entire ceramic assemblage. Because of the unimodal nature of deposition on a site, this mean usually falls near the midpoint of a site's occupation and is helpful in gauging the accuracy of date ranges found by bracketing. Based on an analysis of 11,394 datable ceramic sherds, I calculated a mean date of 1791 for Camden. This was only one year removed from both the midpoint of 1790 for the documented occupation and 1792 for the bracketed range. The dates derived from the ceramic analysis fit closely with those given in documentary sources. On the surface, the ceramic date seemed only to confirm a fact already known; however, it also provided new information in the sense that it revealed something about the nature of Camden's occupation. The correspondence of the ceramic mean date with the median date of Camden's settlement implied that the archaeological record here formed as a result of increasing deposition and a subsequent decline. This trend indicated that the intensity of the town's occupation followed a unimodal curve, rising to a peak and falling evenly, despite the disruption of the Revolutionary War occupation. Indeed, the fact that the occupation's peak intensity actually came after the war further underscored Camden's continued expansion and growth, a process that declined only with the gradual abandonment of the old town site.

HYPOTHESIS 8: SETTLEMENT SIZE, FORM, AND CHANGE

Although I had used archaeological and documentary evidence to establish the size and layout of Camden and ascertain information about its contents, I had not yet examined changes in the town's form over time. During the 60 years of its existence, Camden had grown from a nucleus at Pine Tree Hill to become a larger planned settlement consisting of a sizable number of buildings devoted to a variety of purposes. The 1781 map allowed me to view the patterning of settlement at one moment, and other documentary materials provided clues to the locations of certain buildings and activities. These documents could give only a partial picture of the changing settlement. But the distribution of artifacts alone was capable of providing a complete and unbiased record of Camden's entire settlement history. If the archaeological deposits retained stratigraphically separate layers laid down progressively over each phase of occupation, then it would be possible to identify those units having occupations associated with each period of Camden's existence. Unfortunately, the nature of the artifact assemblages from the sample excavations limited the extent to which material evidence could be employed to trace progressive settlement spread and contraction. Because all of the artifacts were contained in a plowed zone, the contents of each unit included the sum of all deposition there. These temporally mixed assemblages thus represented the entire range of each unit's occupation. How could I utilize this evidence to determine the time when each part of the site was occupied?

Because of their temporal sensitivity, ceramics once again held the key to determining time, but tracing the flow of settlement would be more difficult than calculating dates for an entire site. Bracketing the assemblage of ceramics from each sample unit offered one possibility, but I felt that the use spans of the ceramic types found in a mixed deposit would not allow me to obtain dates narrow enough to measure chronological variation within the limited time of the site's occupation. Observing the distribution of mean ceramic dates of individual units across the site, however, seemed to offer promise. These dates, which ranged from 1763 to 1819, virtually paralleled the range of Camden's occupation, and when expressed as a frequency distribution, they tended to peak around the 1790 median date of the site (Figure 4.6). If I assumed that these mean ceramic dates also reflected the midpoint of each unit's occupation, then the means of those units with the longest occupations would fall closer to the site median. Their dates could not tell me how early deposition occurred or when it ceased, but the point at which it culminated would indicate whether the greatest intensity of occupation took place before or after 1790. Those units with earlier or later dates were likely to represent shorter occupations that peaked before or after this time. I predicted that most of the town area would exhibit mean dates indicative of its long-term occupation, but those areas with early and late mean dates might also reveal the first areas occupied and abandoned and the last areas to be placed in use. The spatial patterning of these dates might then provide clues to the town's evolution.

My general expectation was that the earliest settlement at Pine Tree Hill occurred in the southern portion of the town and that the latest lay in scattered locations across the site where its last residents lived. Because of the northward movement of settlement, many of the most recent deposits are likely to have been at its northern end. I anticipated that the bulk of the longer-term occupation would have been associated with the consolidated settlement concentrated on

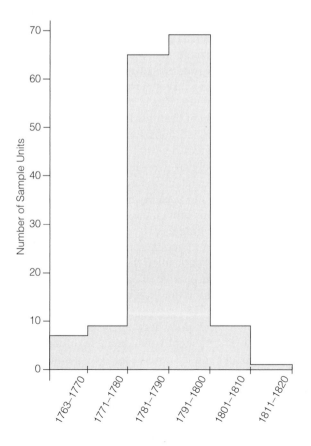

Figure 4.6 Histogram showing the frequency distribution of mean ceramic dates derived from sample units excavated at Camden in 1974–1975. Source: Lewis (1976).

the west side of Broad Street. In order to study shifting spatial patterns of settlement through time, I mapped the distribution of sample units according to ranges
derived from their mean ceramic dates. Using the year 1790 as the midpoint of
the occupation, the lengths of the temporal ranges were determined by calculating one standard deviation (8.31 years) and defining this period on either side of
the midpoint date. This calculation essentially divided the heaviest occupation
into two periods: 1782–1790 and 1791–1798. I placed the units whose mean
dates fell outside these limits into an early range (1763–1781) and a late range
(1799–1819). The SYMAP program produced a contour map that predicted the
patterning of these mean date ranges across the site (Figure 4.7).

The resulting map confirmed some of my assumptions but also produced
some unexpected results. As anticipated, it revealed that the occupation of most
of the settlement west of Broad Street peaked in the 1780s and 1790s. Areas with
pre-1790 dates appeared to be quite extensive, but those occupied after that date
seemed to concentrate closer to the main road, especially toward its northern
end. This patterning seemed to verify the long-term occupation indicated by the
1781 map and later documentary accounts describing residences and businesses
in this area. It implied that the western half of town recovered quickly from the
war and remained a center of activity through the end of the century. The more
restricted distribution of the post-1790 dates also seemed to reflect the shrinking
size of the older settlement around the buildings mentioned in the 1800 descriptions. Areas exhibiting pre-1780 mean dates were small and scattered and perhaps denoted the few areas that were not reoccupied and which did not remain
in use after the war. The distribution of units with post-1798 dates was especially
interesting in that most lay at the north end of the area where concentrations may
have accumulated on the properties of John Adamson and Thomas Dinkins.

Similarly dated areas also occurred east of Broad Street; however, the pattern
here was very different. Instead of being widespread, these areas were confined

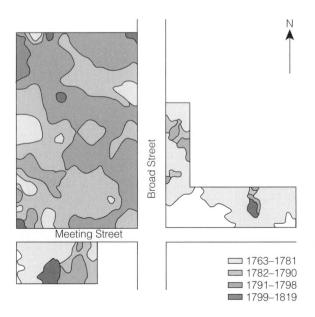

Figure 4.7 The spatial
distribution of mean
ceramic dates at Camden
produced by SYMAP.
These patterns were
based on ceramic data
recovered in the
1974–1975 sampling
excavations. Source:
Lewis (1976).

☐ 1763–1781
▨ 1782–1790
▨ 1791–1798
▨ 1799–1819

to three "islands" amid a sea of units with pre-1782 dates. This suggested that the eastern half of town, unlike its western portion, experienced its heaviest occupation before the Revolution and that Camden's inhabitants abandoned large parts of it after the war. This pattern conformed to documentary descriptions of the area. The 1781 map showed it heavily built up, but turn-of-the-century accounts mentioned only one structure, Dinkins's tavern, on the land included in the sampling excavations. A single restricted area of post-1798 dated units may have been generated by this activity. Although spatially limited, the examination of this portion of Camden implied that its most substantial development occurred early and that much of its area was not put back into intensive use following the Revolution, when activity gravitated to the west side of town or northward to the public square.

The area south of Meeting Street presented a picture of an extensive pre-1780 occupation, perhaps associated with the Pine Tree Hill settlement and the development of the brewhouse square by Joseph Kershaw in the 1770s. Subsequently, settlement became more concentrated in the vicinity of this structure and persisted into the nineteenth century. The distribution of dated units here implied that while the entire area saw heavy use, widespread activity there became more limited with time and was presumably focused on the single structure that dominated this portion of the town.

The results of the sampling excavations provided tantalizing clues to Camden's changing form. My examination of the distribution of mean ceramic dates obtained from individual excavation units revealed spatial patterning that helped me expand the limited information provided by documents to explore the development of the town. Although restricted by the nature of the material data, my analysis suggested broad early growth, uneven expansion after the Revolutionary War, contraction, and abandonment. These tentative conclusions were crucial to understanding Camden's evolving urban landscape and formed the basis for establishing the temporal control necessary for more intensive investigations.

HYPOTHESIS 9: THE IMPACT OF THE REVOLUTION

The results of Calmes's and Strickland's archaeological investigations left no doubt about the British military presence at Camden in 1780–1781. Their work had located and examined several of the defensive works erected around the town along with the palisade wall that defined the spatial limits of the colonial settlement. Although the outlying defensive elements constituted the defining aspect of the military base at Camden, the greatest intensity of activity seems to have taken place in the town itself. Soldiers were quartered in the town and prisoners of war were temporarily incarcerated there. The British established a central hospital at Camden, and supplies, munitions, horses, wagons, and all the other equipment to support the army's operations in the backcountry, as well as the invasion of North Carolina and Virginia, were secured behind the protective palisade that surrounded the town (Stedman 1794; Kirkland and Kennedy 1905). This intensive occupation, albeit of short duration, is likely to have been confined to the settled area, with the greatest amount of activity taking place in those areas used most heavily. I realized material evidence could occur anywhere

on the site but would be present in the heaviest concentrations in places of intensive use, such as barracks, administrative buildings, and the hospital. Because
these structures were among those represented on the 1781 map, I assumed that
the distribution of military artifacts would identify those structures used during
the military occupation.

The sampling excavations produced a total of 44 military artifacts, nearly all
of which lay in the western portion of the town site. Consisting of gun parts,
ammunition, and uniform components, the group represented portable items
liable to have been lost by their owners as they moved about in the course of
their regular duties. As a consequence, their distribution probably reflected frequency of use as much as storage. Many of the items were individual finds that
were scattered over the site in a pattern that indicated the soldiers' movements
occurred predominantly among the larger buildings along Broad and Meeting
Streets. The appearance of military items in the western and northern portions of
the town indicated that the encampment also extended across the entire palisaded area and implied that the smaller, regularly arranged structures appearing
on the 1781 map were soldiers' huts and other temporary buildings erected during the occupation (Figure 4.8).

Several deposits of military items stood out and pointed to intensive activity
in the area of Adamson's house and store and an unknown building near the
northern end of town and on the tracts owned by the Kershaw brothers farther
south. The association of these artifacts with the locations of structures known
to have existed before 1780 implied that these structures had been converted to
military purposes and perhaps were the storehouses and hospital mentioned by
contemporary observers. The results of the sampling could not answer this question; however, they clearly identified a focus of future inquiry.

The absence of military artifacts on the brewhouse square and their paucity
on the east side of Broad Street stood in marked contrast to other portions of the

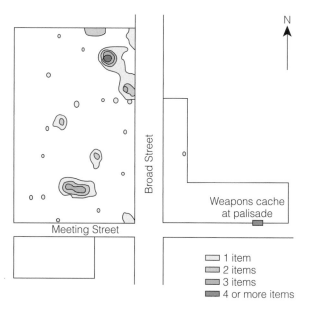

*Figure 4.8 The spatial
distribution of military
artifacts at Camden
produced by SYMAP.
The patterns shown are
interpolations derived
from data obtained in the
1974–1975 sampling
excavations as well as
earlier investigations
at the town palisade.
Source: Lewis (1976);
Strickland (1971).*

site. Modern disturbance to both areas may have contributed to the situation, but the small buildings assumed to be soldiers' huts on the 1781 map were absent from the portions of these areas that were examined archaeologically. Despite lying within the fortified town, they may have seen less intensive use. The low, wet ground in the southeastern corner of the town was, in fact, noticeably devoid of structures on the 1781 map and appears to have been avoided by the garrison. Although the weapons cache Strickland found earlier was the largest collection of military items recovered at Camden, its origin as a deliberate deposit by those intending to hide its contents made its presence the result of a process quite different from that responsible for the presence of the other military artifacts and did not indicate regular use of that area (Figure 4.8).

The results of the sampling excavations provided clear evidence of Camden's occupation by the British army in 1780–1781, but the uneven distribution of the material evidence showed that the army's presence was not evenly spread across the town site. At this point I could neither identify the nature of the military activities nor the structures where they were carried out; however, the patterning revealed in this initial phase of archaeology indicated the potential for material data to shed light on this dramatic but transitory episode of Camden's past.

SUMMARY

The initial investigations in the settlement of Camden produced a wealth of data that allowed me to examine the extent to which the process of insular frontier colonization influenced the nature and development of this central settlement in the South Carolina backcountry. By employing a research design capable of gathering a representative sample from the entire town site, I was able to examine the colonial settlement's size, form, and content utilizing a number of hypotheses relating to Camden's relationship with the region and the outside world, its function as a central place on the periphery of British expansion in the southern interior, and the manner in which the settlement responded to the evolving economy and other changes associated with the time and place of colonization.

The written record enhanced my ability to analyze the archaeological evidence from Camden but did not dictate the findings. Documentary material assisted this research at several levels: by identifying the site of Camden, by providing analogies to interpret the function of artifacts and assemblages, and by establishing a historical framework for the development of the town. By itself, the written record could not address the focus of the inquiry because it was silent or incomplete concerning the occurrence of the insular colonization process. The archaeological record, however, when adequately informed through analogies derived from documentary sources, uncovered patterning that supported the hypotheses drawn from the model of colonization and provided evidence that Camden arose as a frontier town, fulfilled the roles of economic and social center, and evolved as the backcountry was absorbed into the larger economy.

Although the results of this initial phase looked promising and clearly demonstrated the efficacy of archaeological sampling to produce meaningful data from sites disturbed by plowing, the extremely small sample size collected limited the information this research could gather. I did not intend the sampling excavation to produce a database capable of answering all questions about Camden. Rather,

I employed this methodology to acquire material evidence on a scale that would provide information about the community as a whole. Camden's community, extending into the surrounding countryside, served as the basic unit of organization for the immigrant society and reflected its adaptation to frontier conditions. Examining colonization at this scale not only helped me assess the influence of the insular frontier process in shaping settlement in the backcountry, but it also identified areas where more intensive research was necessary. The sampling excavations succeeded in their purpose of guiding future research at Camden.

In the conclusions of the 1974–1975 report, I discussed the direction of future research and stressed the need for a systematic approach. I recommended that the structure-based activity areas identified in the sampling excavations be used as the basis for further research. Future work might proceed by conducting more intensive sampling in these areas to better trace their boundaries and more accurately define the extent of activities within them. In addition, complete excavation of selected features would expose large areas, providing details about architecture, the nature and distribution of activities, and other information relevant to their function. For comparative purposes, I proposed that work be carried out at areas representing the three general functional activity categories identified in the initial sampling. Although subsequent archaeology at Camden did not take place as soon as I hoped or in precisely the manner I wished, additional investigations relied heavily on the results of the sampling excavations and focused on questions relating to frontier adaptations on a household scale.

5/Enlarging the Scale of Observation

Households on an Evolving Frontier

INTRODUCTION

The sampling excavations at Camden provided material evidence for the role of frontier change in fashioning the form and composition of colonial settlements in the South Carolina backcountry, but their results also became the key to investigating the impact of insular colonization on individual households within these communities. Just as the larger process shaped the town of Camden, the region's evolution affected the manner in which individual households adapted to the conditions they encountered. Anthropologists view households as groups of people who normally live or work together. Often households represent family groups, whose size and organization may vary considerably, or they may include groups of unrelated persons who do not comprise conjugal units and whose presence is linked to their shared tasks, or they may be mixed. Examples of households range from groups of nomadic hunter-gatherers to sedentary farming families to occupants of isolated mining camps. In all cases, the variation observed in households related to how people who live together organize their activities in the context of the larger society of which they are a part.

As the elemental units of society, households have always performed its basic social and economic functions, and their composition and arrangement reflect the society's institutional structure. I expected frontier households, as basic units of British colonial society, to exhibit characteristics arising from societal adaptations to the conditions imposed by colonization. Distinguished by isolation, poorly developed transportation and communications, and the absence of an effective central administrative infrastructure, areas undergoing rapid and extensive expansion developed indigenous social, economic, and political institutions to order production, implement trade, oversee the operation of the colony, and maintain its cultural integrity. In South Carolina's backcountry, the household as the basic unit of economic and social organization provided a context within which production and exchange were carried out and was an integral element of incipient political, religious, and military arrangements on the frontier. The nature of pioneer households would have affected their form and composition, and be discernible through distinctive attributes recognizable in the material record. By examining households at Camden, I hoped to explore the nature of colonization at the most basic level.

In order to study households in Camden archaeologically, I had to first define them spatially. Regardless of a household's composition, the communal arrangement of its residents and their activities confines it to the space regularly used by its members. A household generally includes a dwelling and its associated outbuildings and activity areas. Lying adjacent to one another, they encompass a space that defines the functional boundaries of the household (Laslett 1972; Wilk and Rathje 1982). At Camden, the sampling investigations identified a number of spatially discrete clusters of architectural materials and associated artifact distributions whose layout and proximity to documented structures implied the existence of at least 10 distinct households. The outlying Kershaw House complex, uncovered earlier, and the jail, also separated from the town and examined separately, added two more potential households to those within the early settlement. Each of these units offered an opportunity to examine frontier adaptations at a household scale.

By analyzing households in Camden, I expected to observe the influence of the insular frontier colonization on the smallest units of social and economic organization. To do so, I would have to observe activities in much greater detail than before. Because households represented the context in which a group of people carried out tasks, the composition and organization of their activities were affected on a different level than those conducted on the scale of the community that the households comprised. For example, community-level efforts to facilitate production and trade would involve the placement of mills, warehouses, and roads to improve access to and within a settlement. A comparable adaptation by a household within that community, on the other hand, might focus instead on actual processes of production and on making the size, composition, and arrangement of buildings and work areas accommodate the needs of its member's activities. Founders of a town may favor access to trade in choosing a site, but a resident potter would prefer to locate his kiln close to suitable clay. In examining the households at Camden, I had to consider the manner in which insular frontier colonization was likely to have affected the tasks of individual immigrants and how pioneer households would have adapted to the conditions they faced. Because conditions changed as the frontier society and economy matured, it also became necessary to determine how households would have changed to meet the emergence of a commercial economy in the backcountry.

Colonial households, like the settlements they comprised, can be investigated through the use of models designed to identify and explain their salient characteristics. Such models also provide a basis for deriving material expectations useful in examining households in the archaeological record. I believed that a model for household adaptation on the frontier should focus on the functional role of households in the backcountry and document their change over time. Derived primarily from comparative written evidence, the model emphasized the structure of frontier households and explained how they were affected by the region's transition to a commercial economy. Because economic forces played a dominant role in colonization, I felt that they were likely to have heavily influenced the nature and organization of household activities and their arrangement in space. Consequently, I anticipated that the composition of households would in large part reflect their members' engagement in production and trade, and changes over time are likely to have followed alterations in these functions. Because Camden's households were situated in a central place, they represented only a portion of the activities carried out in the region. These households were not farms or other rural settlements but stores, shops, and town residences, and the model had to take this into account. The model, then, would have to predict the evolution of urban household composition.

FRONTIER HOUSEHOLDS IN THE BACKCOUNTRY

Initial colonial settlement in the backcountry supported an economy characterized by diversified strategies of subsistence and complex networks of regional exchange. Within such a system, households engaged in a variety of enterprises intended to exploit different resources with which to sustain themselves and exchange for other frontier products, finished goods, and services. Rural settlers generally immigrated with the intent of becoming farmers; however, some turned to hunting and herding. Pioneers practiced various strategies that not only supplied their own households but linked them to a wider rural community through an extensive network of exchange. Rather than being guided by external market demand, production was carried out to ensure the survival and success of all. In this context, need controlled production more than price, and distribution usually involved the direct exchange of goods and services without a substantial accumulation of wealth. As a result, frontier production was diverse in nature and regional in scope. Backcountry households grew a variety of cultigens including corn, wheat, barley, oats, rye, peas, flax, hemp, and indigo. They also provided livestock, butter, cheese, pork, beef, tallow, and other products for trade. Although some of these found their way to lowcountry markets, most were intended for regional exchange. The flexibility of unspecialized production on the frontier was well adapted to the needs of a developing region (Meriwether 1940; Kulikoff 1993).

Regional exchange in the interior centered on isolated stores situated in central locations. These stores operated as redistribution points for local produce, conduits for exports, trading posts for exchange with Native groups, and sources of imported items. Samuel Wyly's store at Pine Tree Hill served all these purposes. Other specialized activities such as blacksmithing or milling also took place at separate locations. This form of economic organization resulted in the virtual absence of nucleated settlements during the early days of colonization (Sellers 1934). Dispersed settlements associated with specialized activities would have combined these functions with those of residence and subsistence and constituted multipurpose households. Although the organization of exchange in a regional economy discouraged the accumulation of wealth and the formation of settlements, the appearance of stores laid the groundwork for economic inequality by transferring the management of trade to the hands of a limited number of people. The stores established an infrastructure of central places linked by overland routes, and their locations became the loci for towns such as Camden, whose existence attracted both economic activities and also formal administrative and ecclesiastical institutions as they appeared on the frontier (Brinsfield 1983; Klein 1990).

The organization of the backcountry depended on the household as a central institution during the period of initial colonization. The multiple roles of households in the unfinished society of this developing agricultural region reflected this institution's ubiquitous nature and flexibility as an organizational unit in colonial society. Frontier households accommodated multiple functions, the presence of which were manifested in the composition and distribution of their associated activities. The nature and arrangement of its activities determined the form and content of a household settlement and were likely to be evident in the patterning of its material remains. As an early hub of economic activity in the backcountry, Camden played a central role in the development of central household institutions. Their material remains seemed to offer an excellent opportunity to investigate frontier households.

FRONTIER HOUSEHOLDS AT CAMDEN

The earliest European occupation on the site of Camden was associated with Samuel Wyly's Pine Tree Hill store, and the search for the material remains of frontier households focused on identifying the location of this tract. Situated along the Catawba Path, the store, inn, and related structures are likely to have lain on Wyly's property in what later became the southwestern part of Camden. The lands immediately adjacent to it became the property of Joseph Kershaw and his business partners in 1758. Their store, which superceded Wyly's business, seemed to have been located at or near the site of his establishment. When the partnership dissolved in 1774, Kershaw retained ownership of a tract immediately north of Meeting Street and, together with John Chesnut, continued to operate a store there after divesting himself of surrounding lands. Although the Kershaw-Chesnut store may not have been Wyly's original building, its presence indicated the use of this tract during the early years of settlement and identified the site as the likely location of a frontier household (Meriwether 1940; Lewis 1999b).

If Kershaw's initial household was centered here, it must have generated a material record of its occupation, and I assumed that the composition and distribution of these archaeological remains would reflect the nature of his initial activities at Camden. In spite of Joseph Kershaw's historical prominence as the town's founder, only limited information was available to shed light on his early household. Kershaw came as the backcountry agent of a Charleston firm. As an unmarried manager of the Pine Tree store, his household was likely to have consisted of company employees who were not attached to other households in the surrounding rural community.

This household was apparently not extensive; however, some information about the organization of this enterprise could be gleaned from the text of a sermon by the Reverend Charles Woodmason, an Anglican itinerant minister familiar with Camden and its inhabitants. In discussing the successful rise of Kershaw's future partner, John Chesnut, he described the composition of the store household. In it were three employees: a bookkeeper, a counter clerk, and a chief wagon driver. Presumably there were also laborers who assisted in loading, unloading, and shipping the goods and produce that regularly moved through the Pine Tree emporium. Although at least one of these employees, driver James Chesnut, may still have been a member of his parents' household, the others probably resided at the store. James's brother, John, was taken into this household as an employee while in his teens. Woodmason reported that John Chesnut had been "made one of [Kershaw's] family." Having been taken "under his roof as an errand boy, he had made his bed in the garret. He dined at the same family table" and rapidly worked his way up in the business (Hooker 1953).

The corporate household of the Pine Tree Hill store, comprising a group of largely unrelated male employees under the control of the store's manager, was not untypical of economic enterprises in frontier areas where the number of males was proportionately higher; however, because of the tenuous nature of the links between their members, such households were inherently unstable (Casagrande, Thompson, and Young 1964). The marriage of its head altered the composition of this household by adding a kin-based element whose presence was likely to have had a profound impact on its character. Four years after his arrival at Pine Tree Hill, Joseph Kershaw married Sarah Mathis, the daughter of Samuel and Sophia Mathis, early Quaker settlers who operated a tavern in the vicinity and whose family was also engaged in trade (Kirkland and Kennedy 1905). The link between Kershaw and another early business family enlarged the extent of the store-based household and helped establish its infrastructure for subsequent commercial development.

The Kershaw family grew rapidly in the next decade, enlarging the size of the resident group and altering the function of the store tract. The documents provide few clues to the location of a family dwelling, but given the small size of the early settlement, the Kershaws probably found it convenient to live close by the store. It was only much later in the mid-1770s, after the town had begun to expand systematically along the lines of the 1771 plan, that Joseph Kershaw began constructing his mansion on the east side of Camden. With the Kershaw family living on the store tract with servants, possibly slaves, and other nonrelatives such as John Chesnut, the complexity of the store household increased as new activities were added to its domestic function. Presumably the ensuing changes would have been reflected in the size and composition of the settlement it occupied.

The increasing commercialization of the frontier economy and the growth of Camden in the 1760s encouraged the further evolution of the early Kershaw store household. Many of the employees obtained property and moved off the premises as they formed families of their own. John Chesnut, for example, received an interest in the communal land holdings of Ancrum, Lance, Loocock, and Kershaw on becoming their partner in 1767 and later acquired lots in Camden and rural lands in the surrounding area. The collection of largely unrelated individuals at the store was gradually replaced by a more traditional kin-based household centered around the Kershaw family. This household, together with the activities associated with the store itself, was likely to have characterized the site at the close of the frontier period.

HYPOTHESES FOR FRONTIER HOUSEHOLDS

Camden played an important role as an early focus of trade on the backcountry frontier, and the historical record strongly implied that its initial households were centered around this economic activity. I anticipated that such households exhibited distinctive patterning in the character and distribution of activities carried out there and that evidence would be discernible in the archaeological record. Identifying and analyzing the sites of frontier households depended on my being able to recognize the characteristics of their form and content linked to their function. Conducting intensive archaeological investigations was the next step in exploring the impact of the colonization process on the settlement, and its success depended on my ability to develop hypotheses capable of exploring the nature of frontier households. These hypotheses would serve as the basis for generating archaeological expectations to guide this phase of the research.

Hypotheses relating to frontier households had to recognize that Camden's initial occupation represented both a chronological period and a developmental stage in the community's history. Material evidence early households generated was likely to reflect the site's particular temporal context as well as the presence of a group of activities associated with its multiple roles as a residence and focus of regional institutions. Because of the importance of trade at Pine Tree Hill, I decided to focus the functional analysis on the role of early households as centers of economic enterprises. Based on documentary evidence, it seemed that the Wyly store and the Kershaw establishment that succeeded it constituted the earliest colonial settlement at Camden. For this reason, I directed the intensive archaeological investigations intended to examine frontier settlement toward that portion of the town site where this occupation was likely to have taken place. I anticipated that its material record would provide the following types of evidence (Lewis 1998, 1999b).

1. The frontier period household should consist of a *group of structures and activity areas* in recognizably close proximity to one another.
2. Architectural elements and archaeological deposits associated with the structures should indicate its *origin before 1770,* the approximate time when the backcountry began to transition into the larger commercial economy.
3. The household site should reflect the *dual domestic/specialized nature* of its initial occupation.
4. Material evidence should demonstrate the household's *participation in a regional economy.*

TRANSITIONAL HOUSEHOLDS AT CAMDEN

The introduction of outside capital to fund backcountry enterprises and the improvement of transportation routes linking the region with the entrepôt of Charleston made it possible for entrepreneurs to develop the infrastructure for export trade. The close of the 1760s witnessed a shift in the organization of frontier production that accompanied Camden's rise as a center of milling and warehousing. By 1770 the town was the principal transshipment point for produce and imported goods as well as the location of formal administrative institutions. The British occupation during the Revolutionary War disrupted these activities, but Camden made a relatively rapid postwar recovery and expanded in the last decade of the eighteenth century. Although the settlement south of Bull Street was no longer the center of town, it remained a viable part of the community.

Households of the transitional community differed from those of the frontier in that the kin groups that occupied them increasingly lacked the multiple functions of the earlier period. Economic, political, and religious activities that once were based in homes had begun to move to separate businesses, offices, stores, court-houses, and churches. As a result of the increasing separation of functions, many households became more exclusively domestic or more specialized. Activities also appear to have become more narrowly defined in Camden over time. By the end of the century, its residents were engaged in numerous crafts, trades, professions, and services in addition to the large-scale businesses associated with milling and trade (Schulz 1972). I anticipated that the spatial separation implied by documentary evidence would also be clearly seen in the material record.

The alteration of the frontier economy brought other changes to the nature of households as well. Commercial growth and expanding external trade increased the amount and the variety of imported goods flowing into the interior. At the same time, increasing export sales permitted an accumulation of wealth that noticeably raised its residents' standard of living. These developments affected the material conditions of settlement by permitting conspicuous consumption in the form of larger and more elaborate architecture and the use of a wide variety of finished products. Both developments impacted the material record of Camden during the transitional period.

Accompanying the shift to commercial production was an increase in its scale and the organization of its agricultural base. The introduction of slave labor changed the nature of all economic activity as well as the composition of the population. As the number of free residents grew in response to the opportunities for wealth provided by participation in the larger economy, the number of enslaved people expanded in consequence of the immigrants' increased purchasing power. Even domestic households formed largely on the basis of kinship included a large non-kin component, who might have left a discernible record of their presence.

The sites of several documented households in Camden had been or would be the focus of intensive archaeological research, and the investigation of the areas of several others provided additional evidence regarding the nature of transitional households. Those areas completely uncovered included the Kershaw House and associated buildings excavated by Alan Calmes in 1968 and Robert Strickland from 1970 through 1973 (Calmes 1968b; Strickland 1976; Lewis 1975, 1977) and the Kershaw property, later occupied by Gayeton Aiguier, in the southwestern portion of the town, examined in 1996 through 1998 (Lewis 1999b). Extensive test excavations were conducted in 1998 at the site of the Blue House, home of Dr. Isaac Alexander (Lewis 1999b); Joseph Kershaw's brewhouse south of Meeting Street in 1981; and the site of the early Camden jail, lying north of the town, in 1979 (Lewis 1984b).

Erected as a residence by prominent Camden merchant Joseph Kershaw in the late 1770s, the large structure east of the town became the family residence shortly before the British invasion of the backcountry in 1780. British forces fortified the house as part of the town's defenses, and the commanders of the occupying force, Lieutenant General Charles, Lord Cornwallis and later Lieutenant Colonel Francis, Lord Rawdon, used the Kershaw House as their headquarters. Following their withdrawal the following year, the Kershaw family returned and used the house as a residence until after Joseph Kershaw's death in 1791. The property passed out of the family's hands and saw service as an academy in the early nineteenth century and later as a residence. By the 1850s it lay abandoned, watched over by a caretaker who lived in an outbuilding. In the closing months of the Civil War, it became a temporary storehouse for Confederate supplies to prevent approaching Union troops from destroying the town depot and other public buildings. The house burned during the federal occupation in February 1865 (Lewis 1977).

The Kershaw property in the southwestern quadrant of Camden emerged from the frontier period as the headquarters of the family's commercial enter- prises. Joseph Kershaw's original store was situated at the southern end of the block, and later his brother Ely acquired the tract abutting it on the north. Both operated stores on their properties. Ely Kershaw died in 1780, and the retreating British army burned his store. The old Kershaw-Chesnut store, which is likely to have served as the garrison hospital during the occupation, survived the war and remained standing as late as 1786 when the property was offered for sale. Twelve years later, Joseph Kershaw's tract came into the hands of Gayeton Aiguier, a refugee tin worker from Saint-Domingue, who conducted his business there. The Aiguier household included his family of six and four slaves, one of whom apparently was a skilled craftsperson. His wife remarried following his death, but with his widow's passing a year later, the property was abandoned (Lewis 1999b).

Ely Kershaw's property was apparently vacant when it passed through sev- eral hands following the Revolution and remained so until it came into the pos- session of Margaret Brisbane Alexander, wife of prominent physician, Isaac Alexander, before 1790. Contemporary documents revealed that the Blue House, an adjacent office and shop, and a number of outbuildings existed on the prop- erty. The Alexander household consisted of his family and domestic servants. After Margaret's death in 1805, the property passed to her descendents and Dr. Alexander left the premises in 1807. Although the new owner may have lived there, the property was certainly abandoned by 1815, when this portion of the town site had become a "lonely old field" (Lewis 1999b).

Joseph Kershaw was operating a brewhouse on the block south of Meeting Street by 1770. These structures appeared on the 1781 military map, which shows that the town palisade wall was extended to surround them. Although damaged during the British occupation, the brewhouse and "outbuildings" sur- vived the war and remained in use at least as late as the mid-1790s, after which no mention of it occurred in documents. Throughout its existence, the brew- house would have constituted an industrial household consisting of persons, both free and enslaved, who were engaged in manufacturing (Lewis 1976).

Another non-kin based household centered on the Camden jail, an adminis- trative building completed in 1771 to accommodate Camden's new role as the judicial seat of Camden District. Employed to house prisoners awaiting trial and suspected fugitive slaves, the jail acquired the additional role of military prison during the Revolution. During the British occupation, the jail was fortified to become the town's northernmost redoubt. When it abandoned Camden, the army burned the jail. Unlike the other transitional period households, the jail was sit- uated on a tract of public land, where a second jail was soon built. It was removed in 1812. From 1816 until 1859 a market building stood on the property (Lewis 1984b).

The distinctive nature of these seven households in Camden plainly set them apart from those of the preceding period. Changing economic and social conditions accompanying the closing of the backcountry frontier had dramatically altered the composition and function of urban households. The nature of these households would, in turn, have created an archaeological record likely to reveal evidence of their more specialized roles in a settlement that had taken on a new role in the postcolonial economy. In order to examine the material transformation of frontier to transitional households in Camden, I developed several hypotheses that embodied characteristics likely to have been associated with their function.

HYPOTHESES FOR TRANSITIONAL HOUSEHOLDS

1. Transitional period households should consist of a structure or structures *spatially associated* with an activity area or areas.
2. Architectural elements and archaeological deposits should indicate their *origin or use after 1770,* by which time the transition to a commercial economy was underway.
3. The architecture and contents of each household should bear witness to the fact that it served either *domestic or specialized functions* but not both.
4. The household should exhibit evidence of its wider *participation in the national economy*.
5. The relative affluence of post-frontier property owners in Camden permitted them to *incorporate enslaved persons into their households*. Material evidence should indicate their presence.

To investigate the nature of frontier period households and their response to the economic and social transition that accompanied the frontier's close in the last quarter of the eighteenth century, I needed to examine material data on a much more intensive scale than that employed in the earlier sampling. I identified eight areas at Camden where such evidence could be obtained, either from the results of earlier work or from new excavations based on information obtained in the 1974–1975 sampling of the site. Documentary sources identified the households likely to be associated with each area and provided clues to the extent of their boundaries. Written records also indicated the properties' potential owners or users and the activities in which they were engaged, and they sometimes provided details about the households themselves. Despite the information that the documents supplied, they often remained silent regarding the manner in which the economic and social circumstances of colonization and its aftermath shaped the actual form and composition of households in Camden and organized their activities. This information, which reflected pioneer adaptation on the scale of its most basic residential units, could only come from a comparative analysis of material data from actual examples. The archaeological record created by individual Camden households held the potential to reveal patterning that would help me recognize the extent to which the characteristics proposed in the model actually typified the development of this settlement. The next task, then, was to design an archaeological inquiry capable of examining the nine hypotheses derived from the model.

6/Defining Camden's Households in Space

INTRODUCTION

My study of households in Camden grew out of the results of the previous archaeological work. By the late 1970s, my investigations at Camden had sampled the accessible portion of the eighteenth-century town site and identified several areas likely to contain the remains of early households. Earlier excavations at the Kershaw House site had explored its occupation intensively, but their results were as yet unreported. Over the next two decades, I completed the analysis of this earlier archaeological work and carried out new explorations designed to examine three areas within the town. In addition, construction work unexpectedly uncovered material remains at the site of the Camden jail, providing a limited opportunity to examine another household. These projects together discovered the remains of numerous structures and generated a considerable amount of data about the town's occupation and the nature of the households that comprised it.

Although directed at specific topics, the questions settlement archaeology addressed at Camden were broad enough to employ material data gathered in all the earlier investigations. As often happens with archaeological research carried out under dissimilar circumstances or directed toward specific and differing goals, the methodology that guided the fieldwork at Camden varied between projects. Even though all of the excavators intended to increase our knowledge of the early settlement, their work was not always concerned explicitly with the nature of household composition and organization. Those pursuing questions on other topics, such as the architecture of fortifications, collected evidence appropriate to their interests. Time constraints also limited the scope of some investigations and narrowed the range of data they gathered. These differences, however, did not necessarily make the material evidence generated by these projects incompatible with my research, nor did it preclude the use of their data. The goals of household archaeology focused on understanding residence groups and their activities, and my questions sought to understand how changing household structure reflected the development of frontier economy and society. Answering these questions required information about time, spatial arrangement, and content that could be discerned from evidence collected in pursuit of other topics. The data gathered in the earlier Camden projects, while often limited, were not unusable nor were they inappropriate for the investigation of past households. Each project's goals affected its role in the current research, but all of the past work contributed to the study of household development.

The hypotheses for household form, composition, and change during the frontier and the transitional periods provided an outline for an examination of archaeological evidence from the five areas investigated at Camden. My first task was to identify the remains of specific households in each of these areas and then define them as discrete spatial units. Once I had recognized potential household sites, I could then determine the time of its occupation through an analysis of architecture and other artifacts. This analysis would make it possible to assign each household to a particular period in Camden's historical development. Because the role of households changed as backcountry society evolved from a frontier to a transitional economy, I anticipated that material evidence would reveal variation in the structure and organization of the households assigned to each period. Related to the changing role of households was their participation in an increasingly wider economy. I assumed that the material record Camden's households generated would exhibit evidence of this phenomenon. Finally, I hoped to explore the question of increasing ethnic variation during the transitional period.

The order of this inquiry offered the advantage of introducing each household complex, delineating its boundaries, and describing the layout and distribution of its physical remains prior to evaluating the nature of its contents. Once identified as households, each complex might then be examined with regard to its temporal position and the functional implications of its material remains explored in relation to social organization, economy, and ethnicity. In all phases of this investigation, an examination of historical documentation provided direct information about the complexes' occupations as well as analogies pertaining to their material remains. These sources together with the material record helped me reconstruct the evolution of Camden's households.

This chapter deals with the first aspect of this inquiry. In it I will discuss how investigators examined each of the intensively investigated areas at Camden and how documentary, architectural, and archaeological data were employed to establish the structural basis for households and how this evidence helped identify the time of their occupations. This important information allowed me to define households in time and space. Understanding these parameters establishes a context for the analysis of content and function and is a crucial step in archaeological analysis. My identification of Camden's households and their temporal framework was the necessary first step in investigating the town's development.

THE KERSHAW HOUSE COMPLEX

The earliest household investigations at Camden centered around the Kershaw House complex, situated just east of the town. Alan Calmes's and Robert Strickland's excavations uncovered the principal structure and explored an extensive area around it to examine the Revolutionary War fortifications as well as other features related to the Kershaw occupation. Over the six-year period in which archaeological work took place, the excavations followed several different strategies and each of these affected the data collected. Calmes's work employed the first strategy, which centered on the use of exploratory trenching and unit excavations to discover and delineate architectural features useful in reconstructing the site. His work focused on finding the Kershaw House and associated military defensive fortifications. He began by excavating a 5-foot wide east-west trench until it intersected the footings of the house and then opening a second trench, perpendicular to the first, to establish the limits of this structure. The area assumed to contain the remains of the Kershaw House was then excavated in 10 by 10 foot squares and larger units of varying size. Calmes then extended his excavations west and south of the building in search of adjacent structural features (Figure 6.1). During the course of this 1968 work, he uncovered a portion of the trench for the surrounding palisade, and a large pit lying just outside its southwest angle (Calmes 1968b).

Robert Strickland continued Calmes's architecture-oriented strategy to uncover the remainder of the fortifications, but he later altered it to examine the area surrounding the house. In 1970 he excavated a line of 10 by 10 foot squares to intersect and define the northern and southern limits of the palisade wall, after which he traced the remainder of its course (Figure 6.2). Having identified the boundaries of the military site, he turned to exploring the extensive area it enclosed. The 1971 investigations, however, brought a change in excavation

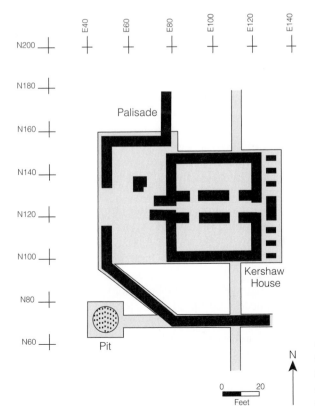

Figure 6.1 Plan of Alan Calmes's archaeological investigations at the Kershaw House in 1968. Source: Calmes (1968a).

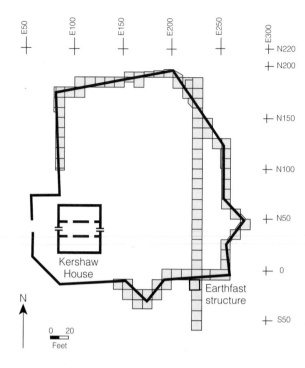

Figure 6.2 Plan of Robert Strickland's 1970 excavations at the Kershaw House. This project defined the shape of the British military palisade surrounding the mansion and its yard. Source: Lewis (1977).

strategies. Rather than focusing on architectural features alone, Strickland sought to locate and investigate all cultural features associated with past occupations at the site. Because cultivation had disturbed material lying near the surface, he concluded that evidence of only general patterning would survive to be discovered in the plowed zone and that far more information could be derived from the undisturbed material evidence contained in pits, postholes, and other intact features that lay beneath it. Given the large area to be explored with limited time and resources, Strickland elected to sacrifice the data contained in the plowed zone by stripping it away to uncover the buried features (Figure 6.3). Consequently he removed this layer from the site to expose the subsurface features, which he then carefully mapped and excavated over the next two years (Strickland 1976).

In 1972 Strickland modified his excavation strategy to examine the area outside the palisade. He sought to determine the spatial extent of the occupation associated with the Kershaw House by discovering features outside its immediate vicinity (Figure 6.4). Of particular concern to him were the graves of American captives who died during the British occupation and were, according to tradition, buried nearby. The proximity of the Kershaw House to the property of John Bartlam, the potter who successfully produced Carolina creamware at Camden in the 1770s, also made Strickland aware of the possibility that evidence of his activity may have extended into this area. Seeking to discover patterning of extensive activities, he abandoned area excavations in favor of exploratory trenches. Slot trenches aligned with the cardinal directions extended the archaeological work to the north, east, and south but uncovered no evidence of burials or pottery making. They did, however, reveal additional architectural features (Strickland 1976).

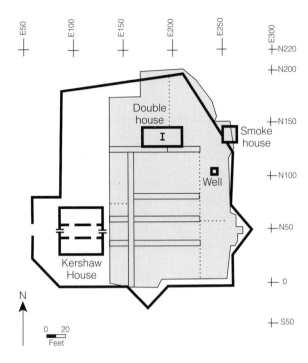

Figure 6.3 Plan of Robert Strickland's 1971 excavations at the Kershaw House. Trenches and area excavations exposed structural features in the palisaded yard. Source: Lewis (1977).

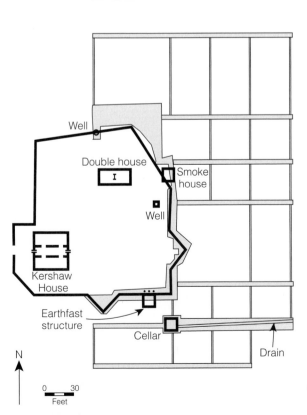

Figure 6.4 Plan of Robert Strickland's 1972–1973 excavations at the Kershaw House. Extensive trenching explored the area around the yard and exposed additional structural features. Source: Lewis (1977).

Strickland's investigations in the vicinity of the Kershaw House uncovered remains of several other major structures that formed a complex of household activity areas. They included a rectangular double house with a central hearth. This structure measured approximately 39 by 19 feet and was large enough to have been depicted with the Kershaw House on the 1781 military map of Camden. Although nothing remained of the building's superstructure, the one-and-a-half brick-wide foundation on which it rested was capable of supporting a substantial frame building. The foundation also indicated that the double house had been rebuilt at least once, and this implied that it had remained in use for an extended period (Noël Hume 1969).

Strickland also discovered a second substantial building southeast of the palisaded enclosure. This 20-foot square brick cellar contained a well in its floor as well as an eastward-sloping drain leading away from the cellar and down the adjacent hillside. This building may have been a spring house, or cooling cellar, where dairy products, fruit, and other perishables were stored to keep them cool (Vlach 1993).

A wooden earthfast structure measuring 16 by 16 feet square was situated just outside the south palisade line (Figure 6.5). Earthfast architecture, a form of construction commonly found in early British settlements in the southern colonies, employed a timber frame set on heavy posts of durable wood set in the ground. Earthfast buildings rested on a series of supporting posts, which formed an outline of their shape. Some, like this one, also had wall studs placed directly in narrow trenches excavated in the ground (Carson, Barka, Kelso, Stone, and Upton 1988).

Several additional architectural features emerged in the archaeological investigations, but none were likely to have been the foci of separate households. The largest of these was the foundation of a 9-foot square brick smokehouse that intersected the northeast diagonal of the palisade. The exploratory excavations

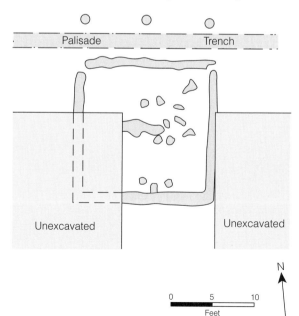

Figure 6.5 Plan of the earthfast structure in the Kershaw House complex. This structure contained a single bay, the walls of which consisted of posts and studs set in trenches. Three postholes aligned with the northern wall imply an overhang on this side of structure. Source: Lewis (1977).

Figure 6.6 Conjectural bird's-eye view of the buildings in the Kershaw House complex as they might have looked about the time of the American Revolution. Illustration by Darby Erd courtesy South Carolina Institute of Archaeology and Anthropology, University of South Carolina.

also discovered a square well, 25 large pits, a ditch, and numerous postholes in the vicinity of the house, and a wall removed some distance to the northeast of it. Later investigations in 1974 located a second well in the north palisade line (Lewis 1975).

The four principal structures near the Kershaw House suggested the presence of as many as four separate households. Their relatively close proximity to each other and the arrangement of the three smaller buildings in a rectangle behind the Kershaw House indicated that they formed an integrated complex. The large mansion building, the cellar, and the double house, all of which had brick foundations shared the same orientation as the town grid. Groups of postholes, representing fence lines and enclosures, shared the alignment of the buildings, revealing a regular and systematic division of space within the larger complex (Figure 6.6). Although the earthfast structure deviated from this alignment by several degrees, its proximity to the other architectural elements tied it to the Kershaw House complex. To analyze these four structures, I designated each of them as a separate focus within this locality.

THE CAMDEN JAIL

Investigations at the site of the Camden jail came about unexpectedly in November 1979 when construction work for a buried gasoline tank on the southeastern corner of Broad and King Streets encountered what appeared to be early structural foundations (Figure 6.7). Because the location of the excavation took place on the tract set aside for the jail in 1771, I was asked to investigate the situation. Construction work had stopped in the meantime because the intended use

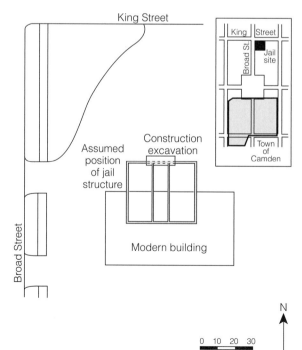

Figure 6.7 Plan of the Camden jail site showing the construction pit intersecting a portion of the jail foundations. Buried well below the present surface, these remains are likely to extend undisturbed beneath a nearby modern building. Source: Lewis (1984b).

of the property violated a city zoning ordinance. The work stoppage allowed me time to inspect the site, prepare maps of the exposed archaeological remains, and collect artifacts uncovered by the construction pit.

Successfully interpreting the nature of the household on this site depended on linking the material evidence uncovered in the construction pit with the historic structure known to have occupied this tract of land. In other words, how did I know that the foundations represented the Camden jail? Documentary records provided the key to understanding the succession of structures built on this parcel of land. Created by the Circuit Court Act of 1769, the Camden Judicial District received funds to erect a court and jail the following year. Built on a lot set aside for this purpose in the 1771 plan of Camden, the jail was completed by 1772. This building was enclosed by a redoubt during the British occupation and burned by retreating troops in 1781. A second jail was built on the same lot after the war and burned in 1812. Following this event, the jail was relocated elsewhere in the town and a market building with a tower was constructed on the old jail lot. A contemporary illustration showed the distinctive form of this structure, and early accounts placed it on the northwest corner of the tract facing Broad Street. A northward shift of Camden's business district in the 1830s and 1840s left the market at the southern periphery of town, and it was abandoned in 1859 in favor of a more central location. Within the next two decades, the old market disappeared and the site remained vacant until the mid-twentieth century, when new businesses were erected there (Kirkland and Kennedy 1905; Lewis 1984b).

The documented presence of only three buildings on the jail tract confined my work to identifying the exposed foundations. Situated near the center of the lot, the buried structure uncovered in the construction pit did not appear to be associated with the nineteenth-century town market. That building lay near the corner of the lot, where exposed brick foundations were still visible on the surface. Their location and the configuration of these remains conformed to documentary descriptions of the market and clearly identified this structure. A process of elimination implied that the buried foundations had to be one of the two jail buildings. As I will discuss later, the alignment of the exposed foundations also suggested that they represented the early structure. I also assumed that the archaeological deposits associated with the foundations were generated by the jail household. Although the nature of this "salvage" excavation restricted my interpretations, I believed that material data collected from this site would provide information about the character of this distinctive household of Camden's transitional period (Lewis 1984b).

THE BREWHOUSE

My first opportunity to carry out intensive archaeological work within the palisaded town presented itself in the summer of 1981 when the University of South Carolina conducted an archaeological field school in the vicinity of Camden. As an element of this field school, I directed limited excavations to determine the accuracy with which the results of the 1975 sampling investigations had been able to predict the location of early structures. I chose the Area 8, which was marked by a single dense cluster of structural material on the western side of town south of Meeting Street (Figure 6.8).

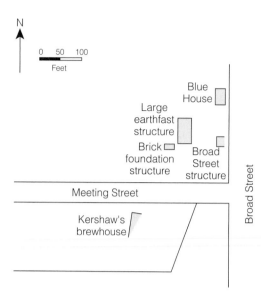

Figure 6.8 Locations of house-holds in the town of Camden identified on the basis of archaeological evidence.

I chose this location for several reasons. First, it possessed a concentration of archaeological materials that was spatially distinct from the others. The SYMAP distribution was confined to a discrete, compact area extending southward from the street that separated it from the rest of the settlement. This patterning suggested a structure or structures that extended back from the street front in a manner similar to those shown on the 1781 map. Second, the uncomplicated chain of ownership of this tract made it possible to associate its occupation with particular people and a specific activity. Documentary records indicated that the "brewhouse square," bounded by Meeting, Broad, Wateree, and Church Streets, was originally part of the jointly owned Pine Tree Hill tract. Joseph Kershaw acquired the land in the 1760s and constructed the brewhouse there. Contemporary observers mentioned the existence of this important colonial industry in Camden before the end of the decade, and Kershaw's records showed that the operation was in his hands by the 1770s. The "brewhouse and out houses" were important enough to have been enclosed by an extension of the town palisade during the British occupation of 1780–1781. Although it was "much injured" by the experience, the brewhouse complex survived and it continued to operate through the 1790s. The structure still stood at the turn of the century, when the property changed hands, but its absence in early nineteenth-century descriptions of Camden imply that it disappeared soon afterward. Finally, because the structural concentration lay on the most disturbed portion of the town site, I thought that its examination would provide a good test of the sampling strategy's ability to predict the nature of subsurface evidence. If archaeological patterning had survived the intrusive activities of a plant nursery intact, they were sure to have persisted under less destructive conditions elsewhere (Lewis 1976).

The field school project investigated a concentration of structural remains uncovered by the sampling project. Finding intact architectural elements, the field school students and I expanded this initial excavation to expose more of the

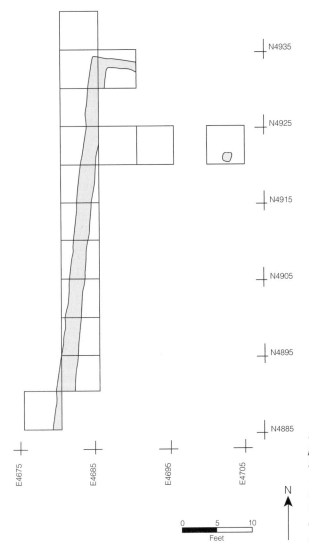

Figure 6.9 Plan of the portion of Joseph Kershaw's brewhouse excavated in 1981. These investigations uncovered a large part of the structure's west wall and a portion of its interior. Source: Lewis (1999b).

structure as well as other features associated with it. This work revealed partially intact brick foundation, a portion of which was exposed and mapped (Figure 6.9). These represented the remnants of a substantial building, the remains of which lay relatively untouched despite contemporary scavenging and later activities associated with the plant nursery. The excavations uncovered portions of a site likely to extend well beyond the area examined in 1981. Although the duration of that project limited the extent of the excavations at this substantial site, the architectural remains and the artifacts associated with them allowed us to gather a great deal of data relating to the brewhouse site. The results of this analysis produced much useful information about structures and activities related to the household that once occupied this locality.

INTENSIVE SAMPLING IN SOUTHWESTERN CAMDEN

In 1996 I began a multiyear project intended to investigate households situated in the southwestern quadrant of Camden. Documentary sources indicated that several households were situated in this area; however, their precise locations remained uncertain. Using the results of the 1975 sampling as a guide, the excavations focused on two structure-based activity areas, Areas 6 and 7. These two areas corresponded roughly to two tracts that had unconnected ownership histories. These were the Kershaw/Aiguier tract, fronting on Broad and Meeting Streets, and the Blue House tract, lying just north of it. Each of these tracts was also likely to have contained separate households that could be examined individually. Before attempting to study such households, the distribution of their structural materials had to be determined more accurately, particularly those in the heavy concentrations near Broad Street. My field assistant Frank Krist and I developed a design for a more intensive sampling that we hoped would allow us to identify more exactly the locations of structures and the remains of additional households around which we could center further work.

Unlike the earlier exploratory archaeology, an intensive sampling was designed to acquire only architectural data. By concentrating on a high-frequency architectural material likely to have accumulated around eighteenth-century structures, the sample could employ small excavated units spaced regularly at closer intervals. Using the grid established for the earlier excavations, Frank and I placed 45 posthole samples at 25-foot intervals. We assumed that the units would yield samples of rubble large enough to measure by weight and yet be spaced close enough together to reveal variation in the artifact's distribution. The amount of brick rubble varied considerably across the sampled area, and clear patterns in its occurrence became visible when its weight by unit was displayed graphically using a computer program called SURFUR (Figure 6.10). This program interpolated values over the area sampled and displayed them as contour lines. By plotting the contours of brick weight frequencies, we discerned three areas of relatively high occurrence.

One concentration of architectural material lay at the north end of the study area and fell within the boundaries of the Blue House tract. It covered a large area extending well back from Broad Street, and its shape suggested the presence of a substantial building or several structures in this vicinity. I felt that such a configuration might well mark the Blue House and perhaps outbuildings associated with its household. Farther south, two additional clusters were visible. The first lay adjacent to Broad Street, and its shape suggested that the building it represented originally continued beyond the cut bank that demarcated the edge of the modern road. Its compact area indicated that a small structure had once stood there. Not far behind it, a much larger concentration of structural material ran roughly in a north-south direction. Situated on the tract first owned by Joseph Kershaw and later by Gayeton Aiguier, the tin worker, these buildings were likely to have been used by either or both of their households.

The results of the intensive sampling greatly assisted my examination of this portion of the colonial settlement. They refined my knowledge of its patterning by providing evidence of the number, size, and location of the buildings that

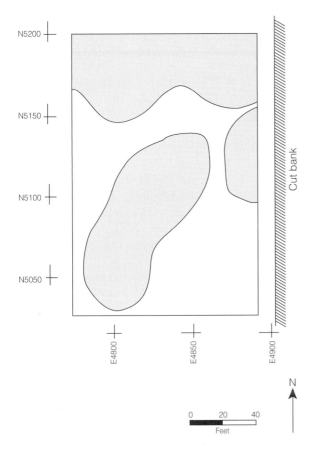

Figure 6.10 Distribution of architectural materials recovered by the intensive sampling excavations conducted in the southwestern part of Camden in 1996. The interpolated patterns created by SURFUR identified general locations of three buildings situated on the west side of Broad Street. The location of the northernmost structure implied that it may have been the Blue House. The other buildings lay on the tract owned by Joseph Kershaw and later Gayeton Aiguier and were likely to represent their occupations. Source: Lewis (1999b).

once existed in Camden and helped provide a context for architectural features discovered in the earlier sampling excavations. On the basis of these results, I conducted a series of large-scale excavations in this vicinity from 1996 through 1998. These projects uncovered several structures and activity areas, the investigation of which allowed me to define and analyze individual households. Although unfinished, this work yielded much new information relating to the origins and later development of the colonial settlement (Lewis 1999b).

THE KERSHAW/AIGUIER TRACT

The key to identifying the households on this large property on the corner of Broad and Market Streets was furnished by the structural remains the sampling excavations located. Data from both samples implied that at least three buildings occupied the tract, but the patterns left by the brick rubble were still amorphous. Although brick rubble was likely to mark the location of nearly all structures, its differential use in a building constructed mainly of other materials could create a deceptive image of its actual size and shape. The structures on the Kershaw/Aiguier tract represented households that spanned 50 years of Camden's history and could have employed different types of architecture. Because building plans were the key to orienting households in space, intensive investigations would be required to define their positions precisely and ascertain their configuration on the site.

I began an examination in the area close to Broad Street. Here the excavation units immediately uncovered a series of large postholes, the layout of which was traced by expanding units outward from this location (Figure 6.8). Features of this type contrasted with the trenches associated with the structure at the Kershaw House complex and verified that the frame of this building rested solely on posts set in individual holes, a feature characteristic of colonial earthfast architecture (Carson, Barka, Kelso, Stone, and Upton 1988). The pattern of postholes revealed the western end of a structure containing a wattle-and-daub chimney at its center. It measured about 17 feet from north to south and extended eastward about 10 feet to a point where the present cut bank on Broad Street destroyed further evidence of the building. Two circular pits lay adjacent to and were probably associated with this structure (Figure 6.11).

Directly behind this building, the excavation units encountered additional postholes aligned in an east-west direction (Figure 6.8). We followed the outline of this structure through additional excavations and uncovered the remains of a second and much larger earthfast building set on posts. It consisted of three bays and measured about 54 feet wide by 28 feet deep and appeared to have no cellar or chimneys (Figure 6.12). Brick rubble from an adjacent building partially obscured its southwest corner.

Close to this large earthfast structure lay brick foundations of a third building, a portion of which had been exposed by one of the 1975 sample units. I expanded the excavations to unearth the remains of a small cellar and adjacent room, together with other architectural elements (Figure 6.8). Although the building's walls had been obliterated by agricultural activity, their footings and lower courses remained intact. Cultural deposits lay undisturbed on the cellar floor within the walls. This assemblage, along with other architectural features, provided important data relating to the activities of the structure's occupants (Lewis 1999b).

The closeness of the three substantial buildings on a tract that was undivided throughout the time of its occupation strongly suggested that they comprised the components of at least one household. Given the multiple activities in which the property's owners were engaged, I felt that the cluster of structures may well have represented several households, and perhaps very different uses. Historical documents tied this property to the frontier period store of Joseph Kershaw and his associates and later to the manufacturing activities of Gayeton Aiguier, the tin worker, in the last decade of the eighteenth century. Because the structures there may have been used in either or both occupations, I would have to determine the association of each building before analyzing the households they represented. Identifying overlapping households on the Kershaw/Aiguier tract would complicate the investigation of this archaeological complex; however, it also offered the potential of examining the earliest occupation of Camden and observing change in the settlement as it emerged from the frontier period.

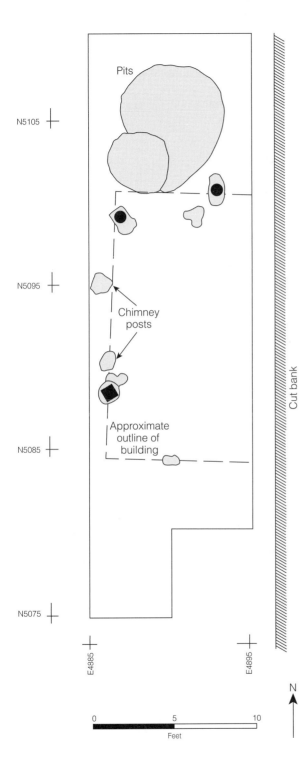

Figure 6.11 Plan of the
excavations at the Broad
Street structure in southwestern Camden. The pat-
tern of postholes revealed
the western end of an
earthfast structure with a
chimney and two adjacent
trash pits. Source: Lewis
(1999b).

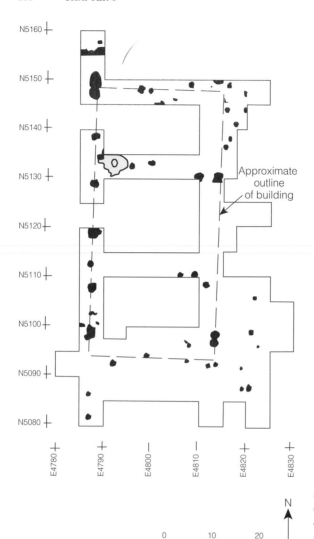

Figure 6.12 Plan of excavations at the large earthfast structure in southwestern Camden. Source: Lewis (1999b).

THE BLUE HOUSE TRACT

In 1997 and 1998 I directed limited excavations in search of the Blue House, the large residence occupied by the Alexander family during the transitional period. Work began at the southern edge of the expansive architectural concentration discovered in the 1975 sampling investigations and delineated more clearly in 1996. Postholes uncovered in this vicinity and a heavy concentration of brick debris at the eastern end of the tract pointed to a building located close to Broad Street (Figure 6.8). We opened an excavation unit to examine this concentration farther. It revealed the edge of the cellar of a collapsed building that extended to the north. This architectural feature appeared to be filled with burned structural debris and other discarded material. Several adjacent units were opened to ascertain the size and shape of this feature, and these excavations showed that the cellar extended northward and eastward and was quite substantial in size.

At this point, it became clear that we had encountered the remains of a large structure on the Blue House tract and that its investigation would require careful planning. Within the limited time available, I adopted a strategy intended to determine the boundaries of the structure as well as its contents. To find the former, I conducted a posthole sample to ascertain the limits of the cellar excavation. The results of this sample revealed that the building's walls once enclosed an area measuring about 35 by 20 feet (Figure 6.13). We also expanded the original excavation unit to investigate the nature of the cellar fill and acquire information about the building's architecture. This excavation continued to the cellar floor and recovered materials deposited prior to the building's destruction (Lewis 1999b).

The results of the initial examination of the building on the Blue House tract marked the beginning of what will be an extensive project to explore this large and complex structure. Despite the limited extent of the current work, it generated a great deal of architectural and material evidence relating to the house and its occupants. I felt that an analysis of data collected in this intensive test excavation held the potential to answer basic questions about the nature of the household once associated with it.

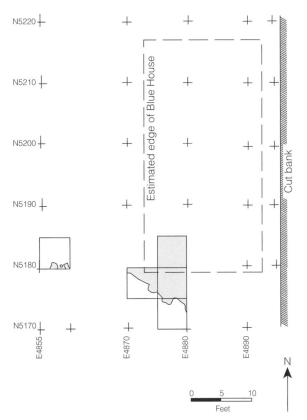

Figure 6.13 Plan of archaeological investigations at the site of the Blue House in southwestern Camden. These excavations located the structure, determined its approximate size, and examined a portion of the cellar. Source: Lewis (1999b).

SUMMARY

Intensive archaeological research in five separate areas at Camden disclosed the remains of 10 separate buildings, each of which was likely to have been the focus of a household and its activities. These buildings included five structures within the palisaded town, the jail lying just to the north, and a cluster of four buildings associated with the Kershaw mansion on the hill east of the settlement. Even though these structures constituted only a portion of the total settlement, I knew from documentary evidence that their owners pursued a variety of enterprises and the households were likely to exhibit functional diversity as well as change in the settlement over time.

Different goals guided the archaeology at each of the household foci and influenced the scope and extent of the excavations. Despite these differences, each project produced a substantial amount of material evidence potentially capable of ascertaining the nature of the past households. This knowledge was crucial to studying the process of colonization because the organization of Camden's households was so closely tied to economic and social change in the backcountry. As frontier settlements evolved, the households in them took on new roles, and the sequential placement of a household became a key factor in its usefulness for examining changes in the larger economic and social milieu. Given the strong association between time and household function, it became vital to learn the correct range of each of Camden's households before analyzing their material remains. I knew that archaeological evidence could yield this chronological information. My next step, then, was to employ these data to organize the households in time.

7/Placing Camden's Households in Time

INTRODUCTION

Archaeological investigations at Camden had uncovered the remnants of 10 distinct households. Although documents allowed me to identify the owners of the historic properties on which they lay, the written sources were much less helpful in linking the households to specific individuals or activities. In the half century that immigrants had occupied the town site, most of the properties had passed through several hands and uses, and were likely to have been home to many whose identities and tasks went unrecorded. The locales on which the households existed experienced sequential occupations and each archaeological deposit might represent any or several of them. Placing the households in time held the key to interpreting the function of Camden's households. Before I could consider examining function, I had to determine the temporal position of each household.

I was fortunate to have several kinds of material evidence that could be used to infer household dates. Certainly artifacts would play a key role. Formed by the constant discard of refuse over time, the archaeological record reflected the artifacts used during the time it was formed. The time of an occupation can be derived by the artifacts present, but the span of the time period identified depends on the rate of change in artifact use. The faster the rate of use changed, the shorter the period that can be measured. The period of Camden's growth as a commercial center was one that witnessed rapid changes in the material culture of British North America. As the colonies became increasingly enmeshed in the Atlantic economy, consumer demand for imported products grew and resulted in a continuous flow of ceramics, clothing, furniture, hardware, and other finished items from the mother country (Breen 2004). This rapid and continuous addition of a wide range of artifacts held great promise for recognizing relatively short periods and helped me calculate the formation and terminal dates of households with some degree of accuracy. Styles in architecture as well as objects crossed the Atlantic and became manifested in building designs and the arrangement of other landscape features. I anticipated that material change would be evident in individual artifacts and their larger contexts and that by examining both I would be able to determine the chronological position of Camden's households.

I began the examination of the households by deciding on an order in which to explore the data at hand. An examination of households began logically with property records. All of Camden's households lay on properties associated with particular people when the first maps were drawn in the 1770s and some tracts had been settled even earlier. In order to place Camden's households in time, I chose to look first at the placement of their material remains within the larger context of the documented property boundaries. Architecture and related land modifications often accompanied the earliest occupation and an analysis of their form might provide clues to initial occupation dates. The archaeological contents of individual household locales offered the richest source of information from which to calculate the span of their occupations. These three types of evidence together would provide the key to arranging Camden's households in order of their appearance.

LOT BOUNDARIES

All of the activity in colonial Camden took place in a world where space was organized according to ownership. Lands in the backcountry, claimed by Great Britain and administered by the provincial government, were granted to private individuals. From these grantees land passed by sale or gift to others, who combined or subdivided it further. The town of Camden was the result of this process. Originally deeded to William Ancrum, the Pine Tree Hill tract became part of a large corporate holding of Ancrum and his partners. Much of the area passed into the hands of the individual partners after being subdivided as a town site in 1771. Because settlement at Pine Tree Hill actually preceded the 1771 survey, the boundaries of early tracts would not have conformed to those of lots in the later town. Although the earliest tracts are difficult to locate precisely, descriptions indicated that their orientation was certainly different from that of the survey. I assumed that these early landholdings would have survived after the town was laid out and their boundaries would appear on subsequent deeds as anomalous lines conflicting with those of later town properties. These nonconforming tracts would identify early properties within which frontier period households might lie.

A study of property transactions in Camden yielded only a single case in which the orientation of a property line conflicted with the 1771 grid. The boundary separated the Kershaw/Aiguier tract and the Blue House tract, situated in the southwestern portion of the town. First documented in 1786, this east-west line bisected later lots at an oblique angle of 3 degrees south of east. They were the only properties in the eighteenth-century settlement that possessed such an aberrant boundary (Figure 7.1). The fact that the southernmost tract was owned by the individual linked to the establishment of the earliest commercial activities at Camden made it likely that its boundaries were laid out prior to the town survey and were important enough to maintain after new lots were demarcated. This implied that Joseph Kershaw had already established settlement and activities in this portion of Camden and that the material remains of the town's earliest households would be located here. The boundaries of all the other

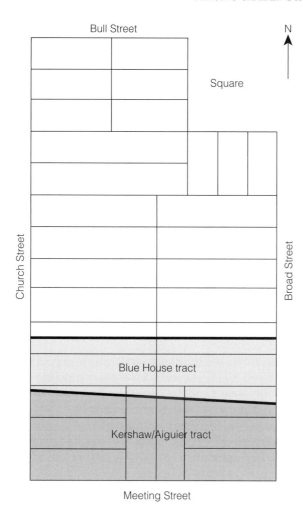

Figure 7.1 Plan of the lot boundaries in the western half of Camden in 1780. The aberrant line separating the Kershaw/Aiguier and Blue House tracts is immediately apparent. It represents the only boundary not conforming to the 1771 town grid and appears consistently in property records throughout the eighteenth century. Source: Lewis (1999b).

properties in Camden either matched the town lot lines or paralleled them, indicating that these tracts had been laid out after 1771. The absence of other non-conforming boundaries suggested that all parts of the town site had been developed later and contained households of the transitional period.

The 1771 survey organized Camden's property lines and roads along a precise grid plan, the form of which was likely to have influenced the orientation of structures built after this time. Given the general practice of aligning the axis of structures in grid-plan settlements parallel to that of the town, I assumed that structures constructed in Camden during the 1770s and later would follow a common orientation linked to that of the town survey (Reps 1965). Existing structures, erected just north of the early settlement during the early nineteenth century, all followed this pattern. Those buildings erected earlier, on the other hand, did not have the town grid to influence their placement and were unlikely to have followed its alignment. They may, in fact, have conformed to the boundaries of the tracts on which they were originally constructed. I felt that the orientation of structures, like that of the tracts on which they sat, might help identify the period in which their households originated and through which their occupations persisted.

ARCHITECTURE

In addition to lot boundaries, the architecture of the buildings uncovered at Camden supported the documented time of their occupations. These excavations encountered 10 structures that had been excavated sufficiently to measure their orientation relative to the town grid. Six of these were aligned with the 1771 survey. They included the Kershaw House and the nearby double house and cellar, the jail, the brick foundation structure on the Kershaw/Aiguier tract, and the Blue House. The alignment of the two earthfast buildings on the Kershaw/ Aiguier property, however, differed from that of these buildings and instead paralleled the angle of the northern boundary line of this tract (Figures 6.5 and 6.9). The similar orientation of the property line and structures argued strongly that these buildings, like the lot they occupied, antedated the 1771 survey and represented the early colonial settlement at Camden (Lewis 1999b). Because the earthfast building at the Kershaw House also shared the alignment of these two structures, it stood out from those that surrounded it. Its distinctive orientation suggested that it too was an early structure (Lewis 1977).

The aberrant axis of the structure on the brewhouse tract also argued that it was constructed before the town grid was laid out. Its divergence from the survey by 8 degrees east of north deviated from the boundary line marking the northern edge of the Kershaw/Aiguier tract as well as the town grid. Its orientation, however, closely approximated the 6 degrees east of north used to define the eastern and western boundaries of several early Kershaw tracts of uncertain provenience but known to have lain somewhere in this vicinity in the 1760s (Figure 6.7). If the brewhouse was an early structure, as one contemporary source mentioned, then it might have been aligned with the boundaries of one of these lots and formed part of Camden's initial colonial settlement.

Although the alignment of structures provided strong evidence for their chronology, further clues to the time of their appearance were found in their methods of construction. Two separate building traditions were evident in the archaeological remains at Camden. The first consisted of earthfast construction, which involved the use of intermittent supports of wood placed in holes in the ground. In addition, past architects also employed solid foundation construction, which provided a continuous or intermittent brick base on which the building was erected. Both types of construction were in use when the South Carolina backcountry was settled, but their appearance in colonial settlements was usually linked to the length of time an area had been occupied. Initial settlers, faced with the need for immediate shelter, erected structures that could be built rapidly using available materials. Although these edifices were often temporary in nature, many were substantial and intended to serve as intermediate buildings until permanent replacements could be constructed.

Earthfast architecture was derived from medieval English building traditions, elements of which were well adapted to frontier settlements such as Camden (Figure 7.2). Ease and simplicity of construction and the ready availability of

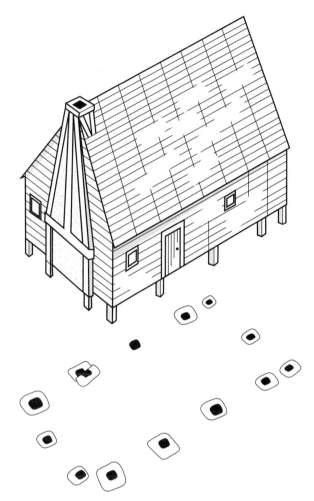

Figure 7.2 An earthfast structure typical of those built in the backcountry in the mid-eighteenth century. This form of architecture employed posts firmly anchored in the ground to support the wooden framework of the building. The archaeological plan is shown immediately below the structure. It consists of a series of postholes, excavated to place the posts, and the darker post molds produced by the posts themselves. Note one of the posts on the back of the building has been replaced, requiring the excavation of a new posthole through the older one. Wooden chimney supports, like those found at the earthfast structure adjacent to Broad Street, are visible at the left end of this building.

wood encouraged its use in the eastern woodlands of North America, where it was firmly established by the seventeenth century. In most British colonies, earthfast buildings were ubiquitous for at least the first quarter century of settlement (Carson, Barka, Kelso, Stone, and Upton 1988). This style of construction accompanied early settlement into South Carolina and typified domestic architecture in the eighteenth-century backcountry. Immigrants employed it extensively in interior frontier settlements, and other examples of earthfast houses have been documented archaeologically. Even later, settlers continued to utilize earthfast construction for impermanent buildings on plantations and elsewhere (Holschlag and Rodeffer 1977; Crass and Penner 1992; Groover 1994). In the absence of permanent building materials, the builders of Camden's early structures would almost certainly have employed this form of architecture.

Although earthfast construction offered initial advantages, the use of brick foundations provided greater structural stability and architectural flexibility, and colonial builders adopted brick as soon as it became available (Figure 7.3). In Camden, the extensive use of brick construction began following the opening of

Figure 7.3 An example of early brick architecture in the South Carolina interior. This storehouse, erected in the 1790s, was located at Pinckneyville in Union County. It is the sole remaining structure at the site of this early settlement.

Joseph Kershaw's brickyard in the1770s (Schulz 1972). Established as a commercial venture as well as to supply materials for his own use, the brickyard's products would have quickly found their way into structures erected during that decade. The availability of brick as a construction material is likely to have brought about a dramatic change in the composition of permanent architecture in Camden, and I reasoned that its presence could serve as a temporal marker for transitional period settlement. The use of earthfast construction, dominant before this time, should have declined rapidly and been confined largely to temporary or insubstantial buildings.

An examination of the Camden structures revealed the use of both earthfast and brick foundation construction and that these methods were generally associated with structures erected during different periods. Earthfast architecture characterized only three buildings: the two structures on the Kershaw/Aiguier tract and the earthfast structure situated behind the Kershaw House. Their 3-degree deviation from the town grid already set them apart from all the others and indicated that their construction predated the 1771 town survey. The last building's proximity to the Kershaw House implied that it was part of this complex; however, its position astride the 1780 palisade indicated that it was not standing at the time of the British occupation. Was it an early pioneer structure incorporated into this complex, or had it disappeared even earlier? The answer to this question awaited the analysis of additional data.

All of the other excavated structures had brick foundation construction. These edifices included the Kershaw House, the double house, and their two associated outbuildings, the magazine, the jail, and the third structure on the Kershaw/ Aiguier tract. Their alignment with the town grid indicated that all had been laid out after 1771. Documentary sources confirmed this supposition for all but the last of these, and its position at the locale of a late eighteenth-century occupation argued for a later building date. The alignment and method of construction of the majority of Camden's structures pointed to the presence of a number of transitional period households, whose distribution reflected the town's expansion over time. The anomalous orientation of the brewhouse's foundations made it the only aberrant brick structure. Although its method of construction argued against an early origin, written evidence showed that a brewhouse predated the 1771 survey. Perhaps the brickyard was in operation before the completion of the survey, or the brick portion of the brewhouse found in the excavations may have been built to conform to the orientation of an earlier structure. Dating the brewhouse would have to await an analysis of the artifacts associated with it.

Architectural data made it possible to identify localities likely to have contained households of both the frontier and transitional periods. It surprised no one that the architectural evidence indicated that the earliest colonial occupation in Camden was associated with the Kershaw/Aiguier tract, first occupied in the 1760s. The inclusion of a later third structure aligned with the town grid also confirmed documents that stated the tract was in use through the transitional period. The brewhouse, situated just south of this property, seemed to mark another focus of early settlement that persisted until the end of the eighteenth century. The early documented origins of the brewhouse, together with its proximity to Joseph Kershaw's store on his adjacent property north of Meeting Street, imply that he developed both together in the 1760s and they formed the core of Camden's early commercial activity. This area would also have supported frontier and later period households. In contrast, the conformance of the structures of the Kershaw House complex and the jail to the orientation of the 1771 survey, combined with the extensive use of brick in their construction, identified them as later buildings likely to have contained exclusively transitional period households. Information obtained from analyzing the period architecture allowed me to establish rough beginning dates of the structural complexes and examine the potential range of their occupations. It also identified ambiguities that required further examination. To define the dates of Camden's households more precisely, I turned to an analysis of additional kinds of artifacts.

ARCHAEOLOGICAL EVIDENCE

Many artifacts could provide clues to the occupation dates of the Camden structures. Because ceramics were ubiquitous and underwent rapid style changes, they offered the greatest potential for gaining the kind of comprehensive information I desired. Consequently, my initial investigation of household temporal ranges rested on an examination of ceramics recovered from each of the structural clusters. As before, I ascertained the midpoint of each occupation by calculating mean ceramic dates for the assemblages from each locality. I then estimated the length of each locality's occupation by comparing these dates to the ranges of all the ceramic types in the assemblage. If the exact date of construction was known, then it could be employed, together with the mean date, to calculate the length of the occupation period more closely. Where possible, I used assemblages recovered from sealed archaeological contexts to determine ceramic dates. Artifacts in such contexts were more likely to have been used together in activities associated with particular households and less prone to disturbance. This does not mean that unsealed contexts were unusable. Rather, agricultural activity on the site mixed material deposited at different times, which made it more difficult to distinguish individual time-sensitive deposits. Indeed, the overlying mixed fill contained the bulk of the material associated with Camden's structural features, and I relied on an analysis of artifacts from the plowed zone to calculate ceramic dates for the entire range of an area's occupation.

Perhaps the most intriguing structural complexes at Camden were those thought to have contained frontier period households. Ceramic collections from the vicinities of the two earthfast buildings on the Kershaw/Aiguier tract, the earthfast structure from the Kershaw House complex, and the brewhouse allowed me to estimate their temporal ranges. The structure closest to Broad Street contained seven construction features and two refuse pits likely to have been filled at the time of the building's use. I calculated a mean date of 1779 from the ceramics contained in these features. If its construction occurred a decade and a half earlier, at the beginning of the 1760s, then it was likely to have remained in use until the early 1790s. Bracketing the date ranges of the ceramic types suggested that the occupation fell between 1762 and 1795. These dates supported my conclusions that this structure contained one of Camden's early households, that it survived the Revolution, but was probably abandoned, and perhaps demolished by the time the Aiguier family resided on the property in the late 1790s. Although its location and early construction date also opened the possibility that this structure was associated with Joseph Kershaw's initial presence at Pine Tree Hill, they provided no clues as to its occupants' identity.

The ceramics from the brewhouse indicated that its occupation had a midpoint of 1786. If the building had been constructed in the late 1760s, as the written record and orientation of its placement attested, then it was likely to have been abandoned just after the turn of the century when documentary mention of it ceased. This period fell within the range of 1762–1815 suggested by ceramic bracketing. This assemblage of ceramic artifacts would have accumulated at the site of a building that appeared during Camden's early period of settlement and remained in use during and after the Revolutionary War. Joseph Kershaw or his employees occupied the brewhouse throughout this period, and it seemed that this locality, like the Broad Street structure, was likely to contain the remains of both frontier and transitional households related to an industrial role.

An analysis of archaeological deposits at the large earthfast structure on the Kershaw/Aiguier tract yielded a mean ceramic date of 1789. I estimated that if this date represented the midpoint of an occupation that began in the 1760s, the structure would have been abandoned around 1810. The ceramic bracket range of 1765–1800, however, implied a somewhat earlier ending date for the occupation, one closer to the time the Aiguier family left the property. The normal quarter-century life span for an earthfast building also argued for a shorter period of service. More than 40 years was an extremely long time for such a structure to be in use, and evidence of frequent repairs suggested that this one probably required a great deal of work to maintain. Like its neighboring earthfast structure, it survived its frontier period origins as well as the British occupation and persisted almost until the time of the old town site's abandonment. I estimated that its households would represent both frontier and transitional periods.

An early mean date of 1776 immediately distinguished the earthfast building from the others in the Kershaw House complex. The closeness of this date to the structure's 1780 destruction, however, suggested that it might have been younger than the architectural evidence indicated. By the 1770s builders in Camden would no longer have been using earthfast construction. The ceramic collection offered a possible solution to this dilemma. Although more than a hundred specimens had been found in the earthfast structure, they comprised only three ceramic types. All were in use for relatively long periods, but their ranges overlapped for only a short period between 1762 and about 1800. This span provided only a rough estimate of time the building was in use, but the beginning date of this range fit comfortably with the time of construction derived from the architectural data. Together, both types of evidence now argued that this structure represented a frontier period building preceding all the others in this locality. Though it persisted as later structures grew up around it, its much earlier beginning date suggested that its initial household existed independently and may represent a distinctive early occupation.

The complex nature of the brick foundation structure on the Kershaw/Aiguier tract made it possible to date this building more precisely than the others. Its remains consisted of a cellar whose walls had been erected in a footing trench that had been filled at the time of its construction. Because the fill placed in the foundation trenches would have contained no artifacts that postdated this event, I could use the fill assemblage to establish a beginning date for the foundation. This date, combined with the mean ceramic date for the structure, could then be used to estimate the time of its abandonment. An examination of the building trench fill revealed that the most recent ceramic type present was John Bartlam's Carolina creamware, introduced about 1774. Its presence indicated that the cellar must have been constructed after this time, but the absence of pearlware in use by 1780 meant the footing trench was closed before that time. The contents of the foundation trench suggested a mid-1770s date that was corroborated by documentary and architectural evidence. When I compared this date to the 1790 mean ceramic date for the entire structure, I arrived at a terminal date in the early years of the nineteenth century. The closing date matched the time at which the property was abandoned at the settlement of the Aiguier estate, and the whole occupation fell within the bracketed range of 1775–1810. Although its occupation overlapped those of the two nearby earthfast buildings, households centered on this structure would clearly have represented the transitional period.

The Blue House was built much later that its neighbors immediately to the south. Its appearance in about 1782 was also well documented. A comparison of this beginning date with the 1795 mean ceramic date derived from deposits in the cellar fill allowed me to calculate a terminal date of 1808, a year after the property passed out of the hands of the Alexander family. This time span agreed with the range of 1780–1810 derived from ceramic bracketing. The close association of the Blue House with the Alexanders assured that it was likely to contain the material remains of their transitional period household alone. Because it was known to have been one of the last houses standing on the site of early Camden, I felt that the end of the Alexander occupation provided a valuable clue to the time of the town site's final abandonment.

The Kershaw House locality presented a more complex picture. Consisting of a cluster of five structures, it was occupied over a period of 90 years. Joseph Kershaw constructed the principal building in the mid-1770s as a family residence, and the transitional period household persisted into the 1790s, when his estate sold the property. Several subsequent owners resided there in the first half of the nineteenth century. For part of this time the house also served as an academy. Written sources indicated that the house lay vacant in the 1850s, by which time it had become dilapidated. This lengthy occupation was likely to have created an extensive archaeological record; however, my ability to observe its entire breadth was limited by the nature of the archaeological investigations there. The differing strategies employed by those conducting the work resulted in the collection of material remains from only a portion of the occupied area. Only the early excavations at the Kershaw House itself retained artifacts recovered from the overlying deposits. Despite the extensive nature of later investigations, their focus on examining architecture and subsurface features ignored the plowed zone overlying the remainder of the Kershaw House complex and excluded the material record it contained. As a result, the recovered archaeological record for the locality as a whole was inconsistent but not necessarily incompatible.

An examination of the entire occupation of the Kershaw House and a comparison of its components depended solely on an analysis of material recovered from subsurface features. Because these features generally clustered around and included portions of individual structures, I combined them into five structural groups. I assumed that each group of features was likely to represent the initial occupation of each building, which began when its construction occurred and continued through its period of heaviest use. A feature group would not necessarily reflect the entire time span of the whole locality's occupation. The overlying deposits at the Kershaw House itself, on the other hand, offered an opportunity to observe its whole history.

An analysis of the ceramic collections from the Kershaw House alone yielded a mean date of 1807. Assuming this date was the midpoint of an occupation that began in the mid-1770s, I concluded that the structure remained in service until the late 1830s. This date seemed in keeping with its origins during the Revolutionary War period as well as the long documented period of use it experienced in the antebellum period. When I analyzed the material from the subsurface features, however, a different picture emerged. Ceramics from the features associated with the Kershaw House produced a much earlier mean date of 1788 and a shorter range falling somewhere between 1763 and 1815. Because I knew the house was constructed in the mid-1770s, I could estimate an ending date just after 1800. The absence of whitewares, a common type introduced in 1805, further implied that these deposits dated from the time of the Kershaw occupation and the period immediately following. The earlier and more restricted range of the subsurface deposits seemed to indicate that they were created during the first part of the structure's occupation and further suggested that other features at this locality might also lack material representing the later part of their occupations.

My analysis of the ceramics from features associated with other buildings near the Kershaw House indicated that here the archaeological record provided rough estimates of each structure's occupation. The study revealed that although the buildings were not all constructed at the same time, the ranges of their occupations overlapped. The double house had a mean date of 1786 and exhibited a bracketed range of 1775–1805. An adjacent outbuilding, though not in itself a household focus, yielded a mean date of 1790 and a similar bracketed range. However, the fact that it was constructed over the filled-in British palisade trench, argued that it was built after 1781. The contents of the cellar supplied the relatively recent mean date of 1798. Although its bracketed range of 1780 to 1805 also implied that it too was a postwar structure, its late mean date suggested that the occupation may have extended later.

Finally, the jail site held a sizeable number of ceramics that proved helpful in dating the occupations of this tract. Because they were recovered from the back dirt pile of the machine excavation, however, their context was uncertain. A study of the ceramics disclosed an assemblage typical of the late 1700s but which included several types that originated in the nineteenth century. They appeared to represent material from all of the site's historic occupations. The presence of early ceramic types seemed to corroborate the jail's documented date of origin. This information, together with the collection's mean date of 1808, allowed me to calculate a range of 1772–1844, a period that stretched into the later years of the market structure that lay nearby. Although the circumstances surrounding the jail's discovery made it impossible to address the temporal frame of this structure by itself, it was possible to identify the building's transitional period origin and the locality's persistent antebellum occupation by the composition of the ceramic collection.

A comparison of the occurrence of two ceramic types lent additional support to my conclusions regarding the relative chronological position of the structures. Creamware and pearlware were two fine, molded, hard-paste earthenwares that quickly replaced other ceramics as the dominant tablewares when introduced in the second half of the eighteenth century (Noël Hume 1969). Creamware came into use in 1762 and peaked in 1791. Pearlware appeared in 1780 and reached its peak of popularity in 1805. Because Camden's buildings were occupied during this period, their assemblages contained both wares. I reasoned, however, that the ratio of creamware to pearlware would be higher in the structures whose occupations originated earlier and would decline in those beginning later and lasting farthest past 1780 when pearlware's popularity grew. As expected, the highest percentages of creamware occurred in the earthfast structures on the Kershaw/Aiguier tract and at the Kershaw House complex, and the creamware frequencies dropped to their lowest at the Kershaw House, the jail, and the Kershaw House cellar.

An examination of other classes of artifacts supported the dates derived from the ceramic analysis. Most of these items could not provide as precise temporal information, but they helped define the periods in which the occupations of particular structures occurred. Wrought nails, for example, dominated construction in the eighteenth century until being supplanted after the development of cheaper cut nails in 1790 (Nelson 1968). Because the use of wrought nails spanned the frontier and transitional periods at Camden, I anticipated that they would be found in all of

TABLE 7.1   OCCUPATION RANGES OF HOUSEHOLD FOCI AT CAMDEN

Frontier Period Households	Range	Mean Date
Broad Street structure	1762–1795	1779
Earthfast structure at Kershaw House	1762–1780	1776
Brewhouse	1762–1815	1786
Large earthfast structure	1765–1800	1789
Transitional Period Households	**Range**	**Mean Date**
Jail	1772–1844	1808
Brick foundation structure	1775–1810	1790
Kershaw House	1775–1839	1807
Double house at Kershaw House	1775–1805	1786
Cellar at Kershaw House	1780–1805	1798
Blue House	1780–1810	1795

the structures examined. Buildings occupied after 1800, however, were also likely to have contained cut nails used in repairs. The absence of cut nails in the assemblages of the earthfast structures at Camden corroborated the conclusion that these buildings were indeed abandoned by 1800, and the presence of cut nails in the others confirmed their continued service into the nineteenth century. An examination of artifacts with longer documented periods of use, such as furniture hardware, tableware, stemware, window glass, buttons, and personal items, verified conclusions drawn from the ceramic analysis regarding the temporal limits of each building's occupation. Material evidence from the jail and the Kershaw House reflected their survival until the mid-nineteenth century. Such artifacts as molded bottle glass, introduced after 1820, marked their long postcolonial occupations.

An analysis of artifact assemblages from the structures in Camden provided reasonably exact information about the time of their occupations and affirmed the ranges determined from architectural data. Collectively, the ranges of the 10 households (shown in Table 7.1) represented the entire span of Camden's settlement, from the time of its consolidation as a trading center during the 1760s until the early town site's abandonment in the early nineteenth century. The material evidence also disclosed the very late use of the two structures that were occupied well into the antebellum period. The specific temporal contexts that I identified for each of the Camden localities now provided a framework for arranging the town's archaeological components for further analysis. Knowing their time of occupation helped me not only define historic households in space but examine their nature as products of the frontier and transitional phases of the town's development.

SUMMARY

Earlier I hypothesized that an analysis of the architecture and contents of early households at Camden would delineate the time of their occupations. I anticipated the existence of households representing both the frontier and transitional periods at this colonial settlement. It was important to recognize households from both these periods because each marked a separate phase in the process of colonization and was characterized by significant changes in the structure and organization of the society and economy. The archaeological contexts identified here would play a crucial role in exploring Camden's evolution as a frontier settlement by providing the means by which to examine material evidence for household function during the town's early history.

Intensive archaeological work, guided by the results of the previous sampling excavations, uncovered architectural remains and associated collections of archaeological materials. These data permitted me to locate the remains of 10 structures along with related activity areas. Each appeared to be the focus of a spatially distinct household. Five of the household foci lay within the area the palisade enclosed, and four belonged to the Kershaw House complex immediately east of the town. The jail, removed somewhat to the north, formed the tenth household. Analyses of temporally sensitive archaeological evidence helped me organize these households in time. Their results indicated that the household foci represented both the frontier and transitional periods. The households and their estimated occupation spans are shown in Figure 7.4.

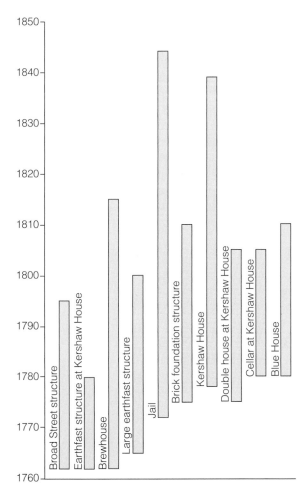

Figure 7.4 Bar chart showing the occupational ranges of household foci at Camden.

A glance at these households revealed that the investigations at Camden contained archaeological contexts whose temporal spans encompassed the range of the town's colonial development. Their occupation periods extended from the time of Pine Tree Hill's founding as a trading center, through its growth as a frontier town, and finally to its expansion as a regional center at the close of the eighteenth century. Indeed, several of the households seemed to endure well into the antebellum period. The fact that archaeological evidence confirmed the presence of early households, as well as those that succeeded them, made it possible for me to explore hypotheses relating to social and economic change within the settlement. The material evidence from each household focus held the potential to address household function, the nature of the economy in which the households participated, and perhaps even changes in the community's social composition. But certain factors complicated my use of these data.

A number of variables influenced the use of the archaeological evidence to examine social and economic behavior at Camden, and I had to consider these factors prior to employing the results of the intensive excavations. First, variation in the extent of the investigations at each focus produced larger collections of the contents of some households but smaller samples from others. In comparing Camden's households, I would have to be aware of the limitations inherent in the results of the restricted archaeological work carried out on several foci when comparing them to others examined more extensively. Second, although some of the households arose early in the town's past, their occupations appeared to continue through later periods. In analyzing the contents of initial households, I would have to allow for the effect of subsequent deposition. Third, all but one of the household foci represent single buildings and associated activity areas. The Kershaw House, however, was clearly the centerpiece of a complex that included other structures lying near it. I had to consider the possibility that additional contemporary buildings may have been subsumed in it when analyzing the Kershaw House household. Bearing in mind the limitations imposed by the archaeological investigations and the nature of the phenomena they encountered, I proceeded to examine and compare the household foci at Camden.

8/Exploring Camden's Evolution on a Household Scale

INTRODUCTION

Having identified a number of Camden's households and placed them in time, I could now explore their content and examine their role in the town's development as a colonial settlement. Camden's households, the early community's basic components, gave me a large-scale context in which to observe broader adaptations to social and economic conditions encountered on the periphery of British expansion. Economic factors drove colonial development and shaped the direction of its change, and I felt that its influence on settlement would have had the greatest impact on the form and composition of households and their change over time. Frontier households played an important role in establishing a production base and were the focal points of a pioneer economy characterized by regional exchange. When the backcountry became more fully incorporated in the broader Atlantic economy, households adapted to the spread of its formal institutions by assuming a more restricted role as foci of domestic and specialized activities. Camden was a focal point for the changes that marked the process of colonization in South Carolina's interior. Its households would certainly have reflected this larger process.

Because my study of Camden's households had implications far beyond their immediate context, it was important that I organize the analysis to address questions of wider scope. Taken together, the 10 household foci contained the material by-products of activities typical of general developments taking place in the backcountry during the second half of the eighteenth century. By comparing their contents, I hoped to discover patterning that expressed variation in the nature of society and economy over time within Camden and also at the broader regional level. I anticipated that a comparison of the archaeological remains of frontier and transitional households at Camden would reveal distinctive patterns in form and composition that relate to the phenomena identified in the hypotheses outlined in Chapter 5. This approach required that I organize the discussion around the following questions: (1) to what degree did the households illustrate the change from multifunctional occupations to those devoted more exclusively to either domestic or specialized activities; (2) how well did Camden's households reflect the nature of the frontier and transitional economies in which they participated; and (3) could I infer the introduction of slave labor during the transitional period by detecting the presence of a population of African descent in these households? I expected the conditions influencing frontier and transitional households would produce distinctive patterning that would allow me to answer these questions.

EXAMINING HOUSEHOLD FUNCTION

Perhaps one of the most marked differences between the structure of a frontier economy and that of the succeeding transitional period is the former's relative isolation and the consequent reliance of its participants on regional production and trade. With a reduced dependence on outside resources, households on the frontier became centers of a broad range of activities and tended to mix domestic and specialized functions. Transitional households, on the other hand, operated in an economy characterized by much more extensive exchange and lesser reliance on the domestic production of diverse goods. Greater access to interregional and overseas trade resulted in a greater dependence on imported merchandise and moved production out of pioneer households and into specialized localities such as stores, ironworks, warehouses, or other spaces devoted to such purposes. Consequently, households of the transitional period became increasingly either domestic or specialized in nature. I anticipated that the material record associated with the frontier and transitional household foci at Camden would exhibit evidence of these functional differences, but first I had to develop material implications that would allow me to observe them.

As I sought to derive archaeological implications for Camden's households, I had to consider the problem resulting from mixed archaeological deposits. Households occupied during the frontier period were not abandoned at its close. Because they remained in use, their localities would have accumulated archaeological contexts containing the remains of both frontier and transitional assemblages. Although they may originally have formed separate deposits, these were largely destroyed by subsequent agricultural activity. With the exception of artifacts recovered from subsurface features, the remains of Camden's early households lay mixed in the plowed zone and did not permit me to separate complete individual household assemblages for analysis. I instead had to discern the functional traits of each frontier household by examining variability within the entire collection from each household focus. To accomplish this, I separated out classes of data that could be linked by analogy to the nature of this household type. Although it was not possible to separate the collective remains of frontier households from those that came later, I was nonetheless able to discern evidence for their presence. This is how I developed material implications for the two phases of Camden's colonial past.

FRONTIER PERIOD HOUSEHOLDS

Perhaps the most visually striking aspect of the early household foci at Camden is their architecture. The earthfast construction of three of the structures clearly set them apart from the ubiquitous appearance of brick in later building. This architectural style told me more than simply the structure's relative age; their attributes could also be linked to use. Earthfast architecture reflected the expediency of colonization in both its form and lack of variation. Based on the English bay of 16 to 18 feet, most domestic earthfast buildings were small, rectangular structures not exceeding 35 feet in length. Domestic structures usually had wattle-and-daub clay chimneys, were erected on posts, and often contained small cellars, features absent from those used for nondomestic purposes. Occasionally special purpose buildings, such as taverns, combined additional bays to attain greater size, but even normally large nondomestic buildings, such as barns, rarely exceeded 50 feet in length (Kelso 1984; Carson, Barka, Kelso, Stone, and Upton 1988). Archaeology had revealed several such early domestic structures elsewhere in the South Carolina backcountry.

Although the similarity of buildings employing earthfast architecture did not lend itself to identifying their function, certain features associated with this method of construction provided clues to the use of the Camden structures. Three earthfast buildings were linked to frontier period households. The Broad Street structure on the Kershaw/Aiguier tract and the one behind the Kershaw House were relatively small and consisted of single bays, measuring 17 by 17 feet and 16 by 16 feet respectively. The former had a wattle-and-daub chimney on one side (Figures 6.5 and 8.1). The configuration of each enclosed space

Figure 8.1 The Broad Street structure on the Kershaw/Aiguier tract in Camden following excavation. The view is toward the southeast with the cut bank and Broad Street on the left. The large pits at the corner of the house are in the foreground. The postholes immediately behind them mark the northern wall and corner of the structure. Its western wall, containing the chimney, extended southward, paralleling the edge of the excavation.

suggested that they were living areas. Neither contained architectural features or artifacts linked to a specialized application, and each appeared likely to have been an early dwelling. But an absence of architectural evidence did not exclude a broader function.

The large earthfast structure measured 54 by 28 feet and was divided into three large bays (Figure 8.2). The absence of cellars, chimneys, or other features normally associated with domestic architecture distinguished it from the others and suggested that it had a special purpose requiring a great deal of interior storage or work space. Indeed, these characteristics and its location near the Catawba Path (Broad Street) made it a good candidate to be the Pine Tree Hill store operated by Joseph Kershaw and his partners. Its close spatial proximity to the smaller contemporary earthfast edifice near Broad Street also introduced the possibility that together they formed a single household cluster linked to the early settlement. If so, the two buildings would have constituted the multipurpose household anticipated for this early frontier occupation.

The partially exposed remnants of the brick foundation at the brewhouse offered only a few clues to its function. The footing trench, from which robbers had removed much of the brick, was wide enough to have supported a one-and-one-half story frame structure. The 50-foot length of the wall exposed in this

Figure 8.2 The large earthfast structure on the Kershaw/Aiguier tract in Camden as seen from the west. The excavation units reveal the outline of the partially excavated structure. The large size of the building prevented its investigation in a single season and excavations here extended over the course of three years. Because the units were refilled at the close of each season's work to protect the fragile architectural remains, the entire structure was never completely exposed at one time.

limited excavation indicated it was subdivided into large rooms, a plan typical of brewhouses (Egan 1989). The presence of perforated paving bricks among the rubble testified more directly to its specialized function. Designed to permit ventilation or drainage, these bricks would have been employed in the floors of malt houses where grain was treated as part of the brewing process (Hurst 1967). Only partially explored, the brewhouse appeared to have been constructed for a special purpose and was one of the earliest industrial structures at Camden. Perhaps an analysis of artifacts associated with this and the other buildings would provide a clearer picture of their households.

Although architectural data provided important clues to how these four frontier period households were used, I needed to examine other data that could help me refine these results. To study function, I needed to identify assemblages of artifacts capable of denoting the mixed domestic-specialized activities typical of this phase of colonization. If the domestic artifacts varied with the significance of these activities in a household, then the relative size of the assemblage they comprised was a key to identifying the building's function. I accomplished this by measuring the relative quantity of ceramics, an artifact likely to have varied with the importance of domestic activities. I assumed that assemblages at domestic households would possess the highest frequencies of ceramics, followed by progressively lower frequencies in households of mixed function and those devoted to specialized activities respectively.

I examined the function of Camden's frontier period households by comparing the size of the ceramic artifact assemblage in each structure with that composed of certain architectural materials that were likely to have been used in all the early buildings regardless of their construction. Window glass was widely available during the frontier period and employed in both wooden and brick buildings. Consequently, I assumed that its appearance in the archaeological record would be similar in every instance. If this assumption were correct, then the size of the window glass assemblages would serve as a relative constant against which I could compare the relative size of the ceramic assemblages for each household to determine the extent of domestic activities there.

To address the question of household function for the frontier period at Camden, I examined the relative size of their ceramic and window glass artifact assemblages. The results of this comparison, shown in Table 8.1, revealed some important differences in the percentage frequencies of the two artifact categories.

Perhaps the most obvious pattern seemed to be the similarity in the frequencies of both artifact categories at the earthfast structures near the Kershaw House and on the Kershaw/Aiguier tract west of Broad Street. The dominance of ceramics implied the presence of a domestic household, but a high occurrence

TABLE 8.1   COMPARISON OF CERAMIC AND WINDOW GLASS ASSEMBLAGES AT FRONTIER PERIOD HOUSEHOLD FOCI AT CAMDEN

Household	Ceramics	Window Glass
Earthfast Kershaw structure	53.2%	46.8%
Broad Street structure	52.0%	48.0%
Large earthfast structure	43.4%	56.6%
Brewhouse	9.8%	90.2%

of architecture also indicated that other enterprises may have been carried out there as well. Although the frequencies, by themselves, did not demonstrate that these households served a dual domestic-specialized purpose, the relative proportions of their artifact assemblages seemed to support the conclusions drawn from the architecture. The large earthfast structure near Broad Street also exhibited artifact frequencies with similar proportions, but its smaller ceramic assemblage indicated a less prominent domestic role. Such a pattern might be expected at a store or other frontier businesses in which people also resided.

Again, the brewhouse stood out as an anomalous area. Archaeological investigations here unearthed an incredibly small ceramic assemblage totaling less than 10 percent. The dominance of architectural material strongly implied that domestic activities were not regularly carried out there and supported the conclusions drawn from the architecture that this structure was devoted to other activities. The presence of a specialized household at this point in Camden's development did not fit my expectations; however, brewing imposed conditions that distinguished it from many other household economic ventures on the frontier. Brewing required large spaces for the storage and processing of bulky and often wet materials. Such areas were not usually conducive to a domestic occupation, and workers generally lived in separate buildings. No one seems to have resided on the brewhouse premises at the southern periphery of the settlement, but the employees were only a short walk away from the Kershaw store. As an early production facility in the regional economy of the backcountry, the brewhouse at Camden may have been organized on a household scale. The distinctive nature of this activity, however, required a spatial arrangement that anticipated the separate living area found in the later commercial economy.

Architectural and archaeological evidence indicated nondomestic activities in two frontier period structures—the large earthfast structure and the brewhouse. This information led me to search for additional data to support this contention. Specialized activities are usually associated with particular tools and materials, and the nature of an activity together with the processes that affect the formation of the archaeological record often determine the form evidence will take. I knew that during the frontier period Camden's economy revolved around two activities—trade and production for a regional market.

Artifacts connected with trade were likely to denote store households. Trade, unlike many production activities such as pottery making or blacksmithing, did not generate a large by-product of waste material. Indeed, successful storekeepers like Kershaw, Chesnut, and their contemporaries would have moved goods and produce in and out of their establishments and left as little as possible to become archaeological deposits. Exchange also did not involve a large number of specialized tools and instruments. Most mercantile paraphernalia such as scales, measuring implements, and other tools were too valuable to be left when business moved elsewhere, and perishable artifacts like account books either remained safe in the hands of heirs or, if discarded or lost, quickly decayed. The material evidence for trade would have to consist of disposable articles associated with exchange and transportation. As a specialized production process, brewing also required distinctive apparatus, but its value and portability greatly reduced the likelihood of its entering the archaeological record. Indeed, the recorded sale of "ye brewing implements" by Joseph Kershaw's heirs in 1794 implied that archaeological evidence of his brewing equipment would not be found on the site of this structure (Kirkland and Kennedy 1905). Brewing also consumed large quantities of raw materials and generated a sizable amount of waste, but the biodegradable nature of both made their recovery unlikely here. Again, I would have to rely on the presence of disposable items involved in beer production.

Two such artifacts helped me differentiate function in these frontier period households. The first consisted of bale seals used to secure the safety of bulk goods shipped in cloth containers. Shippers wrapped loads of general merchandise in bags that could be carried on horseback or by wagon. These containers were employed extensively over often marginal roads or trails in the American interior. Although the organic material of the bales themselves would not survive in the archaeological record, the lead seals that closed the bags or clamped the drawstrings or wires fastening them usually are well preserved. Seals usually accompanied goods shipped to retailers, who unpacked and dispensed the contents of the bags and discarded the broken closures (Noël Hume 1969). Eighteenth-century shippers also transported loose goods in barrels, which left archaeological evidence of their existence. They were sturdy, reusable containers, but barrels frequently suffered damage or simply wore out. Like modern-day shipping pallets, they accumulated at destination points where merchants eventually discarded them. Barrels were also the container of choice for beer and other alcoholic beverages. Fragments of the iron bands that bound the barrel staves in place were durable enough to survive in the ground to mark the presence of these containers. Unearthing seals and pieces of iron bands would provide confirmation of both exchange and production.

Bale seals and barrel band fragments found at the large earthfast structure and barrel band fragments at the brewhouse, together with the absence of both in the other frontier period buildings, identified these two households as foci of specialized activities. The combination of bale seals and barrel band fragments recovered at the large earthfast structure implied that its household was engaged in trade. This evidence strengthened my contention that this was the Kershaw store. The archaeological assemblage from the brewhouse also lacked specialized artifacts linked to production processes; however, the presence of barrels provided strong indirect evidence of the structure's function as a brewery. Finding items that represented only a minor facet of the specialized roles of both structures was consistent with my expectations regarding the material by-products of the activities carried out there. This archaeological evidence supported the conclusions derived from other material evidence.

My analyses of material data allowed me to observe critical differences between the four frontier period households at Camden and link them to adaptations necessitated by conditions encountered in the frontier economy. Households inhabiting the earthfast structures on Broad Street and near the Kershaw House appeared to be residential in nature, but the small yet consistent size of their domestic assemblages implied other activities occurred there. Their architecture and an absence of specialized artifacts corroborated these findings. The smaller domestic assemblages associated with the large earthfast structure and the brewhouse, on the other hand, identified them as sites of specialized activities, and the extremely low frequencies of these artifacts at the brewhouse suggested that it was devoted exclusively to production. All of the household foci except the brew-house exhibited material evidence that supported the assumption that frontier period households were multipurpose in nature, combining living areas with those devoted to diverse production for regional exchange. Their close physical proximity also introduced the possibility that the two earthfast structures on the Kershaw/Aiguier tract were parts of a related household. The specialized role of the brewhouse was more difficult to explain. Although the structure was erected at the close of the frontier period to supply regional needs, its operators clearly carried out extensive production. As the earliest documented manufacturing industry in Camden, the scale of its activities may have encouraged changes in household organization that physically separated the place of work from living areas. The creation of this industry may, in fact, have helped lay the groundwork for Camden's participation in wider trade and signaled the beginning of its shift from a frontier town to a central place. This significant change in Camden's history was certain to have left vestiges in the archaeological record. An examination of transition period households now became the focus of my attention.

TRANSITIONAL PERIOD HOUSEHOLDS

I anticipated that the material record of Camden's six transitional household foci would distinguish them from their predecessors. The regional frontier economy's breakdown altered the structure of production and trade, bringing increased specialization and the separation of work from living areas. This change resulted in a functional shift in households that now became increasingly devoted to either domestic or specialized activities. Because the new roles would have changed the nature of household artifact use, I believed I could distinguish this reorganization of household function through both architectural and archaeological data.

Architectural analysis of the structures revealed formal architectural characteristics that allowed me to assess the likelihood of the six household foci having been associated with exclusively domestic or specialized households. All of the structures sat on brick foundations, whose orientation with the town grid of 1771 reflected the social and political centralization that accompanied Camden's rise as an administrative center. The use of brick foundation architecture permitted greater diversity in form, and the buildings themselves provided important clues to the activities carried out within them.

Perhaps the most extraordinary building of this period was the Kershaw House (Figure 8.3). Excavations uncovered a substantial foundation 47 by 43 feet in size, which was divided into three sections. The two on each side measured 16.5 feet wide, and the one in the center, 10 feet wide. About two-thirds of the way between the front and rear of the house, each side was divided into two rooms. The base of a double hearth marked the location of the wall separating the rooms. The center section extended unimpeded along its entire length and formed a central hallway. Archaeology also exposed the remains of two L-shaped piers that supported a portico extending 14 feet in front of the house as well as a row of piers for an 8-foot wide rear porch (Lewis 1977). This plan was typical of Palladian houses built in both urban and rural settings in eighteenth-century British North America. These structures were known regionally as "double houses." Typically two-storied buildings set on a raised basement, these large,

Figure 8.3 The reconstructed Kershaw House on Magazine Hill east of Camden. Resting on the site of the original structure, this replica was based on archaeological and comparative architectural evidence.

high status dwellings had a central entrance in front, reached by a stairway passing through a two-storied pedimented portico, and a piazza in the rear (Smith and Smith 1917). Several contemporary paintings and an early photograph of the Kershaw House confirmed the conclusions of the archaeology, and the structure's close similarity to a 1768 mansion in Charleston testified to the links between Joseph Kershaw and the economic elite of the entrepôt. The architecture of the Kershaw House clearly identified it as a high status domestic structure that was physically separated from specialized business activities.

The second household foci centered around the double house of the Kershaw House complex. This structure, measuring 39 by 19 feet, rested on a narrow foundation that had been extensively rebuilt and slightly altered, suggesting that the original building had been replaced or significantly modified (Figure 8.4). The foundation's width would have allowed it to support no more than a story-and-a-half frame building. A massive double fireplace base in its center divided it into two rooms of approximately equal size. This form is identified in geographical literature as a "saddlebag house" and saw widespread use for residences throughout the upland South. These buildings were often erected as plantation quarters (Newton 1971), but they may have incorporated kitchen or laundry functions as well (Vlach 1993). Because of its proximity to the Kershaw House, this saddlebag house may well have sheltered those who were employed by this elite family. As such, it is likely to have been the focus of a separate household or households within the complex.

South Carolina Institute of Archaeology and Anthropology, University of South Carolina

Figure 8.4 The excavated double house in the Kershaw house complex. Its remaining brick foundations and the H-shaped base of the central double fireplace are evident, as are several of the builders' trenches. This view from the southeast overlooks a portion of the eighteenth-century town site.

A substantial cellar formed the third household focus in the Kershaw House vicinity (Figure 8.5). Located southeast of the Kershaw House, it measured 18 by 18 feet and contained a circular unlined well in its floor. A 3-foot wide trench extended eastward from its southeastern corner and ran along the slope of the hill for about 140 feet. Its foundation was capable of supporting one-and-one-half stories. The collapse of the walls and subsequent robbing of brick made it difficult to ascertain the nature of the overlying building; however, the interior well and drain were reminiscent of those found in springhouses or other structures associated with specialized food processing or storage (Vlach 1993). These activities implied the building served a nondomestic function and was likely to have been the focus of a task-related household.

Documentary evidence helped identify the remains of the Blue House, the post–Revolutionary War residence of Dr. Isaac Alexander. Situated on Broad Street just north of the Kershaw/Aiguier tract, the building was partially excavated to expose a portion of its cellar. Although incomplete, the archaeology revealed important information about its architecture. Material evidence indicated that the Blue House had been a substantial frame structure, approximately 35 by 20 feet in size, and was set on a brick foundation. The similarity of its construction and dimensions to those found in surviving early nineteenth-century urban dwellings in Camden and elsewhere in the backcountry indicated a residential function for the Blue House. The presence of wall plaster, fittings, and other evidence of a finished interior in the cellar fill supported this conclusion. Architectural evidence clearly identified the Blue House as the focus of another domestic household.

Figure 8.5 The partly excavated cellar near the Kershaw House facing east. The interior well is visible to the left of the balk running through the central part of the structure and the drain exits from its southeast corner.

The architecture of the brick foundation structure on the Kershaw/Aiguier tract helped me identify its specific specialized function. Lying just behind the large earthfast store, its salient feature was its long, narrow form (Figure 8.6). Its two rooms, measuring 8 by 25 feet, exhibited a distinctive configuration likely to be linked to its general use. I found clues to its function by comparing its form to that of other contemporary British structures. An examination revealed that buildings of its size and shape were not commonly found by themselves but were almost always associated with larger ones. They usually served as freestanding kitchens, workrooms, or special purpose areas. Often their interiors were subdivided to accommodate specific tasks carried out there. Its nearness to the large earthfast building implied that it may have originally served as an annex to the store; however, several things implied a separate function (Figure 8.7). First, the structure outlasted the store and its later occupation likely reflected the activities of its subsequent occupant, Gayeton Aiguier, the tin worker. Second, its architecture revealed that substantial changes had been made to the interior. The archaeological investigations uncovered evidence that its eastern room had been modified by the addition of a brick floor and an interior wall to create a specialized work area.

128

Figure 8.6 The brick foundation structure on the Kershaw/Aiguier tract in Camden. This view, looking south, shows the distinctive shape of this narrow building with two rooms. The brick floor occupies nearly all of the eastern room. Just above it the foundations of a stair tower that provided access to the building's second floor are visible.

Figure 8.7 High angle oblique view of the brick foundation structure with the large earthfast structure lying immediately to the northeast. Their close physical proximity implies that the later building was constructed as an annex to the store.

But the precise nature of this activity would become clear only when the artifacts were analyzed.

The architecture exposed by the construction excavations at the jail site provided the most comprehensive information about its function. A comparison of its partly revealed remains with the form, size, and layout of contemporary buildings of identical function allowed me to recognize similarities that identified the Camden structure. Because the Camden jail was built according to a common plan adopted in 1770, I anticipated that it shared elements with others erected in conformance with the Circuit Court Act of the previous year. Documentary sources showed these to have been rectangular two-story edifices built over a cellar. Their floor plan included two rooms divided by a hallway. Archaeological excavations at the backcountry jail at Ninety Six, South Carolina, uncovered the remains of such a facility, and their configuration provided a model for interpreting the one at Camden. An examination of the two pit profiles revealed the robbed footing trenches for an exterior wall as well as two intersecting interior walls whose width and configuration matched those of the Ninety Six jail (Figure 8.8). These architectural elements, together with evidence of the building's destruction by fire, clearly identified this specialized structure as the Camden jail (Lewis 1984b).

An examination of architectural characteristics helped me distinguish transition period buildings erected to house specialized activities from those that were primarily domestic. These results seemed to confirm my prediction that activities associated with these two broad functions had become more spatially separated by this time, a change that I felt would also be evident in the composition of the artifact assemblages recovered from individual structures. To examine this assumption, I first measured the relative importance of domestic activities at each household. Following the procedure employed in the analysis of the frontier

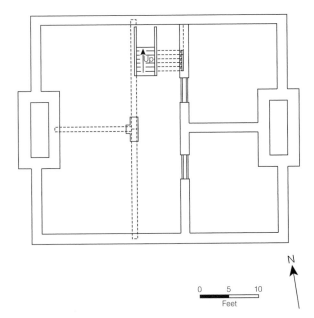

Figure 8.8 Plan of the jail at Ninety Six, South Carolina. The layout and dimensions of this building corresponded closely to those of the foundations discovered in Camden. Source: Holschlag, Rodeffer, and Cann (1978).

N

0   5   10
Feet

TABLE 8.2   COMPARISON OF CERAMICS AND WINDOW GLASS ASSEMBLAGES
AT TRANSITIONAL PERIOD HOUSEHOLD FOCI AT CAMDEN

Household	Ceramics	Window Glass
Kershaw House	69.9%	30.1%
Double house	58.3%	41.7%
Cellar	23.1%	76.9%
Blue House	75.3%	24.7%
Brick foundation structure	48.9%	51.1%
Jail	Insufficient data	Insufficient data

period households, I compared the relative amounts of ceramics and window glass in the household assemblages. I assumed that the relative proportion of ceramics would be markedly higher in the domestic structures, but be much lower in those that also housed specialized activities. Table 8.2 shows the outcome of this comparison.

The relative size of the two artifact categories varied much as I expected. All three suspected domestic households exhibited a greater percentage frequency of ceramics than window glass, but the relative proportion of the frequencies was not consistent. Although the size of the ceramic assemblage in the Kershaw House and the Blue House was uniformly high and exceeded that recorded at the two frontier period domestic household foci, this assemblage was substantially smaller at the double house. The relatively high percentage at the two structures presumably reflected an absence of specialized activities and illustrated the expected separation of domestic activities in the transitional period. The lower ceramic frequency at the double house, however, suggested that other activities may have also taken place in this building. Its proximity to the family mansion made it likely to have been the home of Kershaw family servants. House servants were often quartered in buildings also housing laundering, small-scale production, maintenance, or other activities related to the larger house. The close association of domestic and nondomestic activities was reminiscent of the arrangement found in frontier period households and may have accounted for the smaller ceramic assemblage at this locale.

The artifacts from the brick foundation structure, on the other hand, showed the patterning anticipated in nondomestic buildings. The small size of its ceramic assemblage supported my contention that this was a specialized activity area. The similarity of its artifact frequencies to those exhibited by the nearby earthfast structure also implied that, like the earlier frontier period building, its household also had a domestic component. Its existence may have resulted from a residential occupation on the Kershaw/Aiguier tract during its transitional period commercial use, culminating with the Aiguier family's arrival in the late 1790s. Although not actually housed in the brick foundation structure, they could easily have contributed the domestic refuse that accumulated around it.

The cellar in the Kershaw House complex yielded the smallest ceramic component of all the transitional period structures examined. Because this low frequency of domestic material resembled that observed at the brewhouse, I concluded the detached cellar also represented a specialized activity area, presumably related to processing or storage. These activities would have tied it to the larger role of the complex in the Kershaw family enterprises. The cellar's artifact assemblages alone, however, provided few conclusive clues to the nature of this building.

Unfortunately the circumstances surrounding the examination of the jail site made a comparison of ceramics and window glass impossible there. Because construction machinery had uncovered the structure prior to my examining the site, I could not screen the fill removed from the pit, and my investigation was confined to making a surface collection of exposed artifacts in a limited time. Under these conditions, I acquired a representative collection of ceramics but could not systematically retrieve less-conspicuous artifacts. Therefore, their presence was poorly recorded. The absence of architectural materials eliminated a critical component of my functional comparison and restricted my use of artifacts to examine function at this household focus.

In five of the six transitional period household foci, the results of a comparison of artifact assemblages identified the same functional distinctions derived from the analysis of architecture. A marked increase in the size of the ceramic component on the three domestic sites seemed to reflect the anticipated loss of specialized activities accompanying the decline of the regional economy and the transferring production, processing, and other commercial activities from living areas to separate buildings. Fewer ceramic fragments and a relative increase in the architectural assemblage also revealed a spatial concentration of specialized functions in two of the remaining households. I was unable to ascertain their actual nature because ceramic and architectural artifacts alone could not identify the activities associated with them. I could not compare these assemblages in the jail household, but an analysis of intact architecture there had already provided the necessary evidence to determine its function. I would have to rely on additional artifact analyses to interpret the nature of the remaining two specialized occupations.

An analysis of the artifacts recovered from the undisturbed floor of the brick foundation structure on the Kershaw/Aiguier tract helped me identify the exact nature of its last specialized function. The first clues came from the configuration of the building's interior. The long narrow shape, lack of fireplace, and the presence of an added interior wall at one end of the enclosed room resembled the layout of tin-working shops described by Denis Diderot's *Encyclopedia* (1970), a useful eighteenth-century source illustrating contemporary trades, professions, and other crafts. His plates depicted a shop with an unfinished interior in which workers used hand tools to mark, cut, and shape sheets of tin (tin-plated iron), which they then assembled into finished products. Workers completed the first stage of this work on a raised platform at one end of the room, then used anvils, swages, and other tools mounted on the floor to form pieces and prepare them for assembly. Finally, using the continuous heat provided by raised, portable braziers, they soldered components into completed objects. The artifacts distributed across the building's brick floor also bore testimony to tin-working operations illustrated by Diderot (Figure 8.9). Debris included fragments of files and iron molds, used in cutting and shaping tin plate, as well as more than a hundred irregular cut pieces of left over tin. Fragments of slag and bits of melted lead, generated by workers assembling finished items, provided evidence of the last stages of the tin-working process (Lewis 1999b). Clearly the brick foundation structure was the workshop of Gayeton Aiguier.

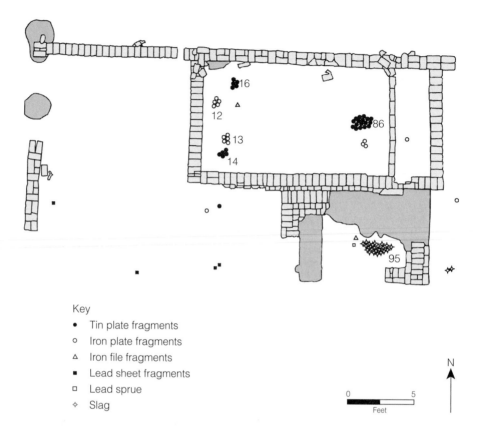

Key
- • Tin plate fragments
- ○ Iron plate fragments
- △ Iron file fragments
- ▪ Lead sheet fragments
- □ Lead sprue
- ◇ Slag

N

0 ————— 5
Feet

Figure 8.9 Distribution of tin-working artifacts at the brick foundation structure used as a shop by Gayeton Aiguier. Because this structure was abandoned following Aiguier's occupation, the remains of his activities remained undisturbed on its floor and in the surrounding area. Source: Lewis (2003).

The evidence for Gayeton Aiguier's occupation left no doubt about the function of this building and the nature of the specialized household centered there, but its intactness also reflected the distinctive manner in which its archaeological record was formed. There were several reasons for this. Certainly, the sunken shop floor protected the assemblage from subsequent agricultural disturbance, but deposits did not persist in the Kershaw House and its nearby cellar, which were similarly shielded from the plow. An examination of documents produced information that helped explain why the Aiguier shop differed from the others. Its uniqueness grew out of conditions surrounding its abandonment, circumstances that ensured the preservation of contents. When most deserted buildings are vacated, their tenants remove their belongings and other things of value. As a result, building sites generally contain only refuse and items no longer useful. Why was the Aiguier shop different? An important clue came from the records of the Aiguier estate.

Probate documents revealed that Gayeton Aiguier died suddenly in the closing months of 1798, and that his wife Elizabeth, left with four children, soon remarried. Under English common law, her property would normally be subject to her new husband's control. Perhaps realizing that her poor health might jeopardize her children's inheritance, she executed a legal agreement that guaranteed her belongings would pass to them. Following her death a year later, the property went into probate. When the new widower appeared to neglect his duties with regard to his wife's estate, the probate court stepped in to supervise its management. Its intervention not only ensured the estate's proper disposition, but protected it from reuse or pilferage. Except for the removal of salable goods, the Aiguier shop was untouched and the material contents of its last occupation remained intact, even after the building's subsequent abandonment and destruction (Lewis 2003).

The cellar in the Kershaw House complex was more difficult to interpret. I had no documents to provide clues to its use, and despite extensive excavations at the structure, the archaeological remains yielded little information regarding function. The lack of a recognizable artifact assemblage, such as that found in the Aiguier shop, implied that no substantial by-products were generated by the activities carried out there. One group of objects, however, provided a clue to the building's use. Among a collection that consisted of generally non-diagnostic architectural items and domestic artifacts was a large number of iron strap fragments. These distinctive artifacts were barrel components, and their presence suggested that this building had been a storehouse. Although I found no evidence of the barrels' contents, their presence indicated a specialized function for the building, one that might have involved the shipping of agricultural products or other goods. This activity would have been an integral part of the many commercial endeavors engaged in by the Kershaw family during the transitional period, and the structure represented by the cellar appeared likely to have been devoted to one of these.

Taken together, the material evidence recovered from the locales of six transitional period structures revealed the predicted changes in household function at Camden. Analyses of architectural remains and the assemblages of artifacts associated with individual structures indicated that the dual-function households of the frontier period had been replaced by households increasingly devoted to either domestic or specialized activities. The Kershaw House and the Blue House households exhibited distinctive forms of residential architecture together with very high frequencies of artifacts characteristic of a domestic function. Documents revealed that both buildings belonged to high status citizens and served primarily as their homes. The architecture of a third house, situated in the Kershaw House complex, also identified a domestic function, but its plan was also common to structures that contained additional activities related to the employment of their residents. As the focus of a household that likely consisted of Kershaw family servants, it contained a somewhat smaller domestic artifact assemblage than the nearby mansion house.

The structures associated with specialized households also exhibited distinctive material traits that set them apart from the others. Although known only from a limited excavation, architectural details of the jail provided details of its plan. The unique configuration of this structure offered strong evidence for its special function. Complete excavation of the brick foundation structure on the Kershaw/Aiguier tract also exposed architectural details associated with a nondomestic function and suggestive of manufacturing activities. The intact contents of its interior allowed me to determine the nature of its household even farther by providing clear evidence for the building's use as a tin-working shop by its last occupant. The architecture and small domestic artifact assemblage implied that the cellar located in the Kershaw House complex also contained a household devoted to specialized activities. Although its artifact assemblage did not specify a particular function, it did suggest the building's use in trade or other commercial enterprise.

SUMMARY

A comparison of the archaeological evidence obtained from frontier and transitional period household foci in Camden revealed the changing nature of household function during this critical period in the settlement's emergence as a central place in the South Carolina backcountry. Distinctive earthfast architecture distinguished three of the four early household foci in the town and linked them to a building tradition employed in frontier regions of British North America. The artifacts associated with the early households implied that they contained the mixture of domestic and specialized activities expected in a frontier settlement. The brewhouse, constructed of brick and containing evidence of specialized activity, stood in sharp contrast to the others. As an early example of large-scale manufacturing for a regional market, it seemed to represent the emergence of commercial production in this backcountry settlement.

Archaeological investigations also exposed six households exhibiting the separation of domestic and specialized activities characteristic of the shift to a commercial export economy. I had uncovered architectural evidence that clearly separated domestic households at the Kershaw House, the double house, and the Blue House from the three other households devoted to specialized purposes. Artifact assemblages supported this functional dichotomy, disclosing largely household activities at the domestic households. Material evidence also identified a shop devoted to tin working. The unique architecture of the jail left little doubt about its purpose.

The material record chronicled distinct shifts in form and function that characterized the changes accompanying Camden's transition at the close of the frontier period. My findings supported hypotheses that predicted an increase in specialization and greater spatial separation of activities as diverse production for general exchange was replaced by market-driven strategies and outside social and political institutions began to penetrate the isolation of this evolving frontier region. As commerce shifted from largely regional exchange to trade on an international scale, household organization experienced critical changes. The evolution of the frontier economy, however, affected households in other ways as well. Camden's residents participated in an increasingly broader economic milieu and became consumers with access to a much wider array of material goods. Although their access to newly available goods may have varied, their households should have been dramatically affected by these events. My next task was to examine the 10 Camden households for evidence of this transformation.

9/Camden in a Changing Economic and Social Milieu

INTRODUCTION

Changes in the backcountry economy in the second half of the eighteenth century affected colonists' acquisition of consumer goods and altered the material record they left behind. Although never entirely isolated from Great Britain and its global economy, frontier settlements in North America were handicapped by an infrastructure of finance and trade that initially limited the volume of imports and encouraged a reliance on indigenous manufacturing and regional exchange. Increasing investment and improvements in transportation laid the basis for commercial production, which provided credit that allowed colonists to expand their acquisition of imported goods. This growth of purchasing power precipitated a flood of European items into the backcountry (McCusker and Menard 1985). This is not to say that all of Camden's households would have shared equally in the consumption of newly available products. Here as elsewhere in colonial North America, wealth, social class, ethnicity, and many other factors affected consumption (Spencer-Wood 1987). I anticipated that these factors affected the degree to which the households' inhabitants acquired imported items. Although they may not have shared equally in the bounty of imported goods, all of Camden's residents needed to replace worn-out articles, and the availability and low cost of imported wares would have led to their adaptation and increased use. Expanding trade changed the scale of export consumption throughout the backcountry. Earlier I hypothesized that the archaeological record would provide evidence that Camden's households participated in a regional economy and the commercial economy that grew out of it. I now sought material evidence to observe this phenomenon archaeologically.

EVIDENCE FOR A REGIONAL ECONOMY

Camden was the center of an extensive network of regional trade, and many of the products made in the backcountry are likely to have passed through its stores. Unfortunately, evidence of this trade was not easily recognizable in the archaeological record. Many of the artifacts involved in regional trade consisted of biodegradable materials that vanished long ago or were non-diagnostic items whose origin would always remain unclear and would probably be unrecognizable in the archaeological record. To observe the early economy in the back-country, I had to find distinctive artifacts that were substantial enough to have preserved well and that had been manufactured in numbers sufficiently large to allow their frequencies to be observed and measured archaeologically. Several familiar types of ceramics fit these criteria and helped me document Camden's participation in the regional economy.

Three regional ceramic traditions arose in the South Carolina backcountry during the frontier period, and I had observed the presence of all three in the results of my earlier sampling excavations. They were the River Burnished wares exchanged by the resident Catawbas, the pottery produced by the Moravian colony in North Carolina, and John Bartlam's fine ceramics made at Cain Hoy and Camden in South Carolina. All circulated in the regional economy of the frontier, and I believed that the occurrence of each type in household contexts would vary with the nature of its role and the time of its use.

The excavations recovered River Burnished wares from all of the household foci at Camden, and its presence clearly indicated the participation of Camden's residents in regional trade. Although never comprising more than a small percentage of the ceramics used, the widespread presence of Catawba pottery across the settlement implied that colonists employed it in different contexts and suggested that its use may even have extended later than the frontier period. A comparison of River Burnished wares to the total ceramic assemblage at each excavated locale also revealed that this pottery was deposited more heavily in some places than others. Table 9.1 shows how its distribution looked when I arranged the households in order of ascending magnitude.

I observed a pattern of unequal distribution of River Burnished ware at Camden. In most cases buildings devoted to specialized purposes generally exhibited much higher percentages of these ceramics than those assumed to be solely domestic structures. The lower occurrence of River Burnished ware at domestic households implied that their members generally used it to a lesser extent than

TABLE 9.1   COMPARISON OF RIVER BURNISHED CERAMICS
TO TOTAL CERAMICS AT HOUSEHOLD FOCI AT CAMDEN

Household	River Burnished Ceramics as Percentage of Total
Jail	0.7%
Earthfast structure at Kershaw House	0.8%
Blue House	0.9%
Broad Street structure	2.7%
Kershaw House	3.4%
Large earthfast store	4.1%
Aiguier shop	4.7%
Cellar at Kershaw House	5.7%
Brewhouse	7.3%
Double house	10.5%

persons belonging to households that engaged in trading, brewing, and tin working. How could I account for this?

A possible economic explanation for the greater use of River Burnished ware in specialized contexts lay in its forms and their broad adaptability. More than 900 specimens of these ceramics were recovered at Camden. These fragments appeared to be pieces of pans, cups, flat-bottomed bowls, and globular jars, the most common vessel forms associated with River Burnished ware (Baker 1972; Ferguson 1989; Davis and Riggs 2003). These shapes are characteristic of utility wares, the kind of ceramics used widely for storage, processing, and other purposes associated with specialized activities such as those carried out in manufacturing and commercial buildings.

The differential use of River Burnished ware at Camden may also have reflected their cost. As less-expensive ceramics, they would have been more affordable to low status laborers who worked at and perhaps resided in specialized activity areas. As such, these artifacts are likely to have constituted a substantial part of the culinary wares used in households of mixed domestic and nondomestic function and would have comprised a much greater proportion of the material record these colonists generated.

Both these explanations seemed to account for the greater occurrence of River Burnished ware at the sites of structures devoted to specialized purposes. The distinctive role of River Burnished ware was particularly well illustrated at the double house in the Kershaw House complex, where this pottery made up more than 10 percent of the ceramics present. This structure probably served multiple functions as a living area for the house servants and as a focus for the kitchen, laundry, and other specialized tasks at which they were employed. In this capacity, its role is likely to have encompassed activities that required earthenware vessels connected with washing, storage, processing, and preparation of food and other materials for its inhabitants and their employers. The high frequency of River Burnished ware at the double house and an adjacent smokehouse testified to its extensive use in a low-status household devoted to domestic and various specialized activities. On the frontier, ceramics made by potters of African or Native American origin were often adapted for these purposes, and archaeologists have recognized these unglazed wares collectively as "Colonoware" in British and Spanish North American colonies (Ferguson 1992).

Another factor may also have influenced the distribution of River Burnished ware in one of the Camden structures. Excavations at the jail revealed that the lowest frequency of these ceramics occurred in a specialized activity structure presumably occupied by people of low status. This low frequency was unexpected because it seemed that the jail's role as a place of human confinement would have required substantial quantities of inexpensive utility vessels. To test this assumption I compared the use of River Burnished ceramics at the Camden jail with that from the only other excavated colonial jail in South Carolina. An examination of the ceramic assemblage at the site of the Ninety Six jail indicated that River Burnished ware constituted 3.9 percent of the ceramics there (Holschlag, Rodeffer, and Cann 1978). The higher frequency of River Burnished wares at the Ninety Six jail approximated that found in specialized households at Camden and was closer to what I anticipated at the Camden jail. The Ninety Six jail, however, differed from its counterpart in Camden in one respect that offered an explanation for the latter's distinctive ceramic record. Unlike the Camden jail, that at Ninety Six was used for a much shorter time. As an important military post during the Revolution, Ninety Six suffered extensive damage and its jail was destroyed in 1781. It was never rebuilt. The reconstructed Camden jail, on the other hand, continued in use and enjoyed a substantial postcolonial occupation. During this time the production and use of Catawba pottery diminished as other inexpensive wares took over their role. Because newer ceramics continued to accumulate during the antebellum period, their presence would have markedly increased the amount of non-Catawba wares in the jail's ceramic assemblage and diminished the proportion of River Burnished pottery.

As part of the larger Colonoware tradition in the American Southeast, River Burnished ware represented a distinctive class of ceramics that was used widely but not universally by immigrant settlers. Although the use of Colonoware reflected the integral role of African and Native Americans in the colonial economy, archaeologists have also discovered that the presence of this pottery had further significance as a social indicator. In addition to its economic role as a utility ware and an inexpensive supplement to European imports, Colonoware might also help identify the ethnicity of its users (Ferguson 1992). The association of River Burnished wares with a Camden household composed of people probably of African descent was very likely to have wider significance than simply that attached to its function as household equipment. Because of their broader implications for ethnicity at the double house as well as elsewhere in the settlement, I would look at these ceramics again.

Pottery from the Moravian colony of Wachovia in North Carolina constituted the second ceramic industry in the regional economy of the backcountry. The earlier sampling excavations had uncovered a handful of specimens of it, and additional pieces turned up during the investigation of individual structures. The distribution of Moravian ware in Camden, however, was far from evenly spaced. The brewhouse and the cellar at the Kershaw House complex each yielded a single sherd, which accounted for only 0.1 percent of their total ceramic assemblages. In marked contrast, a total of 15 pieces were unearthed at the Kershaw House. This relatively large quantity of Moravian fragments totaled 1.2 percent of all the ceramics recovered there and suggested a link between this distinctive artifact and the household centered here. The fact that Moravian pottery occurred only in three Camden locales, two of which lay close together and all of which were the property of a single individual, implied a pattern that tied this ware to a particular individual.

It is probably not coincidental that all of these properties were owned by Joseph Kershaw, the merchant largely responsible for extending commercial trade into the backcountry and establishing ties with the recently founded Moravian community hoping to expand its economic base (Thorp 1989). Kershaw's Pine Tree store had received shipments of Moravian pottery as early as the mid-1760s and continued to import it directly from North Carolina during the frontier period. Although Kershaw imported Moravian ware, he was not its exclusive distributor in South Carolina and may not actually have handled it in large quantities. Contemporary documents revealed that its makers sold their products directly to traveling merchants as well as individuals. In addition, much of the Moravians' long-distance trade apparently went directly to destinations as far away as Ninety Six and the entrepôt of Charleston (Fries 1922), where archaeo-logical specimens have been found (Lewis 1984a). As a result, Moravian pottery seems to have remained a minor ware at Camden and its presence in the material record may owe more to its acquisition and use by the town's principal merchant than to its systematic importation for use on a wider scale. Nevertheless, the pres-ence of this pottery reflected this settlement's participation in the exchange of this regional manufacture.

John Bartlam's Carolina creamware had a much greater impact on regional exchange in the South Carolina backcountry. Produced as early as 1770 near Charleston, its production shifted to Camden by the middle of the decade. These distinctive ceramics rivaled the quality of British fine earthenware and appear to have been produced in relatively large quantities and traded widely in South Carolina. The British occupation of the town in 1780 abruptly cut short their manufacture. Bartlam, who remained loyal to the Crown, ceased production and removed to Charleston with the retreating British army the following year and died soon afterward. Although Moravian potters manufactured similar wares in North Carolina after the war, the influx of imported ceramics dominated the increasingly commercial markets in South Carolina's backcountry and greatly reduced the demand for indigenous products and limited the extent to which Carolina creamware circulated in the region.

I believed that the rapid rise and decline of Carolina creamware during the last years of the regional economy would be reflected by its archaeological pres-ence in Camden's households. Although available for only a short time, docu-ments revealed that this ceramic enjoyed a high level of popularity, and it was made in sufficient quantities to provide evidence for the town's participation in regional trade. Overall, Carolina creamware accounted for 4.5 percent of the total ceramics recovered; however, the amount varied considerably from one locale to the next. Table 9.2 indicates how Carolina creamware was distributed among the households I examined.

Two patterns seemed to emerge from these data. First, households with very long occupations had the smallest frequencies of Carolina creamware. It made up less than 1 percent of the total ceramics at both the jail and the Kershaw House. The Blue House, erected after the Revolution, also yielded few of these artifacts. Clearly the near absence of this ceramic testified to the rapid decline in

TABLE 9.2   COMPARISON OF BARTLAM'S CAROLINA CREAMWARE
TO TOTAL CERAMICS AT HOUSEHOLD FOCI AT CAMDEN

Household	Carolina Creamware as Percentage of Total
Brewhouse	10.0%
Aiguier shop	5.9%
Large earthfast store	5.3%
Cellar at Kershaw House	3.2%
Broad Street structure	3.1%
Double house	2.7%
Earthfast structure at Kershaw House	1.6%
Blue House	1.1%
Jail	0.7%
Kershaw House	0.3%

its use following the close of Bartlam's Camden factory. Variation in the frequencies of Carolina creamware among the remaining households revealed a second pattern, namely that those identified as specialized all exhibited relatively larger amounts of the ceramic. Even the occupants of the cellar in the Kershaw House complex, used mainly after Bartlam's departure, employed this ware more extensively than did the residents of any of Camden's domestic structures.

The reason for the second pattern was uncertain. As a tableware, Carolina creamware should have been used widely in domestic households, yet it was deposited in much larger frequencies in those specialized households that spanned the period of Bartlam's production. Its lower occurrence in domestic households might simply reflect the larger size of their total ceramic assemblages and indicate that Carolina creamware, although widely used, played a relatively smaller role than it did in specialized activity households that employed fewer total ceramics. Perhaps the lower cost of these wares made them more attractive to the residents of such households wishing a facsimile of more expensive imported wares. Indeed, its presence at the double house, assumed to have contained a servants' household, may reflect its residents' reduced buying power. In spite of its uneven use, Carolina creamware was popular in Camden and elsewhere during its brief period of manufacture and found wide distribution in South Carolina's regional economy at the close of the frontier period. The Carolina creamware fragments recovered in the Camden excavations bore testimony to the settlement's role as an important source of its production.

ENMESHED IN A LARGER ECONOMY

By the closing decades of the eighteenth century the South Carolina backcountry had become an integral part of the Atlantic economy, the scope of which encompassed Great Britain's American colonies and linked them more closely with Europe, Africa, and Asia. Camden's settlement spanned this transition, and I anticipated finding material evidence for its impact at the household level. Although some of these households originated in the frontier period, all persisted into the transition that followed and were likely to have been altered by the expansion of trade, the penetration of outside institutions, and the increased wealth generated by commercial production. These changes altered the material culture of Camden's residents by enlarging the volume and diversity of imported goods and increasing the sheer number of artifacts in use. I had already observed the effect of this phenomenon in the elaboration of architecture and the appearance of specialized buildings in Camden, and I believed that these changes would also be evident in the nature of the archaeological record. By noting the occurrence of some objects and changes in others, it should be possible to discern the economic changes that marked the close of the frontier in Camden.

Immigrants in the backcountry had always imported ceramics. The archaeological record of the early settlement at Pine Tree Hill was characterized by the ceramics of the second quarter of the eighteenth century, but the presence of locally made pottery indicated that the amount of European wares was less than adequate to satisfy colonists' needs. As commercial exchange enveloped the backcountry, the volume of imported ceramics and other goods increased markedly over time and brought a decrease in the need for indigenous products. This change should have altered the material culture of Camden's households, and I anticipated that their entry into the broader economy could be detected by examining ceramic assemblages.

The temporal sensitivity of eighteenth-century British ceramics helped me observe the growth of imported ceramics in Camden. The industrialization of ceramic manufacturing in the last quarter of the eighteenth century dramatically expanded the availability of low-cost fine earthenwares, while their enhanced marketing as high status wares effectively promoted sales (Miller 1984). These distinctive ceramics appeared at about the time of Camden's transition and their presence would identify this period. Their availability and desirability were also likely to have ensured the wide use of fine earthenwares, and I expected that they would dominate the archaeological record of transitional period households. Because each of Camden's households spanned a considerable period of time, the impact of the change in ceramic use was likely to vary from one to the other. What form would the pattern of occurrence take?

I realized that all of Camden's households, regardless of the time of their beginning, lasted into the transitional period and would possess a ceramic assemblage from their earlier frontier occupation as well as one that accumulated in later years. Because all households probably kept older items, even after new ones became available, the more recent households may also have had ceramics from the previous period. In other words, I believed that all of the households possessed a collection of *early* ceramics (those produced before the development of fine earthenwares), as well as a group of *later* ceramics (produced afterward). I assumed the output resulting from the activities of each household would have remained more or less constant and predicted that the relative proportion of the early to late ceramics would show a decreasing trend over time. Using the relative sizes of the two ceramic categories as a guide to the chronological order of the households that used these artifacts, I arranged the 10 Camden households as shown in Table 9.3.

I drew two conclusions from these data. First, it was immediately apparent that in all the households ceramics deposited during the transitional period far outnumbered those that had accumulated previously. In each case, fine earthenwares dominated the assemblages, regardless of the time the households were inhabited. Later ceramics occurred almost to the exclusion of all others at the Blue House and jail. Second, I observed a consistent pattern in the variation of relative sizes of the two ceramic categories between households. This pattern

TABLE 9.3   COMPARISON OF EARLY AND LATE CERAMICS
AT HOUSEHOLD FOCI AT CAMDEN

Household	Early Ceramics	Late Ceramics
Earthfast structure at Kershaw House	33.9%	66.1%
Broad Street structure	20.0%	80.0%
Brewhouse	19.9%	80.1%
Double house at Kershaw House	17.3%	82.7%
Large earthfast store	13.4%	86.6%
Aiguier shop	11.3%	88.7%
Kershaw House	10.8%	90.2%
Cellar at Kershaw House	6.2%	93.8%
Blue House	4.6%	95.4%
Jail	2.8%	97.2%

showed that the frequency of early ceramics decreased and that of later ceramics increased directly with the lateness of the occupation. In fact, later ceramics comprised nearly the entire ceramic collections from those households with the most recent beginning dates. My temporal comparison of these ceramic categories clearly showed the increasing dominance achieved by the fine earthenwares introduced as Camden's residents became involved in broader commercial trade. This trend strongly implied the growing dependence on imported goods ceramics made available by the town's entry into the larger Atlantic economy.

I assumed that other material evidence would also reflect the greater availability of imported goods. The use of finished household items manufactured outside the region is likely to have increased as backcountry residents acquired the wealth and credit to purchase quality furniture, housewares, and personal items. Documents indicated that before the 1790s few such items were produced in Camden and that retail manufacturing there did not greatly expand until the second decade of the nineteenth century by which time the old town site was largely abandoned. Consequently, I reasoned that if eighteenth-century finished goods were associated with the excavated household foci, they had arrived as imports, and the extent of their presence would indicate that of external trade.

An examination of the artifact assemblages from each household focus revealed an abundance of finished household items in all of the buildings except the jail. Furniture parts comprised the bulk of these artifacts. These included pulls, plates, ornaments, upholstery tacks, locks, hinges, and knobs. Decorative iron ware and other architectural items also reflected external trade, as did decorated buttons, cuff links, other clothing items, personal articles, and manufactured housewares ranging from pins and thimbles to eating utensils. The presence of these objects attested to the widespread use of imported goods in Camden and implied that its residents had achieved a level of affluence sufficient to acquire them. Their relatively even distribution among households also suggested that imported manufactures were not necessarily high status objects but had become part of the normal component of artifacts in daily use by the town's residents. In addition, the number of imported items and the size of some of them, such as furniture, demonstrated not only that the volume of goods transported had increased but that the shipment of bulky items to the backcountry had become a regular and commonplace practice.

Several coins formed a class of artifacts distinct from the other imported items because they bore witness to the direct role of money in commercial expansion. Two British coins, recovered from a pit in the double house, and a quarter of a Spanish dollar, found at the Aiguier store, offered important clues to the changing backcountry economy. Although specie was known on the frontier, its role was severely restricted by the constraints of a regional economy in which most exchanges involved goods and cash was scarce. In contrast, the residents of colonial commercial centers such as Charleston participated more fully in the larger economy. Currency there took on a much wider role at all levels of exchange. Lying far from sources of British coinage, overseas ports relied heavily on foreign specie as a medium of exchange. Spanish silver coins, whole or cut into halves or quarters, were widely circulated as change in colonial American market centers. A large quantity of Spanish silver coinage was brought to Charleston for this purpose following the capture of Havana in 1763

(Clowse 1971). Presumably this medium followed the subsequent expansion of retail trade into the backcountry. I believed that the presence of coins in transitional period contexts at Camden marked the imposition of a money economy on the frontier.

Although patterning in the occurrence of certain artifact categories supported the changing nature of Camden's colonial economy, it also uncovered variation in the distribution of some items that indicated the town's social composition had not been uniform. In particular, the anomalous presence of River Burnished ware at one structure seemed to have implications for ethnic diversity in the transitional community. The development of such diversity was a critical aspect of Camden's changing economy, and an attempt to discern such variation would conclude my examination of household composition and change.

SOCIAL DIVERSITY IN A CHANGING ECONOMY

Almost all early immigrants to the South Carolina backcountry shared a western European background. The interior townships were created in part to offset the large enslaved African population of the rice-growing coastal lowcountry, and they attracted small farmers whose economic organization and household scale of production precluded the immediate introduction of large-scale slave labor. As a result, the black population appears to have remained relatively small during the period of colonization. By the late 1750s, only 13 percent of the population of the Congaree and Wateree Valleys was enslaved, and their ownership seems to have been confined to a small proportion of the immigrant population (Petty 1943). Only a quarter of the most prosperous residents were slaveholders (Brown 1963). Many free people of African descent also inhabited the backcountry, but evidence of their presence is scanty. The Reverend Woodmason, an Anglican missionary on the upper Wateree reported an abundance of "free Negroes and Mulattoes" living in the rural countryside (Hooker 1953). Black people participated in the trade with the resident Catawbas, and the vastness of the frontier always offered a degree of sanctuary to those escaping bondage (Kirkland and Kennedy 1905; Johnson 1981).

Accounts of Pine Tree Hill remained largely silent on the question of an African American presence in the early settlement; however, the settlement's rise as a commercial center changed things dramatically. The creation of export markets for backcountry crops provided an impetus to enlarge the scale of production and encouraged investment in its infrastructure, including enslaved labor. An accompanying expansion of processing, storage, and shipping further increased the number of laborers in Camden. In 1790 black residents comprised 24 percent of the population in the vicinity of Camden. This number rose to 31 percent in 1800 and a decade later half the inhabitants of Kershaw County were African American (Petty 1943; South Carolina Census 1800, 1810).

The remarkable demographic shift that accompanied Camden's role as a central place transformed the ethnic composition of its population and the structure of its society. I believed that social change of this magnitude would be discernible in the archaeological record of the households examined. It would not be easy to document the arrival and residence of people of African descent because there are no straightforward correlations between ethnicity and artifact use. Detecting the material manifestations of an African American presence required an understanding of the nature of colonial society and their role in it. European and African residents and the Native peoples of the British southern colonies were bound together in a society created by the region's role in the larger world economy. Europe's paramount role, together with the commercial nature of production under the attenuated conditions encountered on the periphery, led to a distinctive society, restructured traditional institutions, and produced innovative solutions.

Large-scale, commercial agricultural production dominated the economy of South Carolina and influenced the structure of colonial society. Established to facilitate the large-scale production of raw agricultural commodities, plantation agriculture introduced factors that shaped the structure of the society it dominated. Plantation agriculture in British America depended extensively on enslaved labor and the incorporation of peoples whose geographical origin and ethnic and racial status set them apart from the Europeans who controlled production and the colonial society the system supported. This society's rigid structure discouraged cultural homogenization of the subordinated groups. Moreover, because it maintained their separate and subordinate status, colonial society actually encouraged the retention of a disparate identity and fostered resistance to acculturation. The inflexible, multiethnic organization of plantation production in a peripheral region created a creole society, the nature of which reflected its specialized colonial economy and its need to accommodate heterogeneous social elements (Adams 1959; Joyner 1984).

Although the plantation system had not yet transformed production in South Carolina's backcountry, the region's economic transition brought with it the introduction of elements of the larger creole society. Chief among them was the important role played by labor relationships based on slavery, which increasingly defined the social structure in both agriculture and domestic life. Recognizing the presence of this division archaeologically required an understanding of how material evidence for ethnicity was expressed in a creole context.

British political control and economic dominance of South Carolina restricted trade with the colony and ensured that its residents utilized artifacts largely of colonial European origin. On the surface, the content of the material record appeared to indicate the widespread adoption of these items and the acculturation of African people to a European way of life. Placing emphasis on the origin of the artifacts ignored their behavioral context, which was a product of their differential interpretation and use by distinctive groups within the larger society. Studies of creole society in coastal South Carolina and elsewhere had revealed the regular incorporation of European artifacts and other elements of material culture into African lifeways (Singleton 1999; Wilkie 2000). To understand the meaning of the material patterning associated with slave settlements, I had to examine how Africans integrated alien artifacts into a creole culture.

The key to interpreting the archaeological record of slavery lay in the knowledge that creolization resulted in using objects commonly understood to have one meaning in other ways. Employing a linguistic analogy, folklorist Charles Joyner (1984) argued that "deep structures" of culture, which are responsible for elements of its patterning, survived even traumatic experiences like the "middle passage" into New World slavery and governed the selective adaptation of new elements. Like a grammar employing new words from a broader lexicon, these structures incorporated both African and European elements into a new colonial culture. By analogy, archaeologist Leland Ferguson (1992) applied this idea to the material culture of American slavery, arguing that artifacts, regardless of their origin must also be interpreted according to the structural context of their users. At Camden, I identified three aspects of material culture through which to explore the African American presence.

SYMBOLIC ARTIFACTS—THE CASE FOR BLUE BEADS

Among the aspects of culture that survived the middle passage to be transformed by the creole experience were broadly based practices and beliefs associated with objects of personal ornamentation. Imported glass beads had traditionally played this role in the portions of western and central Africa, the region from which most of the slaves brought to South Carolina came. Beads served important functions as decorative elements and components of amulets used for protection from harm and illness in animistic religions centered on a spiritual world that required continual mediation by conjurers who relied on their spiritual knowledge and charms to influence all aspects of life. Enslaved people brought their traditional religious beliefs to the New World, where they formed a central institution in African American society. Beads played a major role in religious and magical practices among black people in the rural South. Utilized in charms, beads were selected for their symbolic characteristics, including color. Color symbolism was a central element of western African religious beliefs and appears to have accompanied Africans to the New World. Members of creole society in South Carolina and Georgia associated blue with protection, and this belief led to their employment of blue objects, including beads, for this purpose. Beads are common artifacts on colonial American settlement sites, and archaeologists have found that blue beads are particularly evident on sites linked to people of African descent. The high occurrence of these artifacts led many scholars to conclude that, far beyond being mere articles of adornment, blue beads were a socially meaningful cultural element among creolized African Americans and are thus useful in identifying their presence archaeologically (Stine, Cabak, and Groover 1996).

Beads are extremely portable objects that accompanied their wearers wherever they went and, being easily lost, tend to mark areas most frequented by these people. I assumed that the discovery of blue beads would identify locations of activity that involved people of African descent and reflect their spatial extent. The archaeological investigations at Camden, including the sampling excavations, recovered a small number of blue beads. In fact, they comprised eight of the eleven beads found on the site. I knew that African Americans had become an integral part of the town's population as its commercial role intensified in the closing decades of the eighteenth century. I anticipated that the distribution of these artifacts would help me investigate their role in the community.

The occurrence of blue beads was not widespread, however, and indicated that the presence of African Americans in Camden may have been confined mainly to two areas within the town. Both were properties associated with the Kershaw family, the store tract in the southwestern part of town and the property surrounding the mansion. Blue beads were found at four household locales. In southwestern Camden, the excavations recovered two blue beads at the Aiguier shop and three more at the nearby large earthfast store. Earlier, Strickland had discovered two in the features behind the Kershaw House and a single bead in the cellar at the Kershaw House complex. All of these structures were in use when Joseph Kershaw and his associates were building up commercial businesses where they undoubtedly used enslaved labor. During this time, Kershaw's store must have been a busy workplace for those engaged in gathering and shipping produce and in retail trade. Later when Gayeton Aiguier, the tin worker, resided on the property, his household contained at least four slaves, including a skilled shop assistant named Ipolite (Lewis 2003). Maintaining the Kershaw mansion and the related activities in its vicinity also required a number of servants and workers, and these people almost certainly were enslaved. Men and women of African descent, who lived and carried out numerous tasks in and around the Kershaw house and other nearby buildings, are likely to have lost distinctive artifacts that marked their presence here.

Finding blue beads at two locations belonging to an individual closely tied to Camden's commercial development strongly implied a link between the appearance of African American colonists and the emergence of the transitional period town. Their apparent spatial restriction suggested, however, that slavery was not universal in the emerging central place and that export merchants were the principal slaveholders. Perhaps an analysis of other material data could help me clarify this situation.

ARTIFACTS AND FOODWAYS—COLONO CERAMICS

We have already noted the presence of River Burnished pottery at Camden. Made by Catawba potters who participated in the regional economy growing in the South Carolina backcountry, European colonists used it to supplement scarce imported ceramics. Earthenware vessels remained a widely accepted item for food preparation well into the nineteenth century, and Catawba potters actively marketed their wares to white and black South Carolinians well into the antebellum period (Baker 1972). In the backcountry, traditional cooks continued to use Catawba pots for the preparation of certain food items, particularly okra soup. Longtime Camden resident and collector of recipes, Phinehas Thornton (1845), mentioned this regional preference in his mid-nineteenth-century cookbook.

The similarity of River Burnished ware to the unglazed ceramics long made by African American potters in the lowcountry provided a major impetus to the production of the Catawba ceramics. As plantation agriculture expanded, South Carolina's enslaved population rose rapidly and created a growing demand for earthenwares similar to those they were accustomed to using. Catawba wares fit established African American foodway patterns and black settlers readily adopted this aboriginal pottery. Catawba potters supplemented plantation production of Colonoware in the second half of the eighteenth century. River Burnished ware became a mainstay for food preparation and consumption both on plantations and in urban areas, where cooking was largely in black hands. As an important component of the Colonoware tradition, it retained a market among traditional cooks (Ferguson 1992).

The culinary role of Colonoware in the lowcountry followed the extension of plantation agriculture into the backcountry. Although its initial appearance at Camden reflected use by European immigrants, the persistence of River Burnished ware indicated that it continued to play a role in the transitional period community. One explanation for its endurance may lie in the increasing size of the region's African American population, brought about by the introduction of slave labor that accompanied the expansion of commercial production. Drawn primarily from lowcountry plantations, black people who relocated to the interior would have been familiar with the use of earthenware and are likely to have used River Burnished wares themselves and to prepare food for the households they served. For this reason, I believed that finding River Burnished ware in later Camden households might be an indicator of the town's changing ethnic composition.

The key to the ethnic significance of River Burnished ware seemed to lie in the nature of its distribution. I stated earlier that this pottery comprised the largest portion of the ceramic assemblages in nondomestic structures where immigrants carried out specialized activities. The only exception was the double house in the Kershaw House complex. Ceramic use at all of these locations may have reflected a need for utility wares, possibly for nondomestic purposes, by the members of these households. But it may also have been influenced by household composition, especially during the transitional period when the demand for regionally produced ceramics should have been on the wane in the wake of increased imports. The one thing that the specialized activities of these households shared was the employment of black labor. African Americans involved in brewing, processing, manufacturing, and trade were all members of their workplace households and probably lived nearby. I reasoned that this explanation might account for the prevalence of earthenwares at these locales.

River Burnished ware also helped me tentatively identify the location of an African American household. Because this ceramic served a culinary purpose, I assumed that this class of artifact would be especially evident in domestic households, where activities involving ceramics played a major role. A substantial collection of River Burnished ware in such a household seemed to point toward its having been occupied by black settlers. One transition period household in Camden seemed to fit this description. The double house in the Kershaw House complex exhibited the highest frequency of River Burnished ceramics, greater than 10 percent of the total ceramics present (Table 9.1). The 21.3 percent frequency of these ceramics at the nearby smokehouse was even higher, further indicating an extensive use of this earthenware by the adjacent household. Earlier, an examination of the architecture of the double house had identified it as servants' quarters, probably incorporating a laundry or kitchen. If so, the structure was undoubtedly associated with the nearby mansion and inhabited by enslaved servants of the Kershaw family. The appearance of substantial quantities of River Burnished ware in a transitional period context pointed to an African origin for the structure's residents.

The distribution of River Burnished ceramics at Camden provided helpful clues to tracing the ethnicity of the town's inhabitants in the late eighteenth century. An African American presence in specialized activity households testified to their role in the commercial development of the backcountry, and evidence of a black household at the Kershaw House complex revealed the significant contribution of their activities to the emergence of an elite lifestyle on the frontier.

ARCHITECTURE AND ETHNICITY

In recent years, much has been written concerning African influences on architecture in South Carolina's lowcountry and other regions of the southern Atlantic Seaboard. On the basis of comparative research, scholars have identified characteristics typically associated with slave houses and other structures of the plantation landscape. Archaeologists have uncovered evidence of the earthen floors, wattle-and-daub walls, mud and stick chimneys, thatched roofs, interior pits and root cellars, the end-to-end placement of rooms, and other "African" elements in the remains of multiethnic colonial settlements, including those situated in the backcountry (Ferguson 1992; Vlach 1993). Their work demonstrated the persistence of traditional forms in spite of efforts by Europeans to replace them. I felt that discovering such architectural characteristics at Camden would help identify the presence of people of African descent.

The destructive effects of cultivation had obliterated much architectural evidence at Camden, but architectural features that extended below the reach of the plow offered hope of finding distinctive structural elements. Pits and root cellars were excavated beneath interior floors and served as storage places for root crops, vegetables, and other preserved foods to be consumed over the winter. This class of features was likely to have survived unscathed. Archaeologists have noted that root cellars were commonly found in slave houses in the American South. Absent on earlier pre-slavery sites, they occurred commonly in settlements occupied by people of African descent and are believed to denote their arrival in colonial settlements (Kelso 1984). Cellars have been uncovered beneath the floors of houses in Virginia and both North and South Carolina (Ferguson 1992). Other archaeologists have suggested that subfloor pits may also have served as repositories for ancestor shrines, a hallmark of West Indian houses. Reminiscent of raised household shrines found in West Africa, these may have taken a subterranean form to hide artifacts associated with ancestor worship from disapproving slave owners (Samford 1999). The strong link between subfloor pits and cellars made them a focus of attention in my search for the African American presence in Camden.

An examination of all of the fully excavated structures at Camden revealed that only the double house contained these subfloor pits (Figure 9.1). This building, constructed on a brick foundation and exhibiting other elements of European architecture, contained two large overlapping pits near the end wall of its western room. A third pit lay at the opposite end wall in the eastern room. All were associated with the later occupation of the structure (Strickland 1976). The size and contents of the pits pointed to their having been root cellars. The large number of bone fragments as well as fish scales and egg shells in the pits were typical of the food remains found in food storage areas. The presence of pins, needles, tacks, and two coins implied that the pits also had broader role as places to secret household items and valuables (Kelso 1984). Despite their condition, the remains of the double house revealed architectural practices linked to a

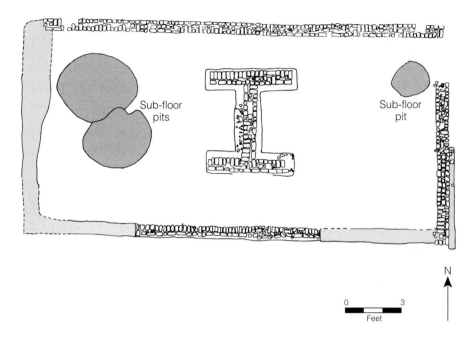

Figure 9.1 Plan of the double house at the Kershaw House complex. The H-shaped fireplace base marks the center wall that divided the structure into two rooms. Note that portions of the brick foundations were removed after the building's demolition and their positions are marked only by the robbers' trench. Source: Lewis (1977).

distinctive ethnic group in the colonial Southeast. These results corroborated the conclusions drawn from the distribution of the River Burnished ceramics and provided additional evidence that this structure was home to an African American household.

SUMMARY

My analyses of archaeological materials recovered from households at Camden revealed evidence of the town's economic transition from the regional economy of the frontier to fuller participation in the commercial economy of the Atlantic world. Because the early frontier occupations continued into the transitional period and their archaeological deposits had been mixed by subsequent cultivation, it had often been impossible to separate discrete temporal components for each household focus. I could, however, examine categories of artifacts whose presence or frequency of occurrence would provide clues to the region's economic organization. To document Camden's participation in the regional economy of the frontier, I observed the distribution of three artifacts produced and exchanged in the backcountry. River Burnished wares traded by the Catawbas, Moravian pottery from North Carolina, and John Bartlam's Carolina creamware all appeared in the remains of Camden's households. Although their pattern of occurrence tied them with earlier households, it also indicated an association with areas devoted to specialized activities as well as a link to the town's most prominent merchant. The relative paucity of imported ceramics that accompanied the widespread use of regionally produced wares characterized frontier households and stood in marked contrast to those occupied later.

The flood of imports and their dominance of the artifact assemblages in transitional period households provided clear archaeological evidence for Camden's absorption in the commercial economy of Atlantic America. Again I turned to ceramics and found that imported fine earthenwares rapidly replaced earlier wares and ushered in a much wider use of this artifact. An expansion of imported finished goods generally paralleled the flood of ceramics in later households and testified to the broader access to consumer goods that accompanied Camden's participation in the larger economy. The emergence of a commercial economy brought with it the use of specie in transactions of exchange, and the occurrence of coins in several later households provided further evidence of this development at Camden.

The study of Camden's households also yielded material corroboration for an important demographic outcome of the settlement's changing role in a region whose economy was increasingly centered around commercial production. The rise of plantation agriculture and the increasing scale of trade brought large numbers of African American people to the backcountry and witnessed their integration as enslaved labor into a new capitalist economy. In the creole economy of South Carolina, surviving elements of African culture took on distinctive forms in a society dominated by Europeans and their artifacts. Expressions of ethnicity emerged through patterns in the arrangement, selection, and use of elements of material culture. These manifested themselves in forms often recognizable in the archaeological record.

Although the archaeological signature of ethnicity is often difficult to trace, my investigation of Camden households revealed distinct spatial patterning in the occurrence of certain artifacts that probably arose from the marked shift in the composition of backcountry society. Based on analogies drawn from historical and ethnographic sources, I examined the distribution of three separate categories of evidence: blue beads, River Burnished ware, and interior root cellars. Of these artifacts, the ceramics were the most numerous and widely distributed, being present to some extent in all of the household locations. Although their ubiquitous nature doubtless reflected their widespread use by all members of the frontier community, the greater frequencies of River Burnished wares in specialized households also suggested a connection with nondomestic activities. Their much higher occurrence at the double house and nearby smokehouse, however, implied heavy use in a largely domestic setting, a pattern anticipated in African American households. Blue beads were found at two locations in the Kershaw House complex and in the vicinity of his stores. These small, personal, and highly portable objects often accompanied their owners and might have been lost anywhere they went. Their distribution was likely to reflect the workplaces as much as the living areas of Camden's early black residents. In contrast, interior root cellars were found at only one location at Camden, the double house in the Kershaw House complex. As non-portable architectural elements constructed within the homes of African Americans, their presence at the double house seemed to identify the ethnicity of this domestic structure's residents.

Although none of these three artifacts were exclusively African, all had symbolic or utilitarian links to African lifeways and have been linked independently to Americans of African descent. By observing the separate spatial distributions of these artifacts, I was able to infer the African American presence at Camden and identify, if only in a very basic way, the association of black people with both domestic and nondomestic activities. The archaeological record implied a substantial number of African Americans at transitional period households in Camden. Further, it confirmed my assumption that material evidence would substantiate this aspect of ethnic diversity during Camden's transitional period and provide clues to the role African Americans played in its changing economy.

10/Camden:
An Unfinished Work

INTRODUCTION

Things are never quite what they seem at first to an outsider investigating a traditional society. In order to understand our observations, we first have to inquire into the meaning of what we see. Similarly, an archaeologist finds past communities filled with secrets that can only be divulged if he or she first knows what questions to ask. Such queries must be derived from a knowledge of the community's structure and composition, its function relative to other communities, and its role in the historical development of the surrounding region. I sought to explore eighteenth-century Camden by examining its role as an emerging focus of economic, social, and political activity in the South Carolina backcountry. As a central place in this evolving frontier region, Camden was a microcosm for elements of the wider process of change, and the settlement's form and content over time were shaped by larger cultural developments. The overriding influence of frontier colonization on the course of Camden's growth made it imperative that my questions about its past focus on the impact of this process.

I have been fortunate that two distinctive but complementary lines of evidence exist with which to study Camden. Like many eighteenth-century settlements, Camden possesses a rich documentary record. Information from documents helped me identify its role as a frontier center and contributed details about some of its residents and their activities, but written sources provided an incomplete account of Camden's past. Two wars, their accompanying occupations, and the normal ravages of time had destroyed a great deal of material relating to the early settlement and its inhabitants. Further, the lives of most of the town's residents probably were not recorded, nor were the mundane details of everyday existence. Fortunately, the sort of past behavior that often went unchronicled manifested itself in another kind of evidence. Archaeological data in the form of features and objects accumulated as a result of the activities of all of the town's inhabitants throughout Camden's entire existence. The composition of the archaeological record and its patterned distribution constitutes a broad and basically unbiased source of evidence from which to examine the settlement.

Because the site of Camden lay intact and relatively undisturbed, its material record offered the potential to provide new clues about the town's formation and growth.

Material evidence presented another way of expanding knowledge of Camden's past, but to employ it effectively, I had to be able to place this kind of data in its larger historical setting. By themselves, physical remnants of the past provide no explanations because they represent only static objects separated from the context in which they once functioned. To understand their meaning, I had to link these physical traces to the behavior that produced them. I set out to establish this link by identifying the significant characteristics of the colonization process and constructing bridging arguments that predicted the form physical evidence was likely to take. My analyses of material evidence revealed spatial and temporal patterning that allowed me to observe the influence of frontier change on the settlement as a whole and on the level of individual households within the town.

The Camden archaeological projects produced a great amount of architectural and artifactual data that I employed to identify the characteristics of colonization at Camden and demonstrate the role of this process in shaping the town's historical development. The content and spatial arrangement of buildings and activities over time illustrated significant changes that accompanied the settlement's metamorphosis from a small cluster of structures at Pine Tree Hill to a diversified social, economic, and political center closely tied to the larger Atlantic world. Material evidence documented its shift from a regional economy characterized by mixed function households to an export-oriented commercial economy in which households devoted to domestic activities separated from those devoted to specialized production and trade. Architecture and the arrangement of buildings also changed as early earthfast structures of generic plan evolved into a multitude of buildings. Their forms distinguished their various functions and their appearance reflected elements of formal style as well as features associated with their particular function. Camden's evolution as a frontier center also witnessed social changes concomitant with a shift toward large-scale commercial production. Two aspects of this change were a marked increase in the differentiation of status in the community and the increase in ethnic diversity brought about by the arrival of enslaved African Americans whose use for labor accompanied the rise of plantation agriculture in the backcountry. Archaeology detailed the operation of a broad process of change on the community level and its effect on the development of the households that comprised it. Information gained from material evidence disclosed aspects of this process overlooked in the written record and helped me understand how Camden's role as a frontier center shaped its early history. Beyond these substantive conclusions, however, the work produced additional results.

METHODOLOGICAL QUESTIONS

Although the archaeology clearly added to our knowledge of Camden's physical form and helped explain its development, it also addressed several methodological issues about the nature of material evidence. The first centered around the *condition of the site of Camden* itself. Over a century and a half of cultivation had obliterated any surface evidence of the old settlement. Agricultural activity had turned over the first foot or so of soil across the site and mixed its contents. This plow zone contained the pulverized remains of all that had remained on the ground or lain just beneath it. Because artifacts no longer lay in situ and the edges of architectural features had become blurred, I had to rely on the patterning of disturbed materials to infer the distribution of structures and activities. Because the accuracy of such patterning governed the success of my work at Camden, I had to be able to evaluate how well it reflected the spatial reality of the vanished settlement.

The early archaeological work at Camden indicated the usefulness of employing plow zone materials as a guide to finding buried remains in the town. Alan Calmes's exploratory excavations rested on the distribution of structural materials to locate the magazine, the Kershaw House, and the northeast redoubt. In each case, these materials had not migrated far from their source and provided a good idea of the location, shape, and content of the buildings they represented. Calmes's results gave me confidence in using plow zone material as the basis for the initial examination of the entire town site. The results of the exploratory excavations conducted in 1974 and 1975 depended entirely on material obtained from the plow zone. Spatial variation in the occurrence of a number of different artifact categories revealed distinct patterns related to the location of structures and different types of activities. Subsequent intensive excavations uncovered intact structural remains of the brewhouse, the Blue House, the earthfast store, the Aiguier shop, and the Broad Street structure at locations first identified on the basis of plow zone materials. My success in finding these buildings demonstrated that the surface mixing associated with plowing did not appreciably alter the spatial distribution of cultural remains. Although the original proximity of artifacts in the plow zone may have been modified, their association remained intact, and the assemblages they formed offered useful information regarding the nature of the settlement and its components.

Although analyses of the archaeological materials contained in the plow zone at Camden were capable of showing the structure and content of the past settlement, the sheer size of the site prevented an explanation of its entire extent. The need to examine the contents of a large area expeditiously led to a second methodological issue, selecting the *means to acquire a representative sample of the site's contents*. My choice of a sample design was influenced by a knowledge of British colonial architecture, settlement layout, activity organization, and other factors likely to have influenced artifact deposition. Despite time and funding constraints, the results of the small sample were comprehensive enough to show the distribution of key material variables across the entire town site. The sample yielded patterning sufficient to answer basic questions about the eighteenth-century settlement and guide further research at Camden.

The results of the sampling excavations at Camden allowed me to recognize building locations and activity areas and supplied data helpful in investigating the form and function of the settlement. The initial sampling of the plow zone gave me the information to evaluate the nature of the early settlement and identify its role in the evolving backcountry. It also influenced subsequent intensive excavations by ascertaining the positions of a number of buildings and activity areas. This allowed me to focus later investigations on areas of more manageable size. In identifying concentrated use areas across the whole site, the sample not only gave me a picture of the entire community, but also allowed me to choose areas likely to represent particular types of households within it. I employed sampling a second time on a larger scale to define architectural patterning in southwestern Camden. Again, it aided me by delimiting the boundary between the activities associated with individual structures and locating the buildings more precisely. Sampling was central to the success of the archaeology at Camden. It made possible an overview of the entire settlement and provided the key to interpreting its component parts.

Because I wanted to examine the process of colonization within a single settlement, I had to deal with the problem of *recognizing behavioral phenomena on different scales of observation*. The ability of sampling to identify material patterning exactly illustrated the relationship between a settlement's function and the spatial arrangement of the structures and activities within it. The nature and distribution of intrasite elements was closely tied to Camden's position as a central place on the frontier, and a search for archaeological evidence indicating the presence of certain components played a key role in identifying this settlement's function. Material evidence on the settlement scale revealed Camden's growth and changing form over time. Through it I could also observe its evolving role as a central place in a regional frontier market system that became enveloped in a wider commercial economy. Analyses on a broad settlement scale relied on general patterning and could only address questions pertaining to Camden as a community. However, the archaeological elements identified at this level of examination were not confined to this scale of investigation. I also found that they offered an opportunity to explore the town's development on the larger scale of its individual households.

In the second phase of the analysis, I focused on the investigation of a regional process manifested at the household level. These households, as components of the central community in a regional social and economic system, were the foci of the various activities characteristic of Camden's development over time. At this larger scale, I could link broad patterns of communitywide form and change to the organization of households and their evolution. By examining patterns of architecture and artifact content, I could document the change from multifunction households in the frontier period to households devoted more exclusively to domestic and specialized purposes. These changes occurred in response to the backcountry's transition to a commercial economy typified increasingly by commercial production and the use of enslaved labor. Recognizing a link between larger-scale patterning and patterning observed at the settlement level was crucial to studying and interpreting households at Camden and to understanding the significance of the household in the broader context of the community.

In order to conduct analyses at either scale, I had to first define appropriate categories of material culture. I could not have addressed questions of trade, status, wealth, ethnicity, or the nature of past activities without first determining meaningful classes of evidence linked to the types of behavior I wanted to observe. *Developing functional artifact classifications* became critical to test all my hypotheses pertaining to Camden's past. Classification is central to archaeological research and involves the ordering or arranging of objects into groups on the basis of shared characteristics, or attributes. In historical archaeology, we can often associate attributes with cultural factors, like decorative elements on ceramics used during a specific time. Classification allowed me to select artifacts appropriate to particular questions at Camden. Analyzing ceramic types of known age permitted me to identify the periods in which people occupied particular households. Similarly, architectural types differentiated by the use of different materials or elements of design helped me distinguish phases of settlement. The employment of earthfast architecture, for example, clearly revealed the frontier origins of three of Camden's structures and helped locate the early Pine Tree Hill settlement.

Some classifications consisted of familiar material categories, but I created others to answer specific questions at Camden. These schemes employed artifacts selected on the basis of their likely association with an activity or function. For example, I compared window glass, a type of architectural material, and ceramics, a common domestic artifact, to measure the relative degree to which household occupations possessed a domestic function. I chose these categories not because either was unique to domestic households or absent where specialized activities took place but because the artifacts were ubiquitous and found in all households. Their presence or absence at a locale was not essential to identify its past function; instead the frequency of each type reflected the relative degree to which domestic activities dominated that function. Problem-specific classifications helped me investigate aspects of frontier change at different scales within the community.

When using classifications directed at narrow questions, I had to be careful not to link complex behavioral categories to simple artifact relationships. For example, ethnicity is a category quite real to those who experience its distinctions but one that is often very hard to recognize archaeologically. To do so effectively requires the construction of bridging arguments tying the use and deposition of artifacts to a particular group. Such is the case with the African American population in colonial America. Because relying on one-to-one correlations results in a somewhat tenuous connection between a group and its physical traces, I relied on the work of several scholars and multiple lines of evidence to detect the presence of members of this ethnic group at Camden. Blue beads don't necessarily translate into black people, but the occurrence of these artifacts together with other material characteristics linked to adaptations by these enslaved Americans can make a strong argument for their presence.

The investigation of Camden, like that of all archaeological sites, required methods appropriate to the questions asked. I designed a methodology to provide information that would permit me to examine Camden's evolving role as a central settlement on the backcountry frontier. The archaeological work approached this question by examining data on two levels: the community as a whole and its household components. Although both addressed the same historical process of frontier change, each examined its impact on a different scale and required distinctive data sets capable of recognizing its presence in the material record. In designing the investigations, I also had to consider the fact that, although Camden was well documented historically, much about the past settlement and its site remained unknown. The uncertain nature of its material remains dictated that the archaeology explore the site to determine its form, layout, and condition before examining its content. The methods employed to study the town site allowed me to accomplish both of these tasks. This work has produced a broad picture of Camden over the last half of the eighteenth century and demonstrated the importance of the frontier process in shaping behavior at different levels of analysis. Archaeological methodology has been a key factor in linking this frontier center to the forces that created and altered it. Despite the success of past projects, there is clearly much more that archaeology can do to investigate Camden's development and bring its details to light. The current projects have just begun to tap Camden's potential as a window to the past.

WHERE DO WE GO FROM HERE?

Archaeology is an evolving discipline and its interests and methods reflect changing concerns about the past and the development of new approaches to address them. In the more than 30 years that have elapsed since excavations were first carried out at Camden, much new information emerged regarding the development of the southern colonies, the evolution of frontier economies, and the role of creolization in forming colonial societies. The southern backcountry has seen a resurgence of comparative research and our knowledge of its archaeological record has mushroomed in the wake of expanded research (Crass, Smith, Zierden, and Brooks 1998; Joseph and Zierden 2002). In the years between my work in the 1970s and the 1990s, historical archaeology changed significantly, but new ideas do not destroy the value of earlier data. Later investigations incorporated new research, and when work resumed at Camden, it built on all that preceded it.

During the intervening years, my involvement with Camden slowed but never ceased. Following the sampling excavations that examined the settlement, larger projects examined settlement spread, explored the brewhouse, documented the jail, and revisited the Kershaw House and the fortifications. These projects provided additional information about the colonial town and helped refine the results of the sampling. They gave me a far better idea of the distribution and contents of buildings and activity areas and identified other patterns in the material record that would be useful in guiding future investigations. Although carried out separately, all of these endeavors contributed to a growing body of data pertaining to the organization of the community and its change over time.

The hiatus between the major excavations of the 1970s and those of the 1990s provided time to evaluate the results of the archaeology in the light of advancements in the discipline and to devise new approaches to exploit the information yielded by the exploratory excavations. During this time, my work had taken me in new directions and I had developed additional interests that grew out of other research. In particular, I had refined my ideas about agricultural colonization and the role of regional variables in this general process. I wanted to test ways of examining the consequences of colonization on a larger scale and felt that a site like Camden would be ideal for this purpose. These interests and experiences gave me additional insights about this settlement that helped me see things I might have missed had the work there been continuous. Sometimes it is worthwhile not to rush.

In some ways, the delays were a blessing. Fieldwork that might have been carried out over the intervening years would undoubtedly have uncovered additional material features and generated a great deal of physical data relating to the colonial settlement. But, given the additional insight and sensitivity that historical archaeology has gained through its intellectual growth with the passage of time, significant evidence might also have been overlooked or destroyed. The absence of large excavations has not been detrimental to the site of Camden. It has been left safe and stable. Structures and other archaeological features discovered there are preserved for future study. Most are reburied with their locations recorded, but some have also been stabilized as interpretive exhibits. Modern exhibits mark the sites of the magazine and the northeast redoubt, and a replica of the Kershaw House overlooks the old town site. All serve as reminders of the past and the role archaeology has played in bringing it to light. But much about Camden's past still eludes us, and insights gained by resorting to its material record are necessary to fill this gap in our knowledge. Designing an approach for accomplishing this task is crucial to the success of future research.

How should we proceed? Camden is a substantial site, too big to completely excavate without a tremendous expenditure of funds and effort. The site must be approached systematically, concentrating on those areas capable of yielding the most useful information about the town's past. This is why I chose to carry out the most recent work on the larger scale of individual households. Archaeologically, these were manageable units that could be excavated within a reasonable time with available resources. Although my examination of the jail site was the result of a fortuitous construction discovery, I selected all the other households because they represented the temporal and functional diversity of the settlement. Their occupations spanned the different periods of Camden's development and included a variety of activities. Investigating these households could reveal information at several levels of inquiry. In this study, I have emphasized how the nature of Camden's households reflected the town's changing role as a frontier center in the backcountry by examining how this process affected their form and content over time. Moreover, the archaeological evidence can also provide a glimpse into the lives of the people who once lived there and whose actions comprised the larger regional adaptations of colonization by observing these changes on a household level. I believe that by concentrating on the household as a unit of analysis, archaeological research can proceed in a systematic manner to investigate the development of this important community.

Archaeology at Camden should remain focused at the household level. We should begin by completing those investigations already begun. Analyses of material evidence from a number of locales in the settlement have already provided considerable information about the households that once existed there, but several of these excavations remain incomplete. Only portions of the Blue House and the brewhouse have been exposed. Both contain additional intact buried architecture and cellar deposits likely to yield information helpful in delineating their form and size as well as the nature of the activities once carried out there. While the large earthfast store building has been nearly uncovered, important features associated with it and the surrounding yard have yet to be examined. The remains of the jail are perhaps the most elusive and intriguing. One of

Camden's most notorious buildings, it lies intact beneath a commercial property north of the historical site. Although buried, this key institutional structure of the early settlement is still unprotected and unexplored. Collectively, the form and contents of all of these structures have helped me examine Camden's evolution as a frontier settlement, but the information the architecture and artifact assemblages have provided represent only part of each locale's potential to contribute to our knowledge of the past. Completing this work must be a priority. But this will only begin the archaeology needed to adequately explore the colonial settlement. Where should we go from here?

Just as the household investigations depended on the results of the sampling, the next phase of the excavations at Camden should emerge from the results of the previous work. But an expansion of the archaeology does not mean simply increasing the area of the site exposed by the shovel. Rather, we should design our future research to answer the questions raised by the recent studies. In other words, the archaeology should be conducted in such a way as to identify and examine locales within this site that are likely to yield material data that can help us expand our knowledge of functional variation within the settlement over time. I have already observed some of the basic changes that characterized Camden's emergence as a frontier settlement and its subsequent transition to a commercial center. These historical developments involved more than simply the shift from functional homogeneity to differentiation and specialization. Several avenues may be pursued to address the implications of this change for the nature of individual households and their archaeological remains.

The first step in expanding our investigations should examine the extent of variation among households during each of Camden's developmental phases. This approach will help us ascertain how the members of specific households adapted to the conditions they encountered on the frontier and afterward. This information should be particularly useful in determining the range of behavior associated with pioneer settlement in the backcountry and will provide comparative data useful for analyzing the structure of colonial society and economy. Such evidence should be beneficial in investigating the manner in which the formal institutions of the transitional period arose within the context of the insular society and regional economy of the frontier.

My examinations of four early households have provided tantalizing clues to the nature of the frontier settlement of Pine Tree Hill. Three structures lay on the Kershaw tract situated in the southwestern part of town. They mark the location of the earliest contiguous settlement here and, as they appear to mark the focal point of the frontier community, they can serve as a base for an expanded study of the initial town. Documents tell us that other early residents of Pine Tree Hill, such as Samuel Wyly, the trader, lived and carried out their activities nearby. The sites of their households can help us gain a fuller picture of the Pine Tree Hill settlement, and their remains will provide a valuable comparison to the buildings already examined. Excavations designed to discover and explore structures and activity areas will allow us to expand our knowledge of the form and content of the early settlement and comprehend its function as a central place on the backcountry frontier. This information can shed light on the structure of frontier society and the lives of Camden's pioneers, but it can also assist the investigation of larger historical trends, such as the appearance of early specialization on the frontier. Understanding the unfolding process of frontier change in Camden has clear implications for interpreting broader regional development.

Although documentary records point to the settlement on the Catawba Path as the original focus of Pine Tree Hill, archaeology has discovered a second early presence near the Kershaw House. An earthfast structure, comparable to those within the town, lay on the location later occupied by the mansion and its out-buildings. Situated on the periphery of the Kershaw House complex, its site was only partly exposed by the excavations there. What it was and why it was con-structed there are unknown, but the questions are intriguing. Given its unique location and early date, extensive excavations in the vicinity of this structure may reveal important information about Camden's earliest colonial inhabitants and a broader perspective on the composition of their households and the nature of their activities.

Just as archaeology holds the key to exploring the frontier beginnings of Camden, it can also be a prime tool in examining growth and diversification dur-ing the subsequent transitional period. Economic development was the principal element promoting the town's growth and should be a focus of further investiga-tion. At present, I have examined three specialized activity households of the tran-sitional period. Of these, two were associated, at least initially, with Joseph Kershaw's enterprises and one was an administrative building. We know from documents that before 1780 Camden's commercial community had expanded well beyond the activities of this single individual. The early partnership of Kershaw and his associates had dissolved and its members, together with many new entrepreneurs, introduced other enterprises into the backcountry. Although many faded into obscurity, some, like John Chesnut, translated their success in trade to commercial agriculture and became wealthy plantation owners. In addi-tion, different specialized businesses, like tin working, arose to take their places along the established general stores. Late eighteenth-century Camden had become a center of diverse retail activity, the nature and extent of which should be observ-able in the material record of its households.

The remains of Camden's households offer a number of opportunities to study the expansion of specialized production and the diversification of domestic life. In order to investigate economic differentiation, our strategy might examine locales associated with documented activities. Presently, only the Aiguier tin-working shop has been fully exposed, but a number of specialized households await our attention. Sampling excavations have already indicated locations likely to be the remains of Ely Kershaw's and John Adamson's stores and John Dinkins's tavern. Kershaw's brewhouse has only been partly uncovered, and the earth still shrouds much information about this industrial structure. The remnants of the jail, whose use spanned a long and turbulent period of Camden's history, appear to lie intact. The jail is the only surviving example of the administrative institutions that marked the town's rise as a center of political authority in South Carolina's inte-rior. All of these structures, and the households they contained, produced archae-ological assemblages that hold the promise of revealing changes in Camden's economic and political structure as well as the extent of its absorption in the larger Atlantic economy.

An investigation of domestic households of the transitional period can help us understand social changes that accompanied the close of the frontier. Here again, the previous archaeological work has provided opportunities to examine the impact of social and economic disparity in a society increasingly enmeshed in a commercial economy. I have already noted the material distinctions that separated the inhabitants of the Kershaw mansion from the nearby servants' household. The locales of John Adamson's house, Thomas Dinkins's house, and the Blue House all present examples of the households of middle-class businessmen and professionals who owned property and were influential in Camden's affairs. We can learn a great deal about the residents of such households from documentary sources. We often know their names, ages, genders, social and economic statuses, their occupations, and sometimes even their business and personal relationships. This information allows us to see the links between these people and the material record they generated. But these were not the only households in transitional period Camden. The rise of commercial production also created a need for labor, most of it enslaved. The poor and enslaved, who did not own land and who remain largely anonymous in the documentary record, also left their mark in the town's material remains. The buildings they occupied and used and the refuse they generated are part of the archaeological record at Camden, and it is often the only trace of their existence. Archaeology holds the promise of discovering and illuminating their past together with that of the wealthier and better-known residents.

Camden's brief military occupation of 1780–1781 interrupted the town's growth, but its repercussions were more dramatic than lasting. Its major impact, apart from the defensive works, was the quartering of a substantial military garrison in the town itself. Documents inform us that the army occupied existing structures as barracks, storehouses, and administrative buildings and it erected temporary edifices as needed. The 1781 map shows seven groups of small structures, carefully organized and laid out, within the palisaded settlement. Their distribution reflects the social hierarchy within each of the units assigned to Camden's permanent garrison and the regular arrangement of barracks typical of an established camp (Brereton 1986). But these records fail to specify the precise military use of existing buildings.

Archaeological evidence of its presence has also been difficult to discern. Only the Kershaw House, used as a headquarters, and the large earthfast store, whose size and location allowed me to infer that it served as the principal hospital, could be tied to the garrison community with any degree of certainty (Lewis 1999a). The archaeological remains of both of these buildings yielded material generated by the military occupation of Camden, and excavations recovered scattered artifactual evidence of the British army's presence elsewhere in the town. But none of the projects were able to identify specific military households. The ephemeral nature of the short-term occupation has made it difficult to study the garrison community, but this should not diminish the importance of this goal. The households of Camden's military occupation deserve attention because of their potential to shed light on the nature of military society during the American Revolution, information that should also have great value for interpreting a dramatic historical episode of Camden's past. Particular effort should be made to identify barrack areas that may be examined in detail to explore questions relating to the nature of their households. Its results can help us address topics as diverse as subsistence and unit composition and will be useful in comparing regular army households with those of militia and other units stationed at Camden. Such information will contribute to our knowledge of the actual people involved in the war in the backcountry and perhaps illuminate their role in the social history of events related to it.

Although the archaeology at Camden has added greatly to our knowledge of the settlement and its households, it has only begun to explore aspects of the frontier community that lay beyond the immediate boundaries of the 1780 town. Perhaps the most intriguing of Camden's early industries was the pottery of John Bartlam. Products of his kiln were evident in the remains of eighteenth-century households and figured prominently in my analysis of economic change, but no evidence of Bartlam's kilns have ever been found. Property records clearly identify his lands in Camden, but an examination of them yielded neither the kilns nor other telltale evidence of this industry (Rauschenberg 1991). Contemporary kiln sites, including those erected by Bartlam earlier at Cain Hoy, have revealed kiln furniture and an enormous amount of wasters, the broken fragments of ceramic vessels that failed during firing. This distinctive material signature of pottery making is glaringly absent at Camden. The investigation of the Bartlam kilns at Camden would tell us a great deal about the evolution of fine earthenware production in the Carolinas and fill in an important gap in our knowledge of its development in the backcountry.

Given the lack of success in locating Bartlam's pottery works within the town, future exploration must be conducted on a broader scope. One possible location is a place called "Logtown." This early cluster of buildings lay about a mile directly north of the old settlement and arose in the 1760s (Kirkland and Kennedy 1905). In the following decade a visitor to Camden mentioned the prolific work of a Logtown potter (Ernst and Merrens 1973). Although not identified by name, this was almost certainly John Bartlam. Unfortunately this locale now lies in a residential area and the site of the kilns may have been long ago obliterated. Should their remains be discovered here, however, they may provide incomparable evidence for this important backcountry industry as well as new information about rural settlement in the Wateree Valley.

Finally, we must remember that Camden did not exist in a cultural vacuum and that its significance has always lain in its role as a focal point for wider regional processes of change. For this reason, future research must look beyond the boundaries of the 1780 town site and consider the linkages between the colonial settlement and the area. Scholars of colonization have always emphasized the regional aspect of colonization processes. Their work has identified variables likely to have shaped the distribution and function of agricultural settlements in newly occupied regions over time. Because such studies have explored processes of frontier colonization in both space and time, their results allow us to observe the phenomena we examined in Camden on a regional scale. This work has already begun. A related project has surveyed landholding patterns in the surrounding Wateree Valley and found strong correlations between rural settlement distribution and the nature of the economy. It disclosed that an early emphasis on placing settlements to take advantage of diverse subsistence and regional trade was replaced by a trend toward selecting locations more suitable for large-scale agricultural production, investment potential, and access to transportation and export markets (Lewis and Krist 1997). The sites of rural households in the Wateree Valley have remained elusive to archaeologists and they still await discovery and study. When available, their archaeological records will provide a valuable database to compare with that from Camden. The results should allow us to link the temporal and spatial aspects of frontier change and explore this process as regional phenomenon.

On a more restricted scale, the Camden of the eighteenth century must also be seen as part of a continuing community. By this I mean that the abandonment of the old town site in the early 1800s did not mark the end of one town and the beginning of another distinct from it. The same people, businesses, and institutions once situated south of the old square on Bull Street relocated northward along streets laid out in the 1771 survey. The once isolated buildings on the old courthouse and jail tracts continued in their traditional roles as new buildings grew up around them in the antebellum period. By this time, the frontier experience was past and the town had slipped into the stable role of an agricultural center and county seat. But the processes of change begun in the previous century were not really over. The agricultural economy of the interior was still forming. The Kershaws, the Chesnuts, the Adamsons, and other families that played dynamic roles in Camden's rise all participated in its continued development, as did more recent immigrants and the descendants of those lesser-known and unnamed residents who made up the colonial community. The ties between Camden's original settlement and its later northward extension, though separated by space, represent a continuity that must be recognized in the design of future archaeological work in Camden. Valuable information about the town's growth is contained in the material record of structures and activity areas lying outside the old town. Consideration must be given to preserving them for study. This is not to suggest that areas outside the historical park should remain untouched or undeveloped. On the other hand, it would be negligent to ignore the potential presence of existing data there and disregard it when development takes place or opportunity arises. The early settlement need not remain historically isolated.

Archaeological remains of Camden's expansion are already known. The site of the jail, so far only partly examined, lay on a tract occupied by a second jail and a later city market. These buildings, situated directly across Broad Street from the recently restored 1825 courthouse designed by the renowned architect Robert Mills, represent an occupation stretching from the 1770s to the mid-nineteenth century. Together they embody all of the changes experienced by the community in its growth from a frontier center to a county seat and an examination of their material remains would contribute much to our understanding of this process of transition as well as to the public architecture that accompanied it.

Where does all this leave us? When I visit the site of Camden today the remains of the old settlement still lie invisible under the sod and the nearby modern community dominates the view stretching out to the north. In some ways the colonial town seems to have vanished forever. But much still remains unchanged from the past. Broad Street, the old Catawba Path, still carries traffic into Camden from the south. It remains the most direct route to Charleston. And the replica of the Kershaw House, erected on the original site in 1977, looks over the site of the old town as it did at the time of the Revolution. The reconstructed redoubts and portions of the town palisade also attest to that brief dramatic moment in the town's history. A generation has grown up since archaeology began at Camden and much work remains to be done. But maybe that is not entirely a bad thing. The delays between excavations have been fortuitous in some ways. They took place during a time in which historical archaeology has undergone a great deal of innovative change. It is a more mature discipline than it was in the 1970s, and its development has given rise to new questions and introduced new approaches to solving old ones. The hiatus has given me the opportunity to rethink the results of the early work and led me to design the recent investigations of Camden's social and economic structure in ways I would not have done earlier. The unforeseen benefit of delay has broadened the potential of the site and perhaps made the prospects for its future investigation that much more exciting. There have always seemed to be more questions to ask of this place, and these have frequently led my inquiry down different paths than the one I originally anticipated following. Indeed, things at Camden have never been as they first seemed. And I suspect they never will be.

Bibliography

Adams, Richard N. 1959. On the Relation between Plantation and "Creole Cultures." In *Plantation Systems of the New World. Social Science Monographs VII.* Washington, DC: Pan American Union.

Alexander, Sarah Thompson. 1850. Camden Fifty Years Ago. Kirkland Papers, Box 2–23. South Caroliniana Library. Columbia: University of South Carolina.

Anthony, Ronald W. 2002. Tangible Interaction: Evidence from Stobo Plantation. In *Another's Country: Archaeological and Historical Perspectives on Cultural Interactions in the Southern Colonies,* J. W. Joseph and Martha Zierden, eds., pp. 45–64. Tuscaloosa: University of Alabama Press.

Arensberg, Conrad M. 1961. The Community as Object and Sample. *American Anthropologist* 63:241–264.

Baker, Steven G. 1972. Colono-Indian Pottery from Cambridge, South Carolina, with Comments on the Historic Catawba Pottery Trade. *Notebook* 4(1):3–30. Columbia: Institute of Archaeology and Anthropology, University of South Carolina.

Baldwin, Robert E. 1956. Patterns of Development in Newly-Settled Areas. *Manchester School of Social and Economic Studies* 24:161–179.

Bivins, John F., Jr. 1973. *The Moravian Potters in North Carolina.* Chapel Hill: University of North Carolina Press.

Blouet, Brian W. 1972. Factors Influencing the Evolution of Settlement Patterns. In *Man, Settlement, and Urbanism,* Ruth Tringham and G. W. Dimbleby, eds., pp. 3–15. London: Gerald Duckworth.

Braudel, Fernand. 1984. *Civilization and Capitalism: 15th–18th Century, Vol. III: The Perspective of the World,* Siân Reynolds, trans. New York: Harper & Row.

Brereton, J. M. 1986. *The British Soldier: A Social History from 1661 to the Present Day.* London: The Bodley Head.

Breen, T. H. 2004. *The Marketplace of Revolution: How Consumer Politics Shaped American Independence.* New York: Oxford University Press.

Brinsfield, John Wesley. 1983. *Religion and Politics in Colonial South Carolina.* Easley, SC: Southern Historical Press.

Brown, Richard Maxwell. 1963. *The South Carolina Regulators.* Cambridge, MA: Belknap Press of the Harvard University Press.

Buchanan, John. 1997. *The Road to Guilford Courthouse: The American Revolution in the Carolinas.* New York: John Wiley & Sons.

Calmes, Alan. 1968a. *Report of Excavations at the Revolutionary War Period Fortifications of Camden, South Carolina.* Camden, SC: Report to Camden Historical Commission.

———. 1968b. The British Revolutionary War Fortifications of Camden, South Carolina. *Conference on Historic Site Archaeology, Papers* 2:50–60.

Carson, Cary, Norman F. Barka, William M. Kelso, Garry Wheeler Stone, and Dell Upton. 1988. Impermanent Architecture in the Southern American Colonies. In *Material Life in America, 1600–1860,* Robert Blair St. George, ed., pp. 113–158. Boston: Northeastern University Press.

Casagrande, Joseph B., Stephen I. Thompson, and Philip D. Young. 1964. Colonization as a Research Frontier. In *Process and Pattern in Culture: Essays in Honor of Julian H. Steward,* Robert A. Manners, ed., pp. 281–325. Chicago: Aldine.

Clow, A. and N. L. Clow. 1958. Ceramics from the Fifteenth Century to the Rise of the Staffordshire Potters. In *A History of Technology, Vol. 4: The Industrial Revolution, c. 1750 to c. 1850,* Charles Singer et al. eds., pp. 328–357. New York: Oxford University Press.

Clowse, Converse D. 1971. *Economic Beginnings in Colonial South Carolina*. Columbia: University of South Carolina Press.

Coclanis, Peter A. 1989. *The Shadow of a Dream: Economic Life and Death in the South Carolina Low Country, 1670–1920*. New York: Oxford University Press.

Cooper, Thomas. 1839. *Statutes at Large of South Carolina,* Vol. 5, Act no. 1702. Columbia, SC:A. S. Johnson.

Corkran, David H. 1970. *The Carolina Indian Frontier*. Tricentennial Booklet no. 6. Columbia: University of South Carolina Press.

Crass, David Colin and Bruce Penner. 1992. The Struggle for the South Carolina Frontier: History and Archaeology at New Windsor Township. *South Carolina Antiquities* 24:37–56.

Crass, David Colin, Steven D. Smith, Martha A. Zierden, and Richard D. Brooks, eds. 1998. *The Southern Colonial Backcountry: Interdisciplinary Perspectives on Frontier Communities*. Knoxville: University of Tennessee Press.

Cronon, William. 1983. *Changes in the Land: Indians, Colonists, and the Ecology of New England*. New York: Hill and Wang.

Cusick, James Gregory. 1995. The Importance of the Community Study Approach in Historical Archaeology. *Historical Archaeology* 29(4):59–83.

Darby, H. C. 1973. The Age of the Improver. In *A New Historical Geography of England,* H. C. Darby, ed., pp. 302–388. Cambridge: Cambridge University Press.

Davis, R. P. Stephen, Jr. and Brett H. Riggs. 2003. The Catawba Project: Research Problems and Initial Results. Paper presented at the 60th Annual Meeting of the Southeastern Archaeological Conference, Charlotte, NC.

Diderot, Denis. 1970. *Diderot Encyclopedia: The Complete Illustrations (1751–1772)*. New York: Henry N. Adams.

Drayton, John. 1802. *A View of South Carolina, as Respects Her Natural and Civil Concerns*. Charleston: W. P. Young; reprint ed. 1972, Spartanburg, SC: The Reprint Co.

Eden, Frederick Morton. 1973. An Estimate of the Number of Inhabitants in Great Britain and Ireland (1800). In *The Population Controversy,* D. V. Glass, ed. Farnborough, NH: Gregg International Publishers, Ltd.

Edgar, Walter B. 2000. *South Carolina: A History*. Columbia: University of South Carolina Press.

———. 2001. *Partisans and Redcoats: The Southern Conflict that Turned the Tide of the American Revolution*. New York: William Morrow.

Egan, Geoff. 1989. Post-Medieval Britain and Ireland in 1988. *Post Medieval-Archaeology* 23:25–67.

Ernst, Joseph A. and H. Roy Merrens. 1973. "Camden's Turrets Pierce the Skies": The Urban Process in the Southern Colonies. *William and Mary College Quarterly,* 3rd ser., 30:549–574.

Faden, William.1780. *Map of South Carolina and a Part of Georgia . . .* Color map on 4 sheets 136 x 123 cm., scale ca. 1:320,000. London.

Ferguson, Leland G. 1989. Lowcountry Plantations, the Catawba Nation, and River Burnished Pottery. In *Studies in South Carolina Archaeology: Essays in Honor of Robert L. Stephenson,* Albert C. Goodyear III and Glen T. Hanson, eds., pp. 185–191. Columbia: Anthropological Studies 9. South Carolina Institute of Archaeology and Anthropology.

———. 1992. *Uncommon Ground: Archaeology and Early African America, 1650–1800*. Washington, DC: Smithsonian Institution Press.

Fox, H. S. A. 1973. Going to Town in Thirteenth Century England. In *Man Made the Land: Essays in English Historical Geography,* Alan H. R. Baker and J. B. Harley, eds., pp. 69–78. Newton Abbot, Devon: David & Charles.

Fries, Adelaide L. (ed.). 1922. *Records of the Moravians in North Carolina, Vol. 1, 1752–1771*. Raleigh, NC: Edwards & Broughton.

Gallay, Alan. 2002. *The Indian Slave Trade: The Rise of the English Empire in the American South, 1670–1717*. New Haven, CT: Yale University Press.

Gould, J. D. 1972. *Economic Growth in History: Survey and Analysis*. London: Methuen and Co.

Gray, Lewis Cecil. 1933. *A History of Agriculture in the Southern United States to 1860*, 2 vols. Washington, DC: Carnegie Institute; reprinted 1958, Gloucester, MA: Peter Smith.

Gray, H. Peter. 1976. *A Generalized Theory of International Trade*. New York: Holmes and Meier.

Greene, Jack P. 1987. Colonial South Carolina and the Caribbean Connection. *South Carolina Historical Magazine* 88:192–210.

Groover, Mark D. 1994. Evidence for Folkways and Cultural Exchange in the Eighteenth Century South Carolina Backcountry. *Historical Archaeology* 28(1):41–64.

Grove, David. 1972. The Function and Future of Urban Centers. In *Man, Settlement, and Urbanism*, Ruth Tringham and G. W. Dimbleby, eds., pp. 559–565. London: Gerald Duckworth.

Holschlag, Stephanie L. and Michael J. Rodeffer. 1977. *Ninety Six: Exploratory Excavations in the Village*. Ninety Six, SC: Star Fort Historical Commission.

Holschlag, Stephanie L., Michael J. Rodeffer, and Marvin L. Cann. 1978. *Ninety Six: The Jail*. Ninety Six, SC: Star Fort Historical Commission.

Hooker, Richard J. (ed.). 1953. *The Carolina Backcountry on the Eve of the Revolution: The Journal and Other Writings of Charles Woodmason, Anglican Itinerant*. Introduction by Richard J. Hooker. Chapel Hill: University of North Carolina Press.

Hurst, D. Gillian. 1967. Post-Medieval Britain in 1966. *Post-Medieval Archaeology* 1:107–121.

Johnson, Michael P. 1981. Runaway Slaves and the Slave Communities in South Carolina, 1799 to 1830. *William and Mary Quarterly*, 3rd ser., 38:418–441.

Joseph, J. W. and Martha Zierden (eds.). 2002. *Another's Country: Archaeological and Historical Perspectives on Cultural Interactions in the Southern Colonies*. Tuscaloosa: University of Alabama Press.

Joyner, Charles. 1984. *Down by the Riverside: A South Carolina Slave Community*. Urbana: University of Illinois Press.

Kelso, William M. 1984. *Kingsmill Plantations, 1619–1800: Archaeology of Country Life in Colonial Virginia*. Orlando, FL: Academic Press.

King, Thomas F., Patricia Parker Hickman, and Gary Berg. 1977. *Anthropology in Historic Preservation: Caring for Culture's Clutter*. New York: Academic Press.

Kirkland, Thomas J. and Robert M. Kennedy. 1905. *Historic Camden, Vol. 1: Colonial and Revolutionary*. Columbia, SC: State Printing Co.

———. 1926. *Historic Camden, Vol 2: Nineteenth Century*. Columbia, SC: State Printing Co.

Klein, Rachel N. 1990. *Unification of a Slave State: The Rise of the Planter Class in the South Carolina Backcountry, 1760–1808*. Chapel Hill: University of North Carolina Press.

Kovacik, Charles F. and John J. Winberry. 1987. *South Carolina: A Geography*. Boulder, CO: Westview.

Kulikoff, Allan. 1993. Households and Markets: Towards a New Synthesis of American History. *William and Mary Quarterly*, 3rd ser., 50:342–355.

Laslett, Peter. 1972. Mean Household Size in England Since the Sixteenth Century. In *Household and Family in Past Time*, Peter Laslett and Richard Wall, eds., pp. 125–158. Cambridge: Cambridge University Press.

Lewis, Kenneth E. 1975. *Archaeological Investigations at the Kershaw House, Camden (38KE1), Kershaw County, South Carolina*. Research Manuscript Series 148. Columbia: Institute of Archaeology and Anthropology, University of South Carolina.

———. 1976. *Camden: A Frontier Town in Eighteenth Century South Carolina*. Anthropological Studies 2. Columbia: Institute of Archaeology and Anthropology, University of South Carolina.

———. 1977. *A Functional Study of the Kershaw House Site in Camden, South Carolina*. Research Manuscript Series 110. Columbia: Institute of Archaeology and Anthropology, University of South Carolina.

———. 1984a. *The American Frontier: An Archaeological Study of Pattern and Process*. Orlando, FL: Academic Press.

————. 1984b. The Camden Jail and Market Site: A Report on Preliminary Investigations. *Notebook* 16 (whole volume). Columbia: Institute of Archaeology and Anthropology, University of South Carolina.

————. 1998. Economic Development in the South Carolina Backcountry: A View from Camden. In *The Southern Colonial Backcountry: Interdisciplinary Perspectives on Frontier Communities,* David Colin Crass, Steven D. Smith, Martha A. Zierden, and Richard D. Brooks, eds., pp. 87–107. Knoxville: University of Tennessee Press.

————. 1999a. The Metropolis and the Backcountry: The Making of a Colonial Landscape on the South Carolina Frontier. *Historical Archaeology* 33(3):3–13.

————. 1999b. Archaeological Investigations in Southwestern Camden: Report of the 1996–1998 Project. Camden, SC: Report to Historic Camden.

————. 2003. The Tin Worker's Widow: Gender and the Formation of the Archaeological Record in the South Carolina Backcountry. In *Shared Spaces and Divided Places: Material Dimensions of Gender Relations and the American Historical Landscape,* Deborah L. Rotman and Ellen-Rose Savulis, eds., pp. 86–103. Knoxville: University of Tennessee Press.

Lewis, Kenneth E. and Frank J. Krist, Jr. 1997. Settlement Expansion in Fredericksburg Township, South Carolina, 1740–1770. *Report to Savannah River Archaeological Research Program, South Carolina.* Columbia: Institute of Archaeology and Anthropology, University of South Carolina.

Lossing, Benson J. 1860. *The Pictorial Field Book of the Revolution,* 2 vols. New York: Harper and Bros.

McCusker, John J. and Russell R. Menard. 1985. *The Economy of British America, 1607–1789.* Chapel Hill: University of North Carolina Press.

McGill, Caroline E. 1917. *History of Transportation in the United States before 1860.* Washington, DC: Carnegie Museum; reprinted 1958, New York: Peter Smith.

Meriwether, Robert L. 1940. *The Expansion of South Carolina, 1729–1765.* Kingsport, TN: Southern Publishers.

Miller, George. 1984. Marketing Ceramics in North America. *Winterthur Portfolio.* Winterthur, DE: Winterthur Museum.

Mills, Robert. 1826. *Statistics of South Carolina.* Charleston: Hurlbut and Lloyd; reprinted 1972, Spartanburg, SC: The Reprint Co.

Moore, John Hammond. 1993. *Columbia and Richland County: A South Carolina Community, 1740–1990.* Columbia: University of South Carolina Press.

Mueller, James W. 1974. *The Use of Sampling in Archaeological Survey.* Society for American Archaeology, Memoir 28.

Nathanael Greene Papers, Papers of the Continental Congress. 1781. Letters, 1774–1789. Microfilm, Roll No. 175, Vol. 2, Item 161. Washington, DC: National Archives.

Nelson, Lee H. 1968. Nail Chronology as an Aid to Dating Old Buildings. *History News* 17(11).

Newton, Milton B., Jr. 1971. Louisiana House Types: A Field Guide. *Melanges* 2:1–18.

Nobles, Gregory H. 1989. Breaking into the Backcountry: New Approaches to the Early American Frontier, 1750–1800. *William and Mary Quarterly,* 3rd ser. 46:641–670.

Noël Hume, Ivor. 1969. *Historical Archaeology.* New York: Alfred A. Knopf.

————. 1970. *A Guide to Artifacts of Colonial America.* New York: Alfred A. Knopf.

Orser, Charles E., Jr. and Brian M. Fagan. 1995. *Historical Archaeology.* New York: HarperCollins.

Otto, John Solomon. 1986. The Origins of Cattle Raising in Colonial South Carolina, 1670–1715. *South Carolina Historical Magazine* 87:117–124.

Peet, Richard. 1970–1971. Von Thünen Theory and the Dynamics of Agricultural Expansion. *Explorations in Economic History* 8:181–201.

Petty, Julian J. 1943. *The Growth and Distribution of Population in South Carolina.* Bulletin 11. Columbia: South Carolina State Planning Board; reprinted 1975, Spartanburg, SC: The Reprint Co.

Ralph, Elizabeth K. and Henry Börstling. 1965. Instrument Survey of Camden, South Carolina, August 2–7, 1965. Camden, SC: Report to Camden Historical Commission.

Rauschenberg, Bradford L. 1991. John Bartlam, Who Established "New Pottworks in South Carolina" and Became the First Successful Creamware Potter in America. *Journal of Early Southern Decorative Arts* 17(2):1–66.

Redman, Charles L. 1973. Multistage Fieldwork and Analytical Techniques. *American Antiquity* 38:61–79.

Redman, Charles L. and Patty Jo Watson. 1970. Systematic Intensive Surface Collection. *American Antiquity* 35:149–152.

Reps, John W. 1965. *The Making of Urban America: A History of City Planning in the United States.* Princeton, NJ: Princeton University Press.

Roberts, Brian. 1973. Planned Villages from Medieval England. In *Man Made the Land: Essays in English Historical Geography,* Alan R. H. Baker and J. B. Harley. eds., pp. 46–58. Newton Abbot, Devon: David & Charles.

Rogers, George C., Jr. 1969. *Charleston in the Age of the Pinckneys.* Norman: University of Oklahoma Press.

Samford, Patricia M. 1999. "Strong is the Bond of Kinship:" West African-Style Ancestor Shrines and Subfloor Pits on African American Quarters. In *Historical Archaeology, Identity Formation, and the Interpretation of Ethnicity,* Maria Franklin and Garrett Fesler, eds. Williamsburg, VA: Colonial Williamsburg Research Publications.

Santee-Wateree Planning Council. 1972. *Historic Preservation Plan and Inventory.* Sumter, SC.

Schiffer, Michael B. 1976. *Behavioral Archaeology.* New York: Academic Press.

Schulz, Judith J. 1972. The Rise and Decline of Camden as South Carolina's Major Trading Center, 1751–1829: A Historical Geographic Study. Master's thesis, Department of Geography. Columbia, SC: University of South Carolina.

———. 1976. The Hinterland of Revolutionary Camden, South Carolina. *Southeastern Geographer* 16(2):91–97.

Sellers, Leila. 1934. *Charleston Business on the Eve of the American Revolution.*

Chapel Hill: University of North Carolina Press.

Shammas, Carole. 1982. How Self-Sufficient Was Early America? *Journal of Interdisciplinary History* 13 (2):247–272.

Singleton, Theresa A. 1999. An Introduction to African-American Archaeology. In *"I, Too, Am America": Archaeological Studies of African-American Life,* Theresa A. Singleton, ed., pp. 1–17. Charlottesville: University of Virginia Press.

Smith, Alice R. Huger and D. E. Huger Smith. 1917. *The Dwelling Houses of Charleston, South Carolina.* Philadelphia: J. B. Lippincott.

South Carolina Census, Population. 1800, 1810.

South, Stanley. 1977. *Method and Theory in Historical Archaeology.* New York: Academic Press.

———. 1993. *The Search for John Bartlam at Cain Hoy: American's First Creamware Potter.* Research Manuscript 219. Columbia: South Carolina Institute of Archaeology and Anthropology, University of South Carolina.

———. 1999. *Historical Archaeology in Wachovia: Excavating Eighteenth Century Bethabara and Moravian Pottery.* New York: Kluwer Academic/ Plenum.

Spencer Wood, Suzanne M. (ed.). 1987. *Consumer Choice in Historical Archaeology.* New York: Plenum.

Stedman, Charles. 1794. *History of the American War.* London: J. Murray.

Steel, Sophie B. and Cecil W. Trout. 1904— *Historic Dress in America, 1607–1870,* 2 vols. New York: Benjamin Blom.

Steffen, Jerome O. 1980. *Comparative Frontiers: A Proposal for Studying the American West.* Norman: University of Oklahoma Press.

Stine, Linda France, Melanie A. Cabak, and Mark D. Groover. 1996. Blue Beads as African-American Cultural Symbols. *Historical Archaeology* 30(3):49–75.

Strickland, Robert N. 1971. Camden Revolutionary War Fortifications (38KE1): The 1969–70 Excavations. *Notebook* 3(3):55–71. Columbia: Institute of Archaeology and Anthropology, University of South Carolina.

———. 1976. Archaeological Excavations at Camden, 1971–1973. Camden, SC: Report to Camden Historical Commission.

Taaffe, E. J., R. L. Morrill, and P. R. Gould. 1963 Transport Expansion in Under-developed Countries: A Comparative Analysis. *Geographical Review* 53:503–529.

Thornton, Phinehas. 1845. *The Southern Gardener and Receipt Book*. Newark, NJ: A. L. Dennis; reprinted 1984, Birmingham, AL: Oxmoor House.

Thorp, Daniel B. 1989. *The Moravian Community in Colonial North Carolina: Pluralism on the Southern Frontier*. Knoxville: University of Tennessee Press.

Vlach, John Michael. 1993. *Back of the Big House: The Architecture of Plantation Slavery*. Chapel Hill: University of North Carolina Press.

Wallerstein, Immanuel. 1974. *The Modern World System: Capitalist Agriculture and the Origins of the European World Economy in the Sixteenth Century*. New York: Academic Press.

———. 1980. *The Modern World System II: Mercantilism and the Consolidation of the European World Economy, 1600–1750*. New York: Academic Press.

Watson, Patty Jo, Steven A. LeBlanc, and Charles A. Redman. 1971. *Explanation in Archaeology: An Explicitly Scientific Approach*. New York: Columbia University Press.

Weigley, Russell F. 1970. *The Partisan War: The South Carolina Campaign of 1780–1782*. Columbia: University of South Carolina Press.

Weir, Robert M. 1983 *Colonial South Carolina: A History*. Millwood, NY: KTO Press.

Wilk, R. and William Rathje. 1982. House-hold Archaeology. *American Behavioral Scientist* 25:617–639.

Wilkie, Laurie A. 2000. *Creating Freedom: Material Culture and African American Identity at Oakley Plantation, 1840–1950*. Baton Rouge: Louisiana State University Press.

Index

Brewhouse, 27, 42, 82, 83, 93–95, 106,
    109, 110, 114, 115, 120–121, 122,
    123, 124, 130, 134, 136, 138, 139,
    141, 154, 157, 158, 160
Brewhouse square, 42, 49, 65, 72, 94, 106
Brick
    artifacts of, 61, 96, 97, 98, 120, 121, 126
    construction with, 31–32, 35, 87, 90, 93,
        95, 98, 100–101, 107–109,
        118–119, 120, 124, 127, 128, 129,
        131, 148, 149
Brick foundation structure, 98, 106, 109,
    111, 127, 128, 130, 131, 133, 146,
    154. *See also* Gayeton Aiguier
British West Indies, 19
Broad River, 28
Broad Street, Camden, 24, 26, 33, 38, 43,
    47, 48, 49, 60, 61, 63, 65, 67, 71, 73,
    92, 93, 94, 96, 97, 98, 100, 107, 119,
    120, 121, 122, 163. *See also* Catawba
    Path
Broad Street structure, 98–99, 110, 114,
    115, 119, 123, 124, 130, 136, 139, 154
Bull Street, Camden, 24, 28, 32, 43, 81, 163
Buttons, 66, 67, 114, 142

Cain Hoy, SC, 8, 136, 162. *See also* John
    Bartlam; Carolina creamware
Calmes, Alan, 32, 33, 34, 35, 36, 40, 82,
    86, 87, 154
Camden
    British occupation of, 25–27, 30–37, 53,
        61, 69, 72–74, 81, 82, 83, 88, 93,
        94, 108, 139, 161
    as central place, 8, 44, 49, 78, 124, 152,
        155, 159
    churches at, 22, 24
    courthouse at, 24, 43, 163
    courts at, 22, 24, 51
    earthfast structures at, 35, 90, 92,
        98–100, 106–107, 108, 110, 111,
        118–119, 120, 122, 123, 124, 127,
        128, 134, 146, 153, 154, 156, 158.
        See also Broad Street structure;
        Earthfast structure; Large earthfast
        structure
    fair at, 22, 24, 51
    fortifications at, 25–26, 30–37, 72,
        86, 157
    historic, 30, 36
    hospital at, 72, 73, 161
    industries at, 28, 162
    jail at, 24, 26, 27, 34, 43, 82, 83, 85,
        92–93, 102, 106, 109, 113, 115,
        129, 131, 133, 134, 137–138, 139,
        141, 157, 158, 159, 160, 163

market at, 22, 24, 28, 51, 93, 113
palisade at, 26, 27, 30, 33–34, 37, 38,
    39, 40, 42, 43, 72, 73, 83, 94,
    108, 163
powder magazine at, 25, 26, 27, 31–32,
    109, 154, 158
redoubts at, 26, 27, 30, 32, 33, 34, 83,
    154, 158
1771 plan of, 21–24, 32, 37, 38, 39, 41,
    47, 92, 93, 104, 105, 106, 108, 109,
    124, 163
1781 military map of, 26–27, 32, 33, 34,
    37, 39, 40, 42, 61, 62, 63, 64, 65,
    69, 71, 72, 73, 74, 83, 90, 94
weapons cache at, 34, 47
Camden District Heritage Foundation, 30,
    31, 32, 47
Camden Historical Commission, 30, 36
Camden Judicial District, 22, 93
Capital investment, role in colonization,
    12–13, 21
Capitalism, 5
Carolina creamware, 59, 60, 88, 111, 139,
    140, 149. *See also* John Bartlam; Cain
    Hoy; William Ellis; Moravians
Catawba Indians, 17, 18, 57–58, 136, 143,
    146, 149. *See also* River Burnished
    ware
Catawba Path, 17, 20, 22, 26, 60–61, 79,
    120, 160, 163. *See also* Broad Street
Cellar, in vicinity of Kershaw House, 35,
    90, 92, 106, 113, 114, 115, 126, 130,
    131, 132, 133, 134, 136, 138, 139,
    140, 141, 146
Cellars, in Camden, 98, 100, 101, 111, 126,
    131, 133, 148, 158
Ceramics, 4, 68–69, 109–114, 121–122,
    130, 131, 140–142, 156. *See also*
    Carolina creamware; Colonoware;
    Creamware; Pearlware; Porcelain;
    River Burnished ware; Rouen faïence;
    Westerwald stoneware; White
    salt–glazed stoneware; Whiteware
    British, 56
    European, 56
    Moravian, 58, 59, 60, 136, 138, 139,
        149. *See also* Gottfried Aust;
        Moravians; Wachovia settlements
    Oriental, 56
Charleston, SC, 12, 14, 15, 17, 19, 21, 22,
    23, 25, 26, 28, 39, 53, 58, 79, 125,
    139, 163
Cheraw, SC, 16, 20
Chesnut, James, 79, 80
Chesnut, John, 19, 25, 41, 67, 79, 80, 83,
    122, 160, 163

Indian trade, in South Carolina, 11, 13, 16
Indigo, 78
Insular frontier colonization, 6–7, 8–10,
    14–17, 38, 43, 44, 50, 76, 77
Ipolite (slave in Aiguier household), 146

Jails, in backcountry. *See* Camden;
    Ninety Six
Johnson, Robert, 14
Joyner, Charles, 144

Kennedy, Robert M., 30
Kershaw, Ely, 19, 25, 41, 42, 61, 63, 65,
    67, 73, 83, 160, 163
Kershaw, Joseph, 19, 20, 21, 25, 30, 31, 41,
    42, 53, 61, 63, 65, 67, 72, 73, 79, 80,
    81, 83, 94, 95, 96, 98, 104, 108, 110,
    112, 120, 122, 125, 138, 146, 160, 163
Kershaw & Company, 19–20
Kershaw House, 20, 21, 26, 27, 28, 30, 32,
    34–36, 37, 39, 43, 44, 63, 66, 77, 82,
    85, 86–92, 98, 102, 106, 108, 109,
    110, 111, 112, 113, 114, 115, 116, 119,
    121, 124, 125, 130, 132, 133, 134,
    136, 138, 139, 146, 148, 150, 154,
    157, 158, 160, 161
  fence lines at, 92
  palisade at, 27, 30, 32, 35, 37,
    87–90, 113
  smokehouse at, 90, 147, 150
  wells at, 35, 92
Kershaw/Aiguier tract, 96, 97–100, 104,
    105, 106, 108, 109, 110, 113, 119,
    120, 121, 126, 127, 128, 130, 131, 133
King Street, Camden, 92
Kirkland, Thomas J., 30
Krist, Frank J., 96

Lance, Lambert, 80. *See also* Ancrum,
    Lance, & Loocock
Land ownership, in Camden, 41–43
Landscape, 16, 17, 24, 72
Large earthfast structure, 98, 100, 110, 114,
    115, 120, 122, 123, 124, 127, 128,
    130, 136, 139, 141, 146, 158
Livestock raising, in backcountry, 15, 78
Lloyd, Margaret, 30
Lloyd, Richard, 30
Logtown, 162
Loocock, Aaron, 41, 80. *See also* Ancrum,
    Lance, & Loocock
Lot boundaries, dating archaeological
    deposits with, 104–106. *See also* Land
    ownership
Lowcountry, of South Carolina, 11–13, 14,
    19, 24, 25, 78, 147, 148
Lyttleton Street, Camden, 32

Manufacturing, colonial, 20, 28, 51, 57–60,
    94, 121, 123–124, 131–132, 133–134,
    136, 137, 138, 146–147, 160, 162
Market Street, Camden, 34, 97
Market towns, in Great Britain, 52, 62–63
Markets, at Camden. *See* Camden
Mathis, Samuel, 80
Mathis, Sarah, 80
Mathis, Sophia, 80
Mean ceramic dating formula, 68–69, 70,
    71, 72, 109, 110, 111, 112, 113, 114.
    See also Stanley South
Meeting Street, Camden, 38, 42, 61, 63, 65,
    72, 73, 79, 83, 93, 94, 96, 109
Mickle, Joseph, 43, 61, 63
Mills, in backcountry, 18, 20, 26, 27,
    77, 78
Mills, Robert, 163
Models, in archaeology, 4, 5, 7–8, 9, 50
Moravians, 58, 59, 136, 138. *See also*
    Gottfried Aust; Carolina creamware;
    Ceramics; Rudolph Christ; William
    Ellis; Wachovia settlements

Nails, 61, 113–114
Native Americans, 13–14, 17, 57, 78, 137,
    138, 144. *See also* Catawba Indians;
    Indian trade; Regional exchange;
    River Burnished ware; Yamassee War
New Archaeology, 4
Ninety Six, SC, 16, 129, 139
  jail at, 129, 137–138
Ninevah, Iraq, 1
North Carolina, 14, 25, 58, 60, 72, 136,
    138, 147

Orangeburg, SC, 16
Osborne, Millard H., 31

Palisade. *See* Camden; Kershaw House
Pearlware, 56, 111, 113. *See also* Ceramics
Pee Dee River, 14, 16, 20, 25
Peripheral areas, in world economy, 5–6
Philadelphia, PA, 23
Pine Tree Creek, 28
Pine Tree Hill, SC, 16, 17–22, 27, 57, 68,
    69, 70, 72, 78, 79, 80, 81, 94, 104,
    110, 116, 120, 138, 140, 153, 156,
    159, 160
Plantations, 4, 11–13, 24, 28, 125, 144,
    147, 150, 153, 160. *See also* African
    Americans; Agriculture
Plow zone, at site of Camden, 35, 44, 47,
    49, 54, 69, 88, 110, 112, 154
Pompeii, Italy, 1
Porcelain, oriental, 56. *See also* Ceramics
Pratt, Charles (Baron Camden), 21